Anthropology of Contemporary Issues

A SERIES EDITED BY

ROGER SANJEK

The Magic City

UNEMPLOYMENT IN A
WORKING-CLASS COMMUNITY

Gregory Pappas

Cornell University Press

Ithaca and London

First published 1989 by Cornell University Press.

International Standard Book Number (cloth) 0-8014-2277-9
International Standard Book Number (paper) 0-8014-9548-2
Library of Congress Catalog Number 88-47935

Printed in the United States of America

*Librarians: Library of Congress cataloging information
appears on the last page of the book.*

*The paper in this book is acid-free and meets the guidelines for
permanence and durability of the Committee on Production Guidelines
for Book Longevity of the Council on Library Resources.*

In memory of my grandfather,
Charles Pappas (1897–1983)

Contents

Illustrations

Foreword

For the second time in this century mass unemployment has hit the Western industrialized world. During the years of the Great Depression the number of unemployed was higher than it is now and the hardship to which the unemployed were exposed was then even greater. Many millions depended for sheer survival on soup kitchens and other forms of private charity. Only in 1935 was a national unemployment law passed in the United States; it reduced the economic misery though it certainly did not eliminate it. What the unemployed wanted then, as now, was jobs, not handouts, on which nonetheless their very survival depended. The Public Works Administration under the New Deal tried to meet their needs, but even at its height it found work for only 4 million people, about one-quarter of those who had been made unemployed.

In the half century that has passed since then, the world has changed enormously. Confronted with the major issues of today—the danger of nuclear catastrophe, the impact of microelectronic technology on the quality of life and work, and the growth of domestic violence—we all too easily overlook the fact that in some respects life is better now than it was then. For a large majority the standard of living has risen considerably, and with it the health of the population. Life expectancy is greater. Most Americans are better educated. Women and blacks are no longer passively enduring their second-class status, even if they still have a long way to go.

Important though these desirable changes are, they disguise rather than reveal one blot on the social landscape: while the majority benefit, the poor do not. The richest country in the world contains millions of people who are deprived, materially and in their dignity as human beings.

Not all of the unemployed live in abject poverty, but all experience a severe reduction in their resources which makes it difficult and often impossible to meet obligations they entered into while still at work. The consequent upheaval in their habitual style of life intensifies the psychological burden that unemployment as a rule entails. Being forcefully excluded from active participation in the economic life of the country, stamped as useless, their skills ignored, isolated from their workmates and deprived of the solidarity and comradeship that emerge in most workplaces even when working conditions leave much to be desired, the unemployed feel abandoned and time hangs heavy on their hands. Only the very strong can avoid demoralization.

Gregory Pappas's study of the unemployed rubber workers in Barberton, Ohio, has above all one great virtue: at a time when the fate of the unemployed is less visible throughout the country than it was in the Great Depression, not only because of their numbers but because of their concentration in certain industrial locations, he has understood how to bring their experiences in their variety vividly before our eyes. He can do so because for him the unemployed remain people with their individual problems, strengths, and weaknesses, not anonymous statistics. Because he has lived in the community and shared the daily life of the unemployed, he can penetrate behind the facade at which less intensive methods of study all too often stop. He can experience in himself and with all the inhabitants—the unemployed and the still employed—how the entire community has changed under the impact of the decline of the tire industry. Thousands have lost their jobs; tens of thousands have suffered some of the consequences.

In its concrete historical and political context, Pappas's work, combining social history with social science, is free from the handicap that keeps much good work in both areas from the public eye: lack of readability. He writes to be read not just by social scientists but by a much wider group of Americans. I hope this book will be widely read and will touch the conscience of the country.

Marie Jahoda

Preface

This book documents the consequences of economic change in the lives of working-class men and women in the wake of the second largest economic downturn of this century. I have focused on the effects of a plant closing in a midwestern industrial town, Barberton, Ohio. The closing of the Seiberling plant of the Firestone Tire and Rubber Company in 1980 eliminated 1,200 jobs. Barberton is the home of second- and third-generation factory workers who once had a modicum of affluence and security. The plight of the displaced workers and their responses to changing conditions are the subjects of this book.

My intention has been to portray these people neither as passive victims of overwhelming forces nor as free agents in a changing market. These opposing perspectives often color public debate and academic discussion of unemployment. One view emphasizes structure and the other agency; the two are often seen as opposites. Theories of agency give priority to analysis of strategies and action; structural theories explain social reality in a language of victimization. One of the major theoretical contributions of Anthony Giddens is his formulation of the "duality of structure," which serves to unify these voluntaristic and deterministic theories.

By the duality of structure I mean that the structural properties of social systems are both the medium and the outcome of the practices that constitute those systems. The theory of structuration, thus formulated, rejects any differentiation of synchrony and diachrony or statics and dynamics. The identification of structure with constraint is also rejected: structure is both enabling and constraining, and it is one of the specific tasks of social theory to study the conditions in the organization of social systems that govern the interconnections between the two.   [Giddens 1979:69–70]

This ethnography explores the formulation of structure and agency by bracketing them into separate but complementary sections of the book. The first half of the book presents structural considerations associated with unemployment: the declining standard of living in a failing economy, labor-market difficulties during a regional depression, and experiential categories associated with the psychological deprivation of unemployment. These are the structural issues that people experience as constraints and perceive as resources in their day-to-day lives. The second half of the book emphasizes the ways in which people adapt to constraints, mobilize resources, and become actors. I examine the activities of individuals and groups in turn in an effort to understand the strategies of actors as they creatively respond to the conditions of their lives. A historical analysis, pivotal between these two major sections, provides both an explanation for the structural changes that have taken place and a setting in which the actions of individuals and groups can be understood.

I am at odds with two prominent positions. When I was writing this book, one of the positions, laissez-faire, found a voice in the highest offices in the land. President Reagan and his advisers repeatedly blamed the unemployed for their unemployment. Unemployment insurance, they claimed, kept people from looking for work (cf. Lekachman 1984). It seemed to escape our leaders' notice that not enough good jobs were available and that the standard of living had declined for many working-class people. This structural limitation on the prospects of these people went largely unrecognized.

Second, I find inadequate the belief that satisfactory solutions exist in programs designed to meet the needs of the unemployed. This "human services" approach examines the ways in which individuals differ in order to plan interventions and to provide for basic needs. Its advocates stress the improvement of job-seeking skills, the removal of psychological barriers to finding a job, and efforts to help the unemployed deal with the loss of a job. An explicit "grief model" to describe the reaction to job loss has been proposed (Strange 1977; Tiffany, Cowan, and Tiffany 1970).

Although their perspectives diverge in many respects, the laissez-faire and the human-services theorists both tend to reduce the problem of unemployment to the level of the individual, ignoring the broader social context. By skirting the structural issues, they misinterpret many of the experiences of the unemployed and overlook large-scale changes in the economy.

I began my research in Barberton by making informal inquiries during the winter of 1981 among acquaintances who had lost their jobs at the Seiberling plant. I moved to Barberton in April 1981 and lived there until September, when I returned to medical school. I went back to Barberton in May 1982 and stayed until October 1983. I maintained active contact with the community until August 1984.

I was raised in a small town near Barberton. My father worked as a doctor in Barberton for many years, and connections through my parents greatly facilitated this investigation. Having gone to high school nearby, I was familiar with the geography and history of the area. A few of the former Seiberling workers had been my schoolmates.

Many kinds of materials went into the writing of this book. I collected oral histories, mailed a survey questionnaire to the 612 workers who had lost their jobs and had not been granted retirement benefits when the Seiberling plant closed, and conducted formal interviews with forty-five former Seiberling workers. Among the various sources, participant observation was most important in my investigation. Living in Barberton for an extended period of time, I learned the shared knowledge of the community, its culture. My experiences in the community allowed me to look beneath the surface reality depicted by journalists and statisticians.

An anthropologist would like to be everywhere and observe surreptitiously, like a fly on the wall. I routinely scanned the local newspaper for announcements of public functions and became a familiar face at the meetings of the Men's Democratic Club, the local unions, the city council, and local hospital physicians. I was a frequent visitor at the international headquarters of the United Rubber Workers in Akron and marched on Solidarity Day in 1981 in Washington, D.C., with its members. A large part of my time was spent working with a grass-roots political organization of unemployed people. I helped campaign for a school levy and served on committees for the local United Way. At the Barberton Food Pantry, a center for the distribution of free food, I handed out federal surplus cheese and butter to the unemployed. Part-time work at the local hospital's emergency room enabled me to see at firsthand the health problems of the unemployed. I drank countless cups of coffee in an all-night diner with people who spent their days looking for work. I came to know some of these people well, joining them at church, sharing evenings at bars, and playing in summer softball and bowling tournaments. I waited in line with them as they filed for unemployment benefits.

Throughout the text, names and some minor points in personal stories have been changed in order to conceal the identities of my informants. I use real names only in chapter 7, where many of the individuals discussed are public figures. I have reported in intimate detail on people whom I came to know well and count as friends, and I hope that these pages will cause them no embarrassment. The honesty with which I try to tell their stories should reflect only the openness with which they shared their lives with me.

Allan Young supervised my graduate education in anthropology at Case Western Reserve University, and I am indebted to him for his strong guidance of my thinking on the problems addressed in this book. I am also indebted to Ida Susser for her direction of my fieldwork. I thank Roger Sanjek for his thoughtful comments and encouragement. To Dean Daniel Horrigan, Case Western Reserve University School of Medicine, I give thanks for his support of my efforts to pursue a dual degree.

This research would not have been possible without the support and cooperation of the United Rubber Workers. I thank Carl Dimengo of the research department in the international office and Joseph Albanese, former president of Local 18. Additional support came from the Graduate Alumni Fund of Case Western Reserve and the Cleveland Urban Area Health Education Center, for which I am grateful.

Many other persons were helpful in important ways. I thank Ronald Swanger, George Herin, Christine Hayword, Phyllis Taylor, Maria King Constantinidis, and Joyce Kessler. Without the support and encouragement of Joy Marshall and Joseph Frolkis I might not have been able to complete this project. I am most grateful to Janice Tandler for editing and commenting on the many drafts and to Nancy Stone for supplying the photographs that illustrate the book.

My chief debt, of course, is to the people of Barberton and the former Seiberling workers who allowed me to examine and share in their lives. My thanks go to Richard Kepler, Charles Lemon, Rebecca Lemon, and Nancy Fazino for allowing me to participate in their efforts to improve their community.

Finally, I thank my parents, Paul Nick and Despina Pappas.

G. P.

Adams-Morgan, Washington, D.C.

The Magic City

[1]

Parade: An Introduction

Labor Day, 1982

"Stray Cat Strut" blares from the horns of the Barberton High School Marching Band. The musicians are dressed in purple and white, the school colors—purple uniforms with white braids on the shoulders, white tassles on purple hats, and white, high-stepping boots. I count no fewer than twenty-five baton troupes marching today, each in its colorful uniform. Most of them are led by girls dressed in sequined leotards, twirling two and three batons at a time. Behind them the younger girls march, some gangling, others plump, none seeming quite to fit into her costume. The youngest in the troupes can't be over five years old. They sometimes march, sometimes wander off, and wave tiny batons.

I work my way down through town toward Wooster Road, walking in the direction opposite to the parade. There are unicyclists, miniature motorcycles, fire engines from all the surrounding communities, groups of clowns, horses, cowboys and Indians, scores of antique cars driven by men with beards and ladies in bonnets. I stop to look at people, then walk into a bar for a drink and watch the parade from the door.

The sidewalks are crowded. Ten thousand people are expected to attend today. Many wear paper hats that say "Celeste." It is an election year. Richard Celeste, the Democratic candidate for governor of Ohio, is not here, but everyone is certain he will carry Barberton. The Republican candidate, Clarence Brown, is walking down the street, shaking hands and waving. Congressman John Seiberling and his wife walk in the parade, greeting the people. The name is well known in Barberton, and not only because this Seiberling is a congressman. Someone inside a bar yells out, "Hey, Seiberling! Seiberling! Remember the rubber shops! Hey! Seiberling!" Local political candidates sit on the backs of convertibles like beauty queens.

There are fewer floats than there were in previous years. The El Grotto Shrine (a fraternal organization) has a comical entry, a float with crepe-paper palm trees. Seated on it are twenty overweight men wearing robes and burnooses and blowing on desert flutes. On the Body Builder's Gym float, well-greased men and women display their physiques. Another float passes, entered by CODE (Committee Opposed to Destruction of the Environment). As in years past, Reiter Dairy's Rosie, the twenty-foot-tall model cow, is in the parade. Local ambulance companies and fire departments drive by in a motorcade with their sirens blasting.

Many of the local merchants drive decorated cars, advertising their businesses. The Slovene Heritage Society has an older lady dressed in a traditional costume sitting on the back of a convertible. The Barberton High School football team, the Fighting Magics, ride on a long flatbed truck, all with mock-fierce faces. Behind them runs the school mascot, the symbol of the Magic City: a large white rabbit with a magician's hat. Miss Junior Hemisphere sits like a large plastic doll in a lavender lace gown that must be four feet across.

The parade lasts over two hours. For the finale an armored tank, half as wide as the street, rolls by, its turret in full motion. Whirling around, the cannon barrel knocks tree branches down to the street. Children run screaming into their mothers' arms.

By focusing on community rituals, anthropologists have examined the essential structure and contradictions of a community (Gluckman 1958:2). The Labor Day parade has been a tradition in Barberton for more than thirty-five years and embodies much of the city's history. Labor Day is an occasion for community celebration, with bandstand concerts, raffles, speeches, and a fireworks display.

Beneath the excitement and glitter of the event are the crucial issues that face this struggling city. Barberton is an industrial working-class town, with second- and third-generation factory workers who once had a modicum of affluence and security. Now, after a massive wave of plant closings and layoffs, there simply are not enough jobs to go around. Many of the remaining jobs are insecure, low-paying, and without benefits. A way of life that included financial stability, health insurance, and homeownership is disappearing. Unemployment has lowered the standard of living, reduced the tax base, and brought great personal tragedy.

The history of the parade tells the story of the economic transformation and the tilt in political power that has taken place. The Labor Day parade in Barberton was first held in 1947 at the instigation of the Barberton Joint Labor Committee, an organization representing the many unions in the city (*Barberton Herald* 4 September 1947). Local 18 of the United Rubber Workers (URW), the bulwark of organized labor in Barberton, provided the leadership and inspiration for the first parade and for subsequent ones. The parade was an expression of their CIO tradition of civic action and political participation—a symbol of working-class power in red, white, and blue. Over the years the festival attracted thousands of spectators and many political aspirants, including Hubert Humphrey and Richard Nixon.

In 1980 Firestone Tire and Rubber closed its Seiberling plant in Barberton, and URW Local 18 was disbanded. The labor community, in disarray, could no longer sustain the tradition of the parade without the leadership of the rubber workers. Profound changes had occurred: factories had become obsolete, profits had not been reinvested. The closing of the Seiberling plant was part of a series of plant closings and permanent layoffs in the region. Few new facilities have replaced those lost. In Summit County, in which Barberton is located, more than 50,000 were unemployed in 1982. For the displaced workers there is little hope of a return to previous conditions, since there are no plans to reopen the plants. Many unions have been weakened by loss of members, and others have been broken by companies no longer willing to deal with unions (Bureau of National Affairs 1982; Gotbaum 1984).

In 1980 the parade was taken over by the Jaycees, representatives of the Manufacturers' Association, a potent opponent of labor in Ohio. The mayor now pays for the fireworks; he sees the parade as a way to

[3]

please the citizens. The festival has become an opportunity for local industrial leaders to promote a "new era of labor-management relations," which has brought with it lower wages and aggressive attacks against unions. The significance of the parade has changed dramatically. In fact, in 1982 the event was publicized not as the Labor Day parade but as "the Mayor's Fall Festival" (*Barberton Herald* 10 August 1982).

The face of the parade has also changed. Local unions no longer march with the elaborate floats they once entered. Photos of past parades show re-creations of the Statue of Liberty in tissue paper and a huge model of the historic handshake titled "AFL Joins the CIO." The world-famous welders of the Babcock and Wilcox factory once displayed their art atop floats. In 1982 not a single representative of any union participated. As one former rubber worker commented, "There's no labor in the Labor Day parade any more."

The changes in the Labor Day parade are part of a disturbing transformation that is taking place in Barberton and in other communities like it all over the United States. Economic insecurity has overtaken a large segment of the American population. This book attempts to answer three questions about factory shutdowns and the troubles they bring to a community. First, what are the effects of job loss on the conditions of the everyday life of the displaced worker? Second, what events caused so many factories to close? The history and culture of such communities as Barberton have provided their members with resources and traditions for handling the problems they now must face. So third, how do people use these resources to deal with the consequences of job loss?

With regard to the effects of shutdowns on the lives of workers, we want to know how the workers have fared economically. We want to know how they have looked for jobs, whether they have been able to retrain or relocate, how unemployment has affected their psychological well-being and that of their families. Consequences in these areas of workers' lives reflect structural changes in society, including labor-market opportunity, income distribution, and the cultural system of values. Individuals are caught up, knowingly or unknowingly, in a process of great magnitude and worldwide significance. An explanation of industrial decline deepens our understanding of the consequences for everyday life in Barberton. In the history of the great rubber companies can be seen the events that led up to the closing of the Seiberling plant. The history of the people of Barberton, their traditions, expectations, and resources, also has a bearing on the way the community has responded to this decline, and creates a context in which to understand responses to change.

In examining the community's responses to the plant closings, we must take into account not only institutions and forces beyond the control of the individual but also the way people actively respond to and influence the circumstances of their lives. That is, social analysis must complement the consideration of structure with the consideration of agency (Giddens 1979:49). The individual responses range from despondency to focused anger. Churches, philanthropic groups, and government agencies all have mounted programs that attempt to meet the needs of the unemployed. The unemployed themselves have organized in response to the situation. Which of these responses have succeeded and which have failed?

Answers to these questions are frequently offered by major opinion makers, presumably the people who know. The informed reading public relies on such writers to tell them about the working classes. Prominent economists have suggested that people would rather receive unemployment benefits than work (Feldstein 1973), implying that enough job opportunities exist. We read that crime may cause unemployment rather than the reverse (Wilson 1983). Social analysts bemoan the weakening moral fiber of the American people (Etzioni 1983) but fail to note that the economic base of entire communities has disappeared. This distorted image has been projected in part because many commentators on working-class life are fundamentally estranged from the people about whom they write.

Other studies of unemployment, though sympathetic to workers, err in another direction. They depict displaced workers as the passive victims of overwhelming forces. They offer little understanding of the ways in which workers resist and oppose those forces (Buss and Redburn 1983a, 1983b; Strange 1977), nor do they show that the actions of workers can themselves reproduce the conditions of their own domination.

Social scientists have a long tradition of studying the working class through participant observation, that is, by living among them, con-

[5]

ducting lengthy personal interviews, and sharing their experiences.[1] A new generation of ethnographers has built on that tradition by emphasizing the relationship of the everyday life of working-class people to broader political and economic conditions. They have also described the problems and prospects of collective action by these people (Susser 1982; Gavanta 1980; Edwards 1979). Unemployment has not been a primary focus of recent ethnographer, however.

The classic studies of unemployment, made during the Great Depression, still provide inspiration for contemporary work. Social science as a distinct enterprise was in its infancy, and the study of unemployment as a specific field of study was newly recognized (Garraty 1978). *Marienthal* (Jahoda, Lazarsfeld, and Zeisel 1971), circulated in mimeograph during the thirties, is a forerunner of modern community studies and examines an Austrian village, all of whose residents became unemployed with the closing of the local textile mill in 1929. It is a story of desperation. While the authors make many perceptive observations about the psychological consequences of unemployment, they had a broader intention that set them apart from the psychological tradition of Vienna, out of which they had come. It was their objective to study "the community, not unemployment and the individual."

Robert and Helen Lynd had a unique opportunity to study unemployment during the Great Depression in the United States. In 1925 they did research for a community study of a midwestern industrial town, reported in *Middletown* (1929). *Middletown in Transition* (1937) documents the same Indiana town ten years later, during the depths of the Depression. The Middletown studies focus on the town as a whole and situate the working class in terms of its relationships to the dominant class of merchants and company owners.

Edward Wight Bakke's major works, *The Unemployed Worker* and *Citizens without Work*, both appeared in 1940. In these studies of the unemployed in New Haven, Connecticut, Bakke concluded that unemployment insurance allowed people to remain "geared into" society. Unemployment insurance was a safeguard against social disintegration. The effects of unemployment on the worker were analyzed as a "loosening of those economic bonds which hold him to the productive ways

---

[1]See, for example, Berger (1960), Gans (1962), Komarosky (1964), Liebow (1967), Kornblum (1974), and Stack (1974).

[6]

of men in society" (Bakke 1940a:1), an idea generalized in sociological theory as the problem of order. This concept is thought to have originated from the work of Emile Durkheim (Parsons 1960; cf. Giddens 1975), but the problem of order in social science might also be traced to the widespread concern of the time that society was on the verge of collapse (Giddens 1975:43–46). In the United States unemployment peaked at 25 percent, precipitating fundamental changes in American political history. In Europe the depression was much worse. The collapse came first in Germany with the rise of fascism.

Plant Closing and Unemployment

By 1982 mass unemployment had reemerged as a major social issue. Unemployment rose to its highest level since before World War II, and an estimated 12 million people were out of work—10.8 percent of the labor force in the nation. It was not, however, a really new phenomenon. After 1968 a pattern was established in which each recession was followed by higher levels of unemployment during recovery. During the depth of the 1975 recession, national unemployment rose to 9.2 percent. In 1983, when a recovery was proclaimed, unemployment remained at 9.5 percent nationally.

Certain sectors of the work force have been more heavily affected than others. There was a 16.9 percent joblessness rate among blue-collar workers in April 1982, and unemployment in the construction industry climbed to 19.4 percent (Bureau of National Affairs 1982). The automotive, steel, and rubber industries were hardest hit; 25 percent of workers in the rubber industry were idled. Ohio suffered dramatic losses in manufacturing jobs from 1970 to 1983 and continued to lose at a slower pace between 1983 and 1985 (Cleveland Council of Unemployed Workers 1986a). What is distinctive about this downturn is the great number of jobs lost to plant closings. The recessions of the seventies were characterized by temporary layoffs, but the plant closings of the eighties have meant the permanent loss of thousands of jobs—20,000 in the rubber industry alone.

The Akron area witnessed the near-total dismantling of its local rubber industry. For many years Akron was called the Rubber Capital of the World, boasting 65,000 blue-collar jobs in the rubber industry in

1950. By 1980 more than 29,000 of those jobs had been lost (Ohio Public Interest Campaign 1980). Since 1978 eight major facilities in the Akron area have been shut down, with some 7,000 jobs eliminated. On 20 March 1982, the last automobile tire rolled off the production line in Akron (*Akron Beacon Journal* 15 March 1982).[2]

It is often noted that the number of jobs has risen steadily, although not in proportion to demand. This observation obscures the facts about the nature of the new jobs, which are primarily in the service sector and are characterized by low wages, poor benefits, no unions, and insecurity. Involuntary part-time jobs have grown at an alarming rate, over 5.8 million in 1986. In Ohio a mild recovery between 1983 and 1985 brought 330,000 new jobs, which included 118,600 in retailing and another 147,000 in service industries. The average workweek for these jobs was 28.4 hours, at an hourly wage of $5.44 (Cleveland Council of Unemployed Workers 1986b). Many of the people who hold these jobs are, in the current phrase, "underemployed" (Gordon 1972). Unemployment and underemployment have become major problems for the working class. While monthly unemployment figures rise and fall, these underlying problems have persisted over a long period. Mild recoveries merely distract our attention from them.

The monthly unemployment figures of the Bureau of Labor Statistics are very accurate estimates based on a large national sample contacted through a household survey. The magnitude of the problem, however, is not accurately reflected in the monthly index, which is reported in newspapers and on television. The monthly index includes only people who are not working and who are looking for a job. Not included are those who have given up looking, part-time workers who would prefer full-time employment, or students who remain in school because they cannot find work (Sullivan 1978). It is estimated that when such people are taken into consideration, more than 20 million additional jobs are needed (*AFL-CIO News* 11 July 1983). The index also counts only those unemployed during a given month. A count of all the people who were unemployed at some time in 1982 reveals that 24 percent of the work force was affected (*Monthly Review* June 1983).

[2]The last passenger tire was made at the Seiberling plant in Barberton. The last truck tire was made in 1982 by General Tire before the closing of its Plant 7. Today a few airplane tires and a few experimental road tires are made in Akron (interview with Carl Dimengo, Research Department, URW International, Akron, 10 March 1986).

It is also important to understand the distinction between the monthly unemployment rate and the number of workers who filed for unemployment benefits. The number who filed for benefits is the number of those who actually received checks. Only one-third of the people counted as unemployed were receiving unemployment insurance between 1981 and 1983, however (Roberts 1984).

We cannot know accurately the number of persons unemployed in Barberton because the statistics are collected on a county-by-county basis. More than 40,000 people were unemployed in 1982 in Summit County —14.3 percent of the work force. Working-class people are concentrated in the southern half of the county, in and around Barberton; the county figures therefore probably underestimate the magnitude of unemployment in Barberton itself.

Five large plants have closed in Barberton since 1979 and approximately 5,000 jobs have been lost (Brooks 1983). The first large factory to close was the Seiberling plant. In a large-scale reorganization, the Firestone Tire and Rubber Company decided to close five of its tire plants nationwide. On 19 March 1980, the closing of the Seiberling plant in Barberton was announced as part of that reorganization.

The Seiberling plant had for many years been the second largest employer in the city. The plant's work force was approximately 75 percent male and 25 percent female; 20 percent of the workers were black, a much greater proportion than in the population of Barberton itself. At the time of the closing 1,219 jobs were lost, including 987 blue-collar jobs. Two hundred and thirty-two of the workers received early retirement benefits. Those who did not qualify for early retirement faced uncertain futures; two years after the shutdown, 20 percent had found comparable jobs, 40 percent had found jobs that were insecure and low-paying, and 40 percent were unemployed. National studies of displaced workers reveal similar findings.

Barberton, the Magic City

Barberton became known as the Magic City because with rapid industrialization, it grew like magic. Barberton is thirty-five miles south of Cleveland. It is 7.9 square miles in area and shares its northeastern border with Akron. By 1960 its population peaked at 33,805.

[9]

The 1980 census found 29,751 people living within its borders (U.S. Bureau of the Census 1982). Barberton is now regionally known for its depressed economy. A newspaper magazine feature asked the question "Can the Magic Ever Come Back?" (Henson 1983).

Though Barberton is adjacent to much larger Akron, it has a distinct identity. It has its own city government, health department, courts, schools, and hospital. The population is fairly homogeneous in occupation; most of the people have been connected with manufacturing in some way. It would be a mistake to claim that the people of a single town are representative of an entire country's working class, but Barberton is probably as representative as any American industrial town is likely to be. Nothing stands out to make Barberton extreme or unusual among factory towns. It is not a one-factory town; no one ethnic group predominates. The former Seiberling employees are typical of the once-comfortable industrial workers who have been severely affected by the recent recession.

Barberton has the look of a factory town. The large plants dominate the skyline. Adjacent to the factories are neighborhoods of modest homes with small yards. To the outsider Barberton might appear stunningly boring, but for its people the town is a source of great pride. The housing is noticeably homogeneous. Most people live in modest two- or three-bedroom bungalows. There are approximately 8,000 unattached single-family dwellings in Barberton, with a median market value of $34,900 in 1980 (U.S. Bureau of the Census 1982). Among the houses are many small churches and corner bars. Apartments constitute 11 percent of the housing units. There are a few trailer parks and two low-income projects. The older of the two federal housing projects, the Norton Homes, has 219 units and was built in the early fifties. The other, the Van Buren Homes, has 230 units and was built in 1965.[3]

Residents recognize various neighborhoods in town: Snydertown, Austin Estates, "around the lake," the West Side, the North End. Snydertown, the southern end of town, has the poorest housing and the highest concentration of blacks, who constitute 4 percent of Barberton's population. The Austin Estates development has the most recently built, highest-quality houses in town. These are the homes of Barberton's white-collar workers. In 1980 the median market value of

[3]Interview with Michael Gavin, Planning Department, City of Barberton, 19 October 1982.

[10]

The Ohio Brass Company plant, one of five factories closed in Barberton since 1980

the homes in the census tract that includes the Austin Estates was $47,500. When people in Barberton want to make a point about privilege, they refer to Austin Estates, although its residents are far from wealthy.

The ethnic neighborhoods have almost completely lost their identity. Ethnicity in general has declined in importance in Barberton. Although foreign-born residents never exceeded 7 percent of the population, there were at one time immigrants from thirty-one countries, many having their own churches and social welfare clubs. The largest group was the Italians, followed by the Slovenians (Yugoslavians) and the Slovaks (Czechoslovakians). Today ethnic churches, notably the Slovenian and Slovak, still offer ethnic food and polka dancing at their festivals, but otherwise little about these churches is distinctive. Italians in Barberton have been almost completely assimilated. The West Side retains some ethnic character, primarily through its older residents, but there are no longer any foreign-language-speaking neighborhoods. A Sokol Center (Czech) operates a private bar, and the Slovene center has a bowling alley popular with the older men in town. There are no truly ethnic restaurants or shops in Barberton.

Perhaps the largest group with a common heritage and identity consists of the West Virginians. The large number of migrants from Appalachia inspired a popular joke during World War II: "Hitler wants to know how West Virginia took over Akron without firing a single shot." People from West Virginia, Kentucky, and Tennessee came to the area in great numbers in search of work. Some still maintain contact with relatives in other states, making visits on holidays to ancestral farms. A homogenized cultural identity referred to as "country" exists in a particular style of cooking, a preference in music, and an inflection in speech.

In addition to its factories and high school athletic teams, Barberton is known for its numerous "chicken houses." These are family restaurants that specialize in chicken dinners, most frequently patronized after church on Sunday. Barberton is sometimes called the Chicken Capital because it has so many of these establishments, which outsiders discourteously refer to as "redneck restaurants."

Barbertonians today are thoroughly proletarianized. The efforts of these workers to hold their lives together when the work disappeared are in reality the struggles of an industrial class displaced by historical changes that they did not recognize until they were engulfed by them.

[12]

[2]

Fragile Affluence

The image of the affluent worker is one of the most enduring in American social commentary. The growth of wealth in the United States in the post–World War II era, and of the number of people who have benefited from it, is unprecedented in the history of the world (Bowles, Gordon, and Weisskopf 1983). In Barberton, as in other American working-class towns, a modicum of affluence was possible for many. Two cars, two televisions, a house in a suburb, a refrigerator and a freezer, and health insurance were realizable dreams for the workers in large union shops like the Seiberling plant. The more frugal could have a substantial bank balance. The sting of unemployment was thought to have been largely eliminated by unemployment insurance; job loss was no longer dreaded as it had been by the previous generation. It became widely believed that unemployment did not necessarily mean impoverishment (Ginzberg 1968, Levitan 1971). The idea that the working class would disappear completely was popular; many observers envisioned its gradual "embourgeoisement." Some commentators (Illich 1978) began to regard unemployment as a luxury of the twentieth century.

Despite the persistence of poverty and the many studies casting doubt on the reality of the affluent worker, the image remained with us (Berger 1960; cf. Green 1980), perhaps because the working class itself wanted to believe in its own progress. Trying to leave behind their memories of hard times, many workers were led to believe that poverty is the choice of people who do not care to work.

Rubber workers, especially those working for the Big Four—Goodyear, Goodrich, Firestone, and General—were among the most highly paid industrial workers in the United States, ranking just below the auto workers and steelworkers. Seiberling workers were paid a starting wage of $7.85 an hour. The highest-paid workers were the tire builders, who could make up to $33,000 a year if they were willing to work frequent overtime. In 1979 the average annual income at the plant was $20,000.[1] Benefits were generous and the envy of the other workers in Barberton. Getting a job in a rubber shop was the lifelong goal for many, or the end of a long series of inferior jobs. Many of my informants made statements like the one made by Wes Little: "When we got in at Seiberling we thought we had it made."

The Seiberling workers were cushioned from the immediate effects of the regional depression. The United Rubber Workers had negotiated contracts which offered some protection from shutdowns through provisions for extended health-insurance benefits for two years, graduated severance pay based on the number of years worked, and supplemental benefits for older workers not yet eligible for Social Security. The Trade Readjustment Act increased benefit levels through unemployment insurance, provided relocation allotments, and made retraining available to many workers. Despite these advantages, Seiberling workers suffered substantial losses.

Nor has the small-business strategy proven highly successful for the working-class unemployed (Scase 1982). Periods of high unemployment see an increase in the number of small businesses and the number of small-business failures. Many of the Seiberling workers tried to start businesses in such fields as household remodeling, automotive repairs, industrial carpet cleaning, and lawn service. Some of these enterprises were mildly successful, but few became the sole source of support for a family. Small businesses were generally used to augment income from another job.

A new picture of the industrial working class is emerging. The closing of the Seiberling plant is part of a large-scale change that has lowered the standard of living of a large segment of the American population (Sawhill and Stone 1986). The 1980 recession caused a

[1]Interview with Joe Albanese, president, URW Local 18, 6 October 1982.

substantial loss of income for a considerable number of people. There was a 23 percent decline in the income of families experiencing unemployment in 1981. Moreover, 18 percent of those families fell below the poverty level (Terry 1982). For the long-term unemployed, income decreased even more drastically. In Summit County over 7,000 people exhausted unemployment benefits in 1983. Whereas past recessions usually involved temporary layoffs, the downturn beginning in 1980 was marked by shutdowns and the permanent loss of jobs (Bednarzik 1983).

The lowered standard of living is not due simply to the reduction in the number of jobs available. In addition to outright unemployment, there is a more subtle problem with the quality of existing jobs. Changes in the economy have led to a decline in the number of well-paid and secure unionized jobs and a growth in the number of low-paying, insecure jobs. The dichotomy in the kinds of jobs available has been termed the "dual labor market." Many workers who lost jobs in the 1980 recession fell into the second tier of the labor market, to which until recently only minorities and women had been relegated.

The victims of the Seiberling shutdown felt the full brunt of this change in the labor market, as is manifest in their reemployment pattern. Among those who did not receive early retirement, 20 percent found comparable employment, 40 percent found lower-paying, insecure jobs, and 40 percent were unemployed two years after the shutdown. "Comparable employment" was defined very broadly and included any job paying over $7.80 an hour, without consideration of benefits. For some individuals a "comparable" job paid $10,000 less annually.

Many of those in the second tier are now working for minimum wage ($3.35 an hour). The kinds of jobs most of the men and women from Seiberling found were inherently unstable: stockroom jobs in small businesses, home-improvement work, restaurant work. Very few of the workers were able to find unionized jobs. All found themselves at the bottom of the seniority list and thus most vulnerable to layoffs. The labor policy of most employers is still "last hired, first fired." The increased prevalence of involuntary part-time work is a part of this trend. The privileges and security gained through years of service in one company are lost, and workers speak of having to start all over.

It would be a mistake to think that all workers who are unemployed after two years have been continuously out of work. They might better

[15]

be described as skidding from one unstable job to another with bouts of unemployment in between (Ferman and Gordus 1979). Most of these unemployed men and women had worked at some time after the Seiberling closing. They lost jobs for the second and in some cases the third time, a few having gone through yet another shutdown. It would make better sense to consider the 40 percent low-wage earners and the 40 percent not working as one category, the underemployed.

Cutbacks, Losses, and Destitution

During the period following the Seiberling shutdown, families tried to maintain their standard of living by economizing, drawing on their savings, or going into debt in the hope of riding out the recession. However, the recovery never came to Barberton. When I asked Jeff Carey how his family managed the transition to his $4.35-an-hour wage, he answered, "What can you do? You cut back," a reply I encountered again and again. Becky Koegel answered in exasperation, "I keep thinking that we're going to be able to live like normal people again. But I don't know."

After Bob Younger lost his job at the Seiberling plant, he and his family began a long downward slide marked by a major decline in income and by unstable subsequent employment. Initially he and his wife attempted to maintain themselves by cutting unnecessary purchases, forgoing entertainment, and conserving on utilities. It was not until some weeks after his unemployment benefits ran out that Bob got a job with the Occupational Safety and Health Administration (OSHA) as a plant inspector. As chairman of the safety committee at URW Local 18 he had gained some experience in the field of safety. He went from $32,000 a year as a tire builder to $22,000 a year as an OSHA inspector. Bob was very pleased with the job, even though he was earning less and had to drive an hour to work in Cleveland. After nine months with OSHA, the agency eliminated his job. After several months of unemployment, he took a job with the State of Ohio on the Workmen's Compensation Board. He also enjoys the work there, though he has taken still another $10,000 cut in pay and now makes $12,000 a year. This sort of slide is typical of most former Seiberling workers.

Some are forced to live on savings and try to become self-sufficient.

For twenty years Herbert Lesler and his wife, Agnes, lived frugally on his low wages from Akron Porcelain before he got a job at Seiberling. They had been able to save a substantial sum of money during his six years as a rubber worker. "We never lived beyond our means," Agnes told me. A "substantial" sum of money was $10,000. Their savings had gone much more quickly than they had anticipated, however. They owned their home, but there were expenses they had little control over, such as utilities, which continued to climb. They drive their eight-year-old car as little as possible in order to preserve it and save money on gas. The only luxury they feel they can still afford is a telephone. Necessary repairs have been postponed; the kitchen furniture seemed permanently arranged around a bucket to collect water dripping through the unmended roof. Herbert was hoping to find someone to do roof work in exchange for some service he might provide.

They plant a garden each year and freeze most of their harvest to eat during the winter. "We are lucky to have all this land between her mother's and us. We grow a lot of different vegetables and corn. The grandkids wouldn't eat anything but that frozen corn, and we ran out early this year." Herbert had begun to cultivate their half-acre as a hobby. Grocery-store prices continued to rise, although not so rapidly as the year before. Eventually he felt compelled to calculate whether there had been a saving through his efforts. "We come out a little ahead so I still do it. Plus what we grow is so good." Indeed, all their expenses were calculated down to the penny, including the couple of dollars saved on recycling bottles, paper, and cans.

Eddie Wechenbacker told me he had been raised poor and wanted more than anything else to be able to support himself and his family. He had been proud of his income at Seiberling. Now, even with two incomes in the household, they were continually behind on their bills and Eddie worried that he had become poor again.

Eddie slowly began to run out of money as his string of temporary and part-time jobs grew longer. He made money doing daily manual labor where he could find it: mowing lawns, working for small contractors, and chopping wood. He remembers, "I was broke most of the time." Eddie became desperate when he could not pay his rent and in order to survive he had to move in with his girlfriend, Valerie, and her two children.

[17]

For three years Eddie was unable to find steady work. He eventually found a full-time job making $5.50 an hour in a warehouse. He hopes it will last. Valerie runs a small beauty salon, but business has been slow during the last two years. With the low wages Eddie makes at the warehouse and the little money from the business, they find they can afford only necessary food, utilities, and rent. "We just have to hold tight now. Don't go out or anything." Eddie, a handsome man, used to enjoy dressing well. He misses buying clothes and admits that he has not bought a new shirt or pair of pants since he was at Seiberling. Inability to afford gifts for his children from his first marriage was another disappointment. "It hurts not being able to buy your little girl a party dress or an ice cream cone." Valerie's two children, with whom he gets along very well, are similarly denied luxuries.

Eddie considers it a blessing that he has not had any major losses. Nothing has been repossessed and they have not been forced to sell anything. They cannot, however, afford two cars, although Eddie and Valerie both work and would find a second car useful. Replacement of the things that break and wear out is impossible. Their carpeting, furniture, appliances, and clothing are all slowly becoming dilapidated. He once enjoyed taking long car trips, but that sort of vacation can no longer be considered. Now vacations and entertainment have become very simple. "I bought the kids and my Val fishing rods and we all go fishing together. I like things we can all do together." Although he appreciates his simple pleasures, he makes it clear that they are still "holding out for better times."

Orville and May Baker are another couple suffering the humiliation of financial instability. Orville works as a hospital security guard making $5 an hour. He is a huge man with a smooth boyish face that burned with embarrassment as he recounted his family's adjustment to low income. Even with his wife's salary as a part-time bookkeeper at a restaurant, they make only half of what he had earned as a tire builder. May said, "It's so hard to say it, but we are *poor*." The Bakers can barely manage to feed and clothe their teenaged children, and every luxury has been forgone: the piano lessons for their talented son, vacations, hobbies, dining out.

The gap between their income and their needs cannot be bridged through household efficiency, clipping coupons, and canning vegetables. "To be completely honest, we just make it month to month. And I can squeeze a lot out of a penny!" Orville hunts and hikes in the nearby countryside. "You're gonna laugh. But see that berry pie? I picked the berries in the woods. Every little bit helps." Feeding the family is a continuing problem. "You want to see something? Look in the refrigerator. It's usually empty like it is now."

The Bakers dropped out of the food-stamp program. "I just couldn't take it any more," May told me. "The way they look at you at the checkout. And the comments people make in line. 'Look at all that meat!' I came home crying, and Orville said we'd just get along without them." Like many of the couples with whom I spoke, they depend on their parents to help them make ends meet. May's father works at a small butcher shop. "He brings over meat when he can and that really means a lot."

They remain lighthearted about their poverty. Orville had been in the middle of major renovations in the house when he lost his job at Seiberling. The project sat half-finished. Referring to the appearance of the unpainted drywall and unfinished basement bathroom, he told me, "We laugh about a lot of things. We have to!" May related a story to illustrate their good humor. "Joey needed a pair of tennis shoes for gym. He didn't have a lock for his locker, and we didn't want him to lose his shoes! We told him he'd have to wait a couple of weeks and carry the shoes home at night or we could buy the lock and wait for the shoes. I cried when I told him, but he thought it was funny, a lock or the shoes, and we both laughed. We're lucky to have such great kids."

"You came to the right place if you want to hear about cutting back. We've cut till there is nothing left *to* cut," Carole Small told me as she sliced the federal surplus cheese for her family's lunch. Carole and Ron were married a year before the shutdown and now have a three-year-old son. Ron is not working, having lost another job because of a slowdown at the small tool factory at which he had found work after the Seiberling closing. As in the other families, only the essentials are left. "I skimp on food but how much can you cut?" Carole decided to buy clothes for her son and herself at the Goodwill store when it became clear that they would be chronically short of money. Her husband was quick to point out, "There is no sin in that." Ron traded their new car for an older model. In their driveway is a small trailer-camper with a "For Sale" sign on it. "I could afford that sort of thing back then," Ron told me.

[19]

Ron grudgingly admits that they had been forced to borrow from his mother-in-law several times when money was short. Unemployment sapped their savings, and then some unexpected expenses, a high gas bill and an automobile repair, left them unable to pay all their bills. Ron insisted, "We're going to pay it back with the money we get from the income tax return."

The burden of debt and the real possibility of bankruptcy are major worries for some people. Many cars, refrigerators, and stereos were financed by installment debts and now represent a pressing obligation rather than a luxury. A small additional expense such as a doctor's bill, a visit from a relative, or an unexpectedly high utility bill can cause a financial crisis at the end of a month, making it impossible to keep up with bills they easily could have afforded as Seiberling workers. Often a working-class family becomes the victim rather than the beneficiary of its own former affluence.

The most common form of indebtedness among working-class people is the car loan (Sexton 1971). A car is a necessity for a job seeker; failure to keep up with car payments can lead to repossession. Becky Koegel lost her car, which she had bought several months before the announcement of the Seiberling closing. Economic hard times came quickly because she did not receive unemployment insurance. "I tried to keep up with the payments but in the end they took it away. It was such a pretty thing."

The purchase of household items can also put a family in a dangerous financial position. Matt Anderson's family is young, and with high expectations during his ten years as a factory worker, he had bought furniture, a stereo, a television, and a few other luxuries, many of them on installment. Soon after the Seiberling factory closed, Matt found work in construction, but it was irregular and his bills went unpaid. Finally the bailiff visited his house and summoned him to court to face his creditors' charges. The judges gave him a severe warning and allowed him to reschedule his loans. With some credit counseling he was able to continue to repay his creditors and avoid repossession and bankruptcy. In this way the Andersons were able to adjust to their lower, irregular income with some embarrassment but without losses. Matt continues to work irregularly and does not expect to reestablish his credit in the near future.

As their savings disappear and jobs remain scarce, the situation is becoming desperate for Jeff Carey and his wife, Lisa. When I first visited their home it was two weeks before Christmas, and Jeff was about to exhaust his unemployment benefits for the second time. Lisa was busy in a tiny kitchen that opened into their living room. Jeff left the television on during the entire interview, distracting himself from the questions I asked about their household economy. At one point a succulent ham on a splendid holiday table appeared on the screen. "I wish they wouldn't do that. Would you look at that ham," Jeff said. Christmas was poor that year, the food simple.

After he lost his job, Jeff sold his car and bought a "junker." He had managed to pay off some debts, but still it was difficult to pay the bills because so little money was coming in. He told me about the first time their utilities were cut off, and remorsefully recalled how he had once treated his sister when she was going through financial problems. He had laughed when her gas was turned off. He now wishes he had been more charitable. He himself has been utterly demoralized. The end of every month has become a nightmare as the bills fall due and the money runs short. "I just never know where the money's gonna come from. The cash just ain't there." Hounded by bill collectors, Jeff is at the end of his rope and expects the worst. With only his wit still intact, he said, "Chapter Thirteen, here I come."

A maze of legal restrictions surrounds the problem of debt in which some of the unemployed become ensnared. Federal law provides two major options for private citizens' debts, Chapters 7 and 13. The laws establish a citizen's right to bankruptcy and relief from debt. Chapter 7 provides for relief by canceling debt and preventing garnishment of future earnings, creating a bankrupt status. Alienable property is divided among creditors. Chapter 13 provides for the rescheduling of debt payments. The number of personal bankruptcies rises and falls with the business cycle and with the unemployment rate. Personal bankruptcy increased dramatically in Summit County between 1980 and 1984. While there are several explanations for the rise, it is clear that the prolonged recession was an important factor. Some reports suggest that legal reform has taken the sting out of bankruptcy, but according to my informants it remains a painful experience.

Jake and Regina Ryder found themselves in a difficult position after Jake lost his job at Seiberling. Several months before the closing was announced they had bought a house and Regina had had a baby boy.

Jake was twenty-five at the time and Regina twenty-three. They remained in their new house, paying the mortgage note with Jake's unemployment checks while he looked for work. The winter after the closing was very cold, and the cost of fuel oil rose dramatically. In the spring a bill for $900 arrived. Jake's face became grave as he recalled that winter. "It was rough. We were cold, the food stamps ran out every month, bill collectors kept calling. Man, do they make you feel rotten. That fuel bill was the end of it." They had no savings, everything having gone for the down payment on the house.

Jake saw no choice but to declare bankruptcy under Chapter 7. Lawyers' fees were $400, and there was a $90 court fee. The Ryders faced the proceedings matter-of-factly. The judge told them that they had been too young to buy a house and that time would teach them to manage their money better. They had come to think of themselves as poor money managers. "But what is life for, anyway?" Jake asked me. "We like to go out a little. Just for beers. I can't see living like some of those old guys at the shop who would pick up empty bottles to return them for some change. Working and only saving your money."

I had not anticipated the seeming nonchalance with which Jake and another Seiberling worker, George Bastic, talked about bankruptcy. Although I asked in a polite way, George detected my surprise and answered with defensive anger. "You think we used to be this way? I never heard of Chapter Seven before last year. What the hell am I supposed to say? How am I supposed to talk about it?"

Some people avoid the trauma of bankruptcy but meet with another degrading fate: public assistance. After long periods of unemployment, when benefits have been exhausted, many find themselves with no income and few assets. The process of impoverishment can be insidious. Some of the former Seiberling workers remember being quite surprised when they learned that they had run out of unemployment insurance and that the only sort of assistance they were eligible for was welfare. Liz Sutton commented, "I kept thinking there's got to be some kind of program that I'm eligible for. My friends who were still working kept asking me if I'd found anything, but there's nothing but welfare. I couldn't believe that I had to give so much up to get the damn thing, either."

Eligibility criteria for public assistance are complex and continually changing. Many find that they fail to meet all the specifications necessary to qualify. In the state of Ohio, during 1982, a welfare recipient could own a house as long as payments on it did not exceed $160 a month. The value of a car could not exceed $900, and the value of other assets, such as insurance policies, savings, or stock, could not exceed $1,200. Federal welfare under Aid to Dependent Children (ADC) covers families with children whose parents are unemployed and not eligible for other assistance, such as unemployment insurance. Those without young children are eligible for "general relief," welfare paid by the county. These criteria are stringent and the difficult process of application further limits the number of people who actually receive welfare benefits (Susser 1982:54).

A year after his benefits were exhausted, Earl Pedersen was still unable to find a steady job. His wife, Joyce, went to work in a fast-food restaurant for a short time. When she was laid off, the Pedersens applied for public assistance. They survived for one year on welfare until Earl found a job in one of the small plastics factories in Barberton, which he had only recently begun when I first met him in 1982. Joyce remembered, "We fought and fought about it. It was so terrible. But we didn't know what else we could do. So I went down with the babies and signed up."

Earl is a simple man who wants little more than a good factory job and a good family life. He reflected with some bitterness on his life. "My goal when I graduated from high school was to work at Seiberling. My friends all laughed at me. They had big ideas, but that's all they ended up doing was working in factories. But then I couldn't even get that. It was real bad. When I got this job, we called them downtown and told them to take us off the [welfare] list. It was the happiest day of my life. You ever been down there? It's a zoo." Joyce continued, "All we did was fight while we was getting it. But it kept us in the house and we ate. Otherwise I don't know what would've happened."

Health

Health insurance was one of the benefits to which rubber workers had come to assume they were entitled. Eighty-five percent of all private health insurance is purchased through employment-related groups (Monheit et al. 1983). Most workers in the second tier of the

[23]

labor market have no health insurance. For the unemployed and the underemployed, lack of health insurance is a major problem (Lee 1979). Lack of adequate health insurance is a prominent aspect of the decline in the standard of living described here. During 1982 there were an estimated twenty million people, workers and their dependents, in this country who had no form of health insurance whatsoever because of job loss (Congressional Budget Office 1984). Here again the Seiberling workers were more fortunate than most job losers. Their contracts provided extended health insurance coverage for two years after the shutdown (1979–81) regardless of circumstances. The union had won excellent health benefits, which included full coverage for prescriptions, dental work, and optometry. Few were able to maintain this sort of coverage after their policies lapsed.

The precarious situation of being without health insurance creates serious anxiety among the unemployed. Even minor illnesses and discomforts tend to lead to difficult debts. Major illnesses in some cases have led to overwhelming financial problems. Unemployed workers often choose to bear pain and live in fear of the consequences of untreated disease.

Seiberling workers predictably cited inadequate health insurance as one of the important changes in their lives since the shutdown. Tim Herron told me, "Firestone insurance was great. Once we visited relatives in Virginia and our little girl got a bad cut on her leg. We were real worried about going to the emergency room, what it would cost and if our insurance would cover it down there. They're real funny about things like that down there. Well, Firestone paid the whole thing. With the insurance I got now, you never know what they're gonna pay for." Katie Miller commented, "With the insurance we had, when you went to a doctor for something, when you said you worked for a rubber company they treated you real nice. I don't get the same feeling now when I have to go to the doctor."

When faced with low funds and no insurance, people adjust their prescribed treatment to accommodate their budget. While the question of noncompliance with doctors' orders is complex (Haynes, Taylor, and Sackett 1979), it cannot be doubted that inability to afford treatment is a major factor. James Stefancik was diagnosed as hypertensive a number of years ago and took medication for the condition. The medication was paid for with the "prescription card" provided by Firestone health insurance. After the extended coverage had been terminated, however, he had second thoughts about taking it. At that time he made the decision to take the medication "only when it bothers him," either unaware that hypertension usually has no symptoms or unwilling to believe it. On the $5-an-hour wage that he currently earns as a part-time custodian in a church, it is difficult for him to justify the expense of $55 a month for medication. "It doesn't bother me very much and I wonder about these companies, if they don't just want you to keep buying drugs. Can't you just eat the right things and take some kind of herbs?" James's ineffective self-treatment is unfortunately a common strategy among people unable to purchase adequate health care. Failure to control blood pressure explains the higher incidence of heart disease and stroke among this population.

Coping with pain is one of the consequences of loss of health insurance and low income. Wes Little has had no dental work done in the last two years. He has a broken tooth, which aches a good deal of the time, but he cannot afford to go to the dentist. He and his wife, Rita, have trouble keeping up with the doctor bills for their children, and he thinks of himself as coming last. With Rita's job as a registered nurse the family has hospitalization coverage through her insurance but no dental or prescription coverage. I asked Wes if he had considered having a lot of dental work done just before his insurance ran out. He looked at me with a hurt expression and said, "I didn't think of that. I guess I should have, huh?"

At the same time that a growing segment of the population is having to pay for medical care out of pocket, hospitals and doctors are tightening their billing policies in the face of declining revenues. The level of costs remains commensurate with insurance and other third-party payment, however, and has continued to rise. This economic climate has had inevitable consequences for the relations between doctors and their patients.

Doctors vary in their willingness to treat uninsured patients. Luba Szeleny was fifty-three years old when she lost her job. She had for many years been treated for recurrent kidney infections by a local physician. When her insurance lapsed, the physician suggested that she find another place of treatment where the expense would be covered. Luba felt betrayed. "All those years. He was happy to have me when I could pay." Fortunately for Luba, she was a veteran of the

Korean War and could be treated at a veterans' hospital. She drove to the nearest facility, an hour away.

Others have had more generous responses from their physicians. Sally Baines still takes her children to the same doctor. "He knows my husband isn't working and would pay if he was. I really appreciate it. We pay a little something every month or when we can."

When a medical bill remains unpaid, it may be turned over to a collection agency. Dealing with a collection agency can be a demoralizing and enraging experience. Richard Calvino received a telephone call from a medical collection agency while I was in his home. He answered the phone from the kitchen table where we sat, then abruptly stood up and walked with the phone in hand around the kitchen counter and spoke with his back toward me. When he finished the call he said to me, "Man, they must be hard up: seven dollars. That happened while I was still on the insurance, and I told them to bill Firestone. I'm not going to pay it."

John Franklin was highly resentful about an emergency room bill for a broken arm after an automobile accident. "I didn't use to complain about those outrageous doctor bills when we had that good insurance with the rubber company. I figured they went to school so long and all that. Now I just can't see it. What you have to shell out! We got a lot of bills to pay, so I told the guy I'm going to pay five dollars a month but that is all they are going to get."

Delinquent medical bills led to the following unhappy scene, which I witnessed. Jim and Cindy Bott's young son had ears that stood out conspicuously. The Botts had decided to have his ears fixed after the boy started first grade, even though their insurance did not cover the procedure. When the Seiberling plant closed, they had not yet finished paying the doctor's bill. When the remaining bill for $400 was turned over to a collection agency, Jim was frightened and angered by the aggressive approach of the agent and visited the doctor's office to protest. During the pathetic confrontation with the doctor's secretary, Jim raised his voice. When the doctor walked into the waiting room, Jim's voice began to tremble and a tear ran down his cheek. The doctor glanced over the chart and realized he had known Cindy for many years as a clerk at a local store. The doctor dropped the remaining bill.

People who have no health insurance are left with few alternatives. Independent policies are extremely expensive; at more than $200 a month, a family policy is unaffordable for anyone earning a low income. Jeff Carey and his family had had no health insurance for over a year, since he had lost his second job in 1983. "The Firestone insurance had run out and we looked into buying a policy when I was drawing my [unemployment-insurance] check, but there was no way we could afford that." Luckily, they had not had any medical expenses. The children had been well, and routine checkups had been eliminated. "We try and eat right, but that's getting harder. When the girls go out in the wintertime we're a lot more careful that they have a hat and scarf on." Jeff laughed, "You should see them when my wife gets done with them. They look like mummies."

Betty Liston works as a cocktail waitress and earns enough to live on but has no health insurance. The burden of medical bills has increased steadily since she was told that she had an ulcer. Staying healthy is her preoccupation; as she put it, "Well, I heard about stress. I suppose that could have something to do with my ulcer. My doctor tells me to worry less. Worrying won't pay the bills but not worrying doesn't pay them either."

Herbert Lesler has not had health insurance since the Firestone coverage was terminated. He described himself and his wife as "uninsurable." Their ages and past medical histories put them in a high-risk category for which insurance premiums are very costly. Herbert has been treated for hypertension for ten years and continues to see his private doctor when he can. "He has been real good to us and doesn't charge us every time. But the drugs really add up." Agnes Lesler told me, "I just don't go any more. Got all my work done before the insurance ran out." In the six months before their coverage expired, she had four surgical procedures done, including a gall bladder removal, a hysterectomy, biopsy of a benign breast tumor, and a colon-polyp biopsy. The Leslers felt fortunate that her condition had been diagnosed before the insurance lapsed.

A wave of austerity in many institutions (local charities, hospitals, government agencies) has come in the wake of hard times caused by economic stagnation. Assistance to uninsured patients with catastrophic medical expenses has become scarcer as hospitals are less and less able to shift costs to paying patients and community charities can no longer raise the necessary funds. Facing a major medical problem without health insurance can be disastrous.

[27]

Ellen Simpson was divorced from her husband, Artie, a year after he lost his job at Seiberling. When the extended medical coverage lapsed, she found herself and her two small children without insurance. Her former husband worked part-time in the stockroom of a large discount department store and could not afford insurance through the group plan for his dependents. During the three years following the closing, Ellen felt unwell, plagued by a host of vague symptoms: weakness, fatigue, brittle hair, constipation. She worried that she was depressed and that her hard work as a barmaid was causing her health problems. She lost her job and continued to experience these problems while she depleted her savings, unable to find work.

When milk began to flow from her breasts, Ellen became frightened and consulted a doctor, who informed her that she had a potentially life-threatening disease. The possibility of a pituitary tumor had to be ruled out, and $2500 worth of tests and X rays were undertaken. The final diagnosis was severe thyroid deficiency, which fortunately could be managed with inexpensive medications. However, Ellen had no way of paying her medical bills, which she believes will lead her to bankruptcy. She lives in fear that the $10 a month that she pays will not be enough and that the hospital will take away her house. Not to have gone on welfare before her illness episode now seems a great mistake. But she said, "In this town you just don't do that. We were raised that it was bad to ask for help."

Alan Kaiser had exhausted all of his benefits and was unable to find regular work. With a wife and two children to support, he began to do yard work to make money. The mother of a former Seiberling workmate hired him out of sympathy to cut her grass. In an accident with the lawn mower, Alan cut off his big tce. He begged the doctor not to admit him to the hospital, because he knew he had no way to pay the bill. The wound was closed in the emergency room, and the doctor waived the fee. However, surgical attention remained necessary, and Alan, an army veteran, went to a veterans' hospital for the follow-up surgery, thinking it would be free. It had been commonly thought in Barberton that the veterans' hospital could be relied upon as a last resort for medical services for veterans. However, services in the Veterans Administration hospitals have become increasingly difficult to obtain, with increasing restrictions on eligibility. Alan had been unaware of these changes, and was shocked to receive a bill for $2,000 for the surgery.

[28]

Desperate, Alan contacted a lawyer, who suggested that he sue the doctor who had done the outpatient surgery. Their case was weak and never came to court. Next they filed suit against the woman who owned the lawn mower; this suit never went to court, either. Alan, unemployed and facing this and other unpaid bills, saw no alternative but to file for bankruptcy.

Housing

Nothing is more closely associated with the image of working-class affluence than homeownership. During the post–World War II economic expansion, homeownership became possible for many factory workers and was encouraged by the Federal Housing Administration and by government policies that promoted business for small lending institutions and contractors. Today a broad segment of the American working class is finding it increasingly difficult to afford what many consider more a birthright than a dream. The prospect of homeownership has become increasingly illusory, rendered almost impossible by high interest rates, declining housing stock, and the risk of foreclosure (Applebaum, Dreier, and Harrington 1981). Others who have already been paying for homes now find themselves saddled with a financial burden they can no longer bear.

Many former rubber workers in Barberton had expected to buy homes, but those who have not found comparable employment can no longer hope to do so. The changes in the regional economy are reflected in the patterns of homeownership. In 1959, over 67 percent of the housing units in Barberton were owned by their occupants. By 1979 the proportion had fallen to 60 percent, and the decline has accelerated since 1980.

Unstable income among Barbertonians has led to difficulties in home buying. Realtors candidly told me that Barberton is becoming a low-rent district, attracting buyers interested in investing in rental property. The phrase "slum landlord," new to the vocabulary of Barberton, is increasingly heard as the housing stock ages and awareness of the problems of tenants in the city increases.

With the good jobs gone, many homeowners in Barberton have tried to sell their houses to get out from under the burden of a mortgage. Mark Burke put his house up for sale within days of the announcement

[29]

of the Seiberling closing and was able to sell it before he lost his job. "It was the only smart thing I've ever done in my life," he told me. However, because of the glut in the housing market, he was not able to retrieve any of his down payment or the equity he had accumulated from his five years of mortgage payments on the house. The sale price covered only the amount he still owed to the bank, the house's market value having dropped substantially.

After 1979, the housing market in Barberton was flooded. Some people hoped to sell and retire to the South; others wanted to find work in other parts of the country. In 1983, 10 percent of the houses in Barberton were for sale. On every street, on every block, a "For Sale" sign could be seen in one or two front yards. With interest rates high and many people working at low-paying jobs, even the heavily discounted homes could not be sold. The market value of the average house in Barberton dropped by $10,000 during this period.

Betty Liston thought that she could adjust to her lower income by selling her house and then renting a less expensive place. When she investigated, she learned that rents could be higher than her mortgage payments; she had lived in her house for seventeen years and paid only $120 a month on the mortgage, while her sister rented a small apartment with her two children for $200 a month. Betty's problem was how to repair the house, which needed a new roof and major electrical work and was over sixty years old. No such repairs seem possible on the wages she earns as a cocktail waitress. Betty spoke of her concern that her teenage son might never be able to afford a home. "Kids like him might never get a good enough job to afford a house."

The mortgage payment, often the major item in a household budget, cannot be trimmed in any way. Becky Koegel was overwhelmed by her mortgage payments after she lost her job at Seiberling. She had been unable to find work during the three years since the shutdown, and her husband, Hal, had lost his job when the Pittsburgh Plate Glass factory closed. The loss of their house now seemed inevitable.

When they both worked, Hal and Becky jointly earned $50,000 in 1979. They had moved from Barberton to a nearby suburb in 1977, a year after Becky had begun working at Seiberling. For many years before the move, she and Hal had considered moving into a larger and newer house in a suburb. Although they were both over fifty and were industrial workers, she had never earned enough in the plastics factory

Homes adjacent to the closed Seiberling plant

for them to be able to afford a new house. In 1976 Becky got in at Seiberling. With the higher wages she made, they were able to save enough for the down payment on a suburban ranch-style house in Canal Fulton, which they bought for $60,000. Becky told me, "It was a dream house for us. Our old place was kinda run down. We got it at a good price because it wasn't just done. We tried to finish it slowly." Three years later, the driveway remained unpaved, and there were still no shrubs in front of the house.

After the Seiberling shutdown, they hoped to keep the house by living on Hal's salary. Their loan agreement, however, was based on a floating interest rate, so that the monthly payment could change as interest rates changed. When the interest rates jumped from 10 percent to 15 percent in 1981, their house payments increased and Becky missed three payments. The bank demanded $5,000, wiping out their entire savings without reducing their principal. After some desperate efforts, Becky raised the money. The interest rate increased to 16 percent in 1982. Becky put the house up for sale but even at the price of $45,000, the remainder of the mortgage, they could not sell it. They fell behind on their payments again. "When I was working we'd have some extra money and sometimes I'd make a double payment. We figured that it would get us to the point of paying the thing off quicker. Well, now, those double payments don't mean nothin' to the bank. They want their money. I guess they're going to take the house, unless I figure some way out of this."

We spoke in the living room. It was sparsely furnished with a worn sofa, a couple of straight-backed chairs, and a table covered with bills, letters, a paperweight from the Knoxville World's Fair, and a small wire sculpture of a tightrope walker. The walls were unadorned. In the attached dining room was a sewing machine next to a basket of laundry, a set of barbells, and a small cart filled with green plants. Becky sat staring through the large picture window across from the sofa. Her gaze wandered to the large new houses being built on the road and the hilltops that rose above them. "We worked so hard for this. We were hoping to be able to leave something for our kids." Affluence had somehow eluded them.

The number of foreclosures has increased dramatically during the regional depression. A house can become a noose for a family that cannot replace the income they have lost. In Summit County the number of home foreclosures jumped by 70 percent between 1980 and 1981, 286 to 411 houses. Nationally, the 6.19 delinquency rate in the first quarter of 1985 was at an all-time high. Ohio's rate of 7.50 was 21 percent higher (Cleveland Council of Unemployed Workers 1986b). More than 20,000 households in Ohio were behind on their house payments in 1983, and the state led the nation in its foreclosure rate (Talbot 1983). When a debtor is unable to make payments on a home loan, the bank forecloses on the mortgage and the house is eventually sold at a sheriff's sale. This procedure differs from bankruptcy, and the specific laws governing foreclosure vary from state to state (Morris 1983).

When I first talked to George Bastic in 1983, he had two months left before his house was to be sold at a sheriff's sale. He and his girlfriend, Sue, had worked for a summer in Texas in order to save up enough to pay the mortgage; they were two months behind when they left, and the bank, which refused to accept partial payments of a late payment, demanded payment for both months at once. When George and Sue returned from Texas, they had more bad news. The bank had added a late-payment penalty, and the interest rate had gone from 7 percent to 12 percent because they were in arrears. The house payments jumped from $300 to $500 a month. The bank began foreclosure proceedings after they had missed the next three payments, the late fees and overdue payments having exhausted their summer earnings. George learned that he could live in the house without paying anything until it was sold by the sheriff, and so they stayed there, trying to save money for their move, living with the bitterness of their failure to save the house.

George had tried a number of tactics to avoid losing the house. Soon after the closing, he took in boarders, friends from Seiberling, to help pay the note. At one time there were six adults living in the house. He had made money in any way he could—painting, plumbing, clerking—to scrape together his payments. He was accustomed to exerting himself because he had worked at three jobs simultaneously for five years to save enough money for a down payment on the house. He had not wanted to wait many years before he could own a home and had taken advantage of anything that came his way during the better times before the Seiberling closing.

George had also sold most of the furniture a year before when they planned to move to Texas; the proceeds helped pay for the trip. When I visited the house it was almost empty. We sat on bar stools and looked over the long, empty living-dining room, which now held only a mattress and a stereo.

After the trip to Texas, George and Sue listed the house with several realtors, without success. The loan officer at the bank suggested that the realtors were dishonest, and the realtors claimed the same of the bank. George had become exasperated when he discovered that some houses on his street had sold before his, only later realizing that his house was priced too high. George did not expect a profit from the sale, but he wanted to sell at a price that would cover his remaining mortgage. Houses had dropped in price, but his debt had begun to increase as the unpaid interest was being added to the principal.

Now the forced auction of the house would take place, and George, Sue, and Sue's children would have to move. Sheriff's sales take place at the county courthouse, and the owners need not be present. Following the auction, the former owner must vacate the house within thirty days or be removed by force. George and Sue moved a week before the sale. George had rented a house in the country. "The kids will love it. It's way out on a farm, but needs a little work. No one has lived in it for a long time, and the guy is giving me cheap rent if I fix it up." George had arranged with several of his friends from Seiberling to borrow trucks and help him move.

It should be noted that none of the Seiberling workers I spoke with found themselves in a better economic situation after 1980. This is not to say that some were not happier. Alex Davison had found his seven years at Seiberling intolerable and was more relieved by the closing than threatened. He had hated the boring work, the harsh foremen, and the demands of shop-floor politics, but the steady income had kept him from trying something different. The shutdown was a chance for Alex to open a home remodeling business, and training and benefits under the Trade Readjustment Act gave him the basis for his venture. To work for himself, without humiliating supervision, had been a dream he had never really thought would materialize. The business could not sustain his former standard of living, however. A lower and less stable income and incomplete health coverage were the price Alex paid for his new freedom.

[3]

Not Hiring

To the casual reader of newspaper help-wanted ads it may seem strange that so many people remain jobless. The number of ads in the classified section of the Sunday paper seems to prove that there are enough jobs for all who want to work. The ads sound hopeful, even enticing: "HIGH INCOME potential is probably the reason you are looking for a change in career. Does your occupation allow you to earn what you are worth?"; "Looking for self-motivated career-minded person. For confidential interview send resume"; "SUCCESSFUL SALESMAN = $100,000" (*Akron Beacon Journal* 17 July 1983).

Why are so many people not working? The unemployed may not have the right job-seeking skills. Perhaps they cannot put together a convincing résumé. What about those drawing unemployment insurance? Are they sitting at home being paid not to work? Perhaps the unemployed are having trouble adjusting to the new, more technologically oriented economy. Or are they too inflexible, unwilling to relocate to regions that are booming, to go where the jobs are?

The actual experiences of the unemployed suggest a very different set of explanations. The labor market, government agencies, and the other institutions that job seekers encounter create a structure for the disappointment and distress associated with a plant closing in a period of high unemployment.

The Job Hunt

The unemployed waste a lot of time and effort learning how to read the want ads. John Damiani was unemployed for three years after the Seiberling plant closed. I first met him one year after the shutdown, and I asked about his use of the want ads. John is an experienced job hunter. He had a newspaper on hand and turned to the classified ads. He knew by then which ads were repeated week after week, and he could usually weed out the "fakes," as he called them. He spread out the newspaper on the couch between us. "Now listen to this one, it's hilarious." He read, "'IMMEDIATE EMPLOYMENT $400 a week. Your performance is more important than your promises or your past record.' That one is in every week. They want you to sell ladies' dresses door to door on straight commission, no benefits, no expenses—you pay for your own gas."

Even the experienced job seeker can get caught. John related a story about an ad in the Sunday paper that had excited him. On Monday morning he had put on his suit and driven to a large suburban hotel where an interview was to be held in a reserved suite. The ad had offered one job in low-level management at $8.60 an hour, no experience necessary. When he arrived the parking lot was jammed and people were leaving. The manager of the hotel was telling a crowd around the pool that the interview had been canceled because the hotel had refused to let the room be used for interviews. More than a hundred people had responded to the ad. Stories of this kind were common among former Seiberling employees. Only the long lines of applicants were reported in newspaper articles.

Jerry Staruch remembers being hopeful about an opening for a trailer-rental attendant. The ad asked for someone to put on hitches and write up tickets. When he arrived for an interview, the lot was full of men and women, some with their children. First a man came out and told them that anyone with a record of drunk driving should go, and about twenty people left. The remaining applicants filled out a simple form and waited again. Jerry remembers that it was a cold morning, and he had tried to decide just how long he would wait. Finally the man announced that the company wanted people who had experience running their own business.

"Why didn't they advertise it that way, then? I wasted my whole morning and the gas to get out there. A couple of the guys went in and the rest of us just went home. I felt sorry to see those guys that showed up with babies in their arms." It did not occur to Jerry that the new qualification might have been a last-minute attempt to upgrade the job description in order to reduce the number of applicants the company would have to deal with.

Job seekers are also victims of scams. Danny Lawson, my landlord while I lived in Barberton, asked me to refuse a COD package he expected one morning. Unemployed, Danny had answered a newspaper ad and ordered what he thought was a catalogue of job openings. The catalogue cost $26. Before it arrived, he learned that it contained nothing more than out-of-date want ads photocopied from various newspapers. A friend from the all-night diner where Danny spent his long evenings had discovered the truth the hard way and warned Danny.

Newspaper want ads are not the favored source of job leads. Most people I interviewed preferred to turn to their network of friends and relatives. Working people know about their employers' job openings, and friends or relatives can often help the job seeker "get in at" the place where they themselves work. In this way several generations of a family come to work in a particular plant. A personal recommendation from an employee with a good work record is considered valuable; people refer to this sort of support as "standing up for you at work." Bonds established in this way can last for many years. Such people often become what anthropologists call "fictive kin."

David Winchell stopped in to visit and offer a few words of encouragement while I was interviewing Herbert Lesler. Dave and Herbert have known each other for many years, and Dave often drops in for a cup of coffee. Dave helped Herbert get his job at Seiberling; it was the best job Herbert had ever had, and he is still grateful. Over the past ten years their families have become close; their children played together and are still friends as adults. Now David was trying to help again because Herbert had been unemployed for three years. Such personal contacts figure importantly in the way people look for work. Many of those affected by the shutdown now believe that "knowing someone" is the only way to find a job.

Yet seeking a job through one's contacts has led to many frustrations and some unhappy results. Glenn Meden's friend from church was trying to help Glenn get a job at the trucking firm where he worked; the work was dock loading and the wages were high. Every time Glenn saw the friend, the friend told him that there would be an opening very soon. After several months Glenn stopped calling, and the man avoided him. He never asked the man what had happened, but supposed the job had gone to a friend of a foreman. "Everybody's got a friend that needs a job these days."

Jeff Carey hoped that his network would help him find a job. Jeff was desperate—aged forty-five, married, with three children and no job. He had worked for fifteen years in the rubber plant and was a Vietnam combat veteran. This record seemed to matter little to the employers he had approached. Jeff's neighbor managed the gas station at the end of the block and had promised Jeff that he would hire him to replace the young girl who was working at the gas station whenever the job became open. The job involved collecting money from the self-serve customers and paid minimum wage. He stopped talking to the man when a new teenage girl started working at the station. "I won't buy gas there anymore. And you know what I think? I think there's something going on there with those young girls." Jeff is bitter toward his old friend now and is willing to suspect the worst of him.

Another option in the search for employment is registration with the job placement service of the Ohio Bureau of Employment Services. The unemployed must register there in any case in order to receive unemployment-insurance benefits. Some people refer to the office by its initials, "OBES," but it is most commonly called the "unemployment office." The irony is often intentional, the bureau having a very poor placement record.

The local OBES office placed an average of four applicants a week during 1982, when more than 6,000 people were registered every week. Job placement counselors at OBES admit that because few jobs were available, there was little they could do. During the winter of 1982, the State of Ohio reduced the placement service's staff, and the announcement of the cut led to angry public response.[1] In view of the success rate of the agency, however, the decision seemed the most rational allocation of resources.

[1] Interview with Paul Zaleha, director, Norton office, Ohio Bureau of Employment Services, 16 September 1982.

The workings of OBES are a mystery to those who use the service, and there is widespread suspicion that it does not operate fairly. Many believe that OBES employees give jobs to their friends. The bureau has specific criteria for assigning people to jobs that come through the office. If more than one person is qualified for a job, the bureau follows a priority system: disabled veterans, Vietnam veterans, veterans, and veteran families are given priority (Ohio Revised Code 1982). Knowledge of these criteria does little to convince the unemployed that nepotism and corruption are not rampant in the state bureaucracy.

Cynicism and disappointment with the placement service developed from its failure to make placements. Keith Hagen spoke wryly about his experiences at the office. A large chalkboard stands at one side of the OBES office. Job openings posted on it can be seen from the waiting lines. One day the board advertised an opening for a biochemist. The fellow next to Keith laughed. "Yeah, I looked into that one but I turned it down. I'm looking for outside work."

Job seekers rarely use private employment agencies (Sheppard and Belitsky 1966). One man responded when I asked him if he had ever used a private employment agency, "Do I look like a rich man?" Agencies are widely regarded as expensive and ineffective. Some job seekers report bad personal experiences, others have heard discouraging stories. Greg Mitchell refused to pay a $900 finder's fee for a job located for him by an agency. The job was that of assistant manager for a large chain of family-style restaurants. The fee seemed outrageously high to Greg, and he did not have the money to pay it: monthly payments were not acceptable, and the employer was not responsible for the fee. Looking at Greg sitting in front of the TV in his T-shirt and baseball cap, no one could mistake him for anything other than a factory worker. He had done many dirty industrial jobs and endured hard work and it is unlikely that he would have taken to managing a restaurant. His experiences with other agencies were equally frustrating.

Hopes and aspirations are blighted as the job hunt turns into a long series of rejections. It becomes a harsh routine to be lived out in a climate of disturbing uncertainty. Employers usually make no attempt to contact an applicant after they receive a résumé unless they are actually hiring him or her. Applicants do not receive telephone calls to tell them that the job has been filled or polite letters explaining that a better-qualified applicant has been found. Job seekers call to follow up

[39]

on applications only to learn that the opening was filled weeks before. After many such disappointments the unemployed let time pass, assuming the job has been filled.

To deal with the disappointment of rejection, some job seekers blame the stupidity of the prospective employer. Some rationalize that they had no serious interest in the job. One longtime rubber worker said, "I'm not looking for factory work now. There's no future in that." The unemployed move from disappointment to apathy. Over time, being turned down for a job begins to disturb them less and less, and after many rejections some even come to expect it.

Bob Younger told me that he was hurt when the rejections first began. "I took it kind of personal, you know. I remember one place they liked me, I thought. We had those hot-shit résumés. I got on real good with the guy doing the interview. I couldn't believe I didn't get the job. I was real down for a while." As he experienced more and more rejections, his reactions changed. "I finally got to the point I didn't give a damn what they did."

Inevitably some people become discouraged. The prospect of finding a job seems so remote that even the money spent on gas and the effort of preparing yet another résumé seems wasted. Such people have in effect dropped out of the work force; they want work but have stopped looking because they do not believe it is available to them. The Bureau of Labor Statistics counts these people as "discouraged workers" in the same monthly survey that is used to compute the monthly unemployment rate (Bednarzik et al. 1981). Their numbers are not added to the monthly unemployment figures but appear in a separate index. In the summer of 1982 there were an estimated 1.5 million discouraged workers nationally. It is well documented that the number of discouraged workers rises with the jobless rate (Levitan and Johnson 1982).

I spoke with many people in Barberton who might be considered discouraged. John Damiani is one. At the time of our first meeting he was actively seeking employment, receiving benefits, and full of information on job hunting. A year later when I asked about his search for work he bluntly said: "Apathetic; no longer seeking employment," as if he were responding to a sociological survey. He thinks placement and retraining programs were worthless to him and suspects the State of Ohio of wrongdoing. He believes that the programs are designed to

Still unemployed

"shake people off," to discourage them from asking for help. John was suing OBES for allegedly misassigning available jobs. He claimed to know about friends who qualified for minority and veteran status but had been passed over in favor of boys just out of high school. "This guy, Tony Laguardia from the big office, called me and tried to talk me out of the lawsuit. He called me 'paisan.' What the hell is that supposed to mean? He said he would help me."

John thinks that he has been branded as a troublemaker. I talked to him some time later and asked about the pending case. He had become discouraged and had dropped it. "I'm not pursuing it at this time." His suspicions were even worse than before. He believed that OBES employees were cutting a deal with the trade schools or getting jobs for their friends. "Someone is getting paid off."

Three years after the Seiberling shutdown, John had little to say about looking for jobs. "What employer is going to look at you after three years? What are they going to think?" He spoke with the detached amusement of despair and proceeded to tell me of his idea for a TV situation comedy about unemployment, in which he would like to star. John had not worked for three years except for an occasional odd job. All of his benefits had run out the year before. After asking a long series of questions, I still had no idea where he was getting money to live on. His wife did not work, although she was still looking. I finally put the question to him directly. He answered dryly, "I have devised ways of providing for my wife and children." It was obvious that he was conducting some kind of illegal business, and indeed his friends who suspected as much told me so in confidence. Throughout that afternoon people kept coming and going through the kitchen door. He went into the kitchen to speak with them. When someone left, he would return to the living room and say, "Now we can speak more freely." I pressed him to tell me the nature of the business, but he refused.

He commented about the young men who had been in the kitchen. "I feel worst about those kids. That one has a real gift for fixing cars. He will do anything for you. I do my best to help them. But you know what happens if they can't find work. They end up on dope." John told me that unemployment has made him a better person. "At least I have compassion for other people."

Herbert Lesler said, "I've pretty much given up looking. I hope it gets better soon." When the Seiberling plant shut down, Herbert had been working there for six years and was fifty-one years old. His first job had been with Akron Porcelain, where he had worked for twenty years. He had never made more than $4 an hour in all those years, so when his brother-in-law got him in at Akron Towel, he took the job to "better himself." Akron Towel went out of business; his brother-in-law found a job in Arizona. Two weeks later Herbert was hired at Seiberling. "I never even applied for unemployment then. And two weeks later I got another offer from Allied, but you couldn't get a better job than the rubber shops at the time." Jobs were plentiful in Barberton during the sixties. Herbert's highest wage from Firestone was $7.90, and the Leslers had saved up a great deal of money.

Now, a year after his benefits have been exhausted, they continue to live on their savings. His wife said, "He finds odd jobs and picks up a couple of dollars but mostly we try to conserve." He intends to try again to look for work when "things look better," but now it does not seem worth the money it takes for gas. The Leslers canceled their subscription to the newspaper in order to economize, but he borrows the Sunday edition from neighbors to scan the want ads. "I don't see anything out there for me."

Women, blacks, older workers, and the handicapped, as demographic groups, undergo higher levels of unemployment than other segments of the population and figure disproportionately among the discouraged (Parnes 1982, Bednarzik 1983). For them the job hunt is most difficult. An unemployed person may or may not have a sense of these sociological facts. Individuals' awareness of the facts and their willingness to understand that their own circumstances result from discrimination vary. In general it seems that people are hesitant to suggest that they have been subjected to discrimination.

The common view among industrial workers is that reverse discrimination exists—that white males are discriminated against. During interviews, I found that the people most likely to experience discrimination (blacks, women, older workers) did not spontaneously mention the issue. They do, however, have their suspicions. When I probed more deeply about their job-hunting experiences, they would reveal to me the special problems they perceived.

Herbert Lesler is reluctant to claim that he has himself experienced discrimination. It did occur to him that his age—he is fifty-four—was a possible reason for his continual failures to find work. He applied for a

[43]

job opening at Akron Porcelain, hoping that his twenty years of faithful service to that company would help him get in again. They filled the spot with a boy just out of high school. He was angered because he, a proven good worker, was not hired. "Then I thought I had a job at B and C [a local machine shop]. The foreman liked me. He said that he liked the older workers; the young guys in there, they like to blow off steam. They get drunk and miss days." His wife interjected, "But that guy doesn't do the hiring. All they hire there is young kids."

Herbert is aware of the laws prohibiting age discrimination. "I know they can't ask you your age on an application but they always ask what year you graduated from high school. Why do they have to ask you that? Well, how hard is it to subtract eighteen?" Raising his voice ever so slightly, he added, "But how can you prove that kind of thing?" Herbert thought that the additional health cost incurred by older workers was at least one of the factors that led to age discrimination.

Maureen Manning is a beautiful woman with stylishly cut hair. Looking at her seated on the sofa with a cup of tea in her hand, I found it hard to believe that she was disabled. Maureen had been an active woman; she loved to water-ski and had worked as a model while in high school. Work at Seiberling had been a challenge both physically and mentally.

In the months following the closing, while working as a waitress and going to school, she began to notice numbness and weakness in her legs. Her doctors found extensive deterioration of her spine, and six months later she underwent major surgery for fusion of her vertebrae, which has left her with a major disability. "I just couldn't get used to the idea of being a cripple. I can't teach my daughter to ride a bike. I can't even pick her up in my arms."

Her first appeal for Social Security disability payments was turned down, and now she lives with her daughter on a $216-a-month welfare check and food stamps. The court acknowledged that she could not do factory work again, but said that she could do modeling. Maureen laughed. "Have any of those judges ever made a turn at the end of a runway, or been in one of those dressing rooms? I was doing a little modeling before the operation, if you can call it that. I handed out cheese samples in a supermarket. They called me in once a month. That's as close to modeling as I'll ever come again." Her lawyer was appealing the case, and the people at the welfare office encourage her.

[44]

"They tell me, 'Don't give up, you're too intelligent and strong.' They know I could be productive. I know it too. But who is going to hire me? Who wants to be saddled with that kind of medical bill? Tell me who is going to hire a woman with a bad back?"

Maureen remembered a fellow worker at Seiberling who was crippled, stooped 90 degrees at the waist. He had been a great inspiration to everyone in the plant. Maureen said, "He loved that shop, never missed a day of work. I heard that he died the other day. Probably the shutdown killed him." Maureen had seen that during boom times even a handicapped person could find useful work. She had been unsuccessful in finding work after her operation, the disability limiting the kinds of work she could do. She found, as do many of the handicapped, that fewer jobs opportunities in the labor market make an already difficult situation worse (Levitan and Taggart 1977). Still Maureen believes that the constraints on her activity are imposed by others, not by her condition.

With increased competition for jobs, blacks have lost many of the gains they had made in recent years (Harrington 1984b). Don Walker, who is black, told me, "I'm not a racist. I don't say people are discriminating against me all the time. But sometimes things happen that make you think." His father had worked as a film projectionist for the Akron Public Library for many years, and Don knew something about running a projector. When he found himself without a job, he applied for work as a projectionist. At the time that he applied, there were only two blacks in the Projectionists' Union. He was allowed to join and received training, but the union, which also makes work assignments, had not placed him. "The theaters say they like my work but I never get called. After two years I'm still subbing. I haven't got a regular job, and the jobs they give me are all the low-paying places and the ones far out of town." The union, he told me, consists primarily of members of a small group of families. He suspects that the good jobs go to family members and that he has been passed over for a full-time job. Don spends most of his days and nights waiting for calls to do work as a substitute. He offered me a scotch as he poured his second in an hour. "Drinking has become kind of a problem since I'm home so much. I always liked to party, but I never sat around and drank. Now I'm tense and at home all the time, just waiting."

The difficulties of women in the labor market have been well documented (Gordon, Edwards, and Reich 1984), as have their problems with finding work after job loss (Parnes 1982). Lillie Dickerson had had her share of difficulties finding work. She had applied for a job at Seiberling on a dare. Her friends had bet her she couldn't do it. In 1975 Firestone dropped the work rule barring women from jobs that required workers to lift more than twenty-five pounds. The older women in the shop worked primarily in the bead room, which entailed light work and low pay. Lillie took it up for the challenge but also because she knew that she would make a better wage than she was making at the supermarket. She was one of the "new breed" in the shop. Lillie and the other women hired after 1975 saw the new opportunity as their part in the struggle for women's rights, fought out on the shop floor.

Lillie considered herself luckier than some. She found a job in the same supermarket chain after the closing, but she was making even less than she had before she left because of wage cuts in the supermarket industry. Her return to the service sector represents a loss of advances made by some women in the labor market.

Discrimination, discouragement, and frustration are the realities of the job hunt. It is no surprise that people rely on the approaches that have been successful in the past. The mastery of new skills, such as preparation of a résumé, seem to have had small effect on success in the job market. Analysis of the job search itself explains little about the causes of unemployment.

Unemployment Insurance

When people lose their jobs through no fault of their own, their former employers' unemployment insurance, administered by the states, furnishes income for a designated period of time. Since its inception in 1936 there has been much official and public concern that unemployment insurance might discourage the unemployed from looking for work (Adams 1971). In Ohio the benefit level is approximately 50 percent of the former weekly income and ranks among the most generous in the United States (Murray 1974). The experience of the former rubber workers in Barberton with the unemployment-insurance system reveals much about the effects of that system and its meaning for people.

Plant shutdowns entitle former workers to unemployment benefits. In the weeks after an unemployed person registers at one of the offices of the Ohio Bureau of Employment Services, his or her eligibility is determined and benefit payments are mailed out if the worker qualifies under the following guidelines: he or she must have worked for a specified period of time (usually twenty-six weeks during the preceding twelve months), must be able to work, and must be unemployed through no fault of his or her own. People who receive benefits must produce a list of the places where they have sought employment each week.

After an initial determination of eligibility is made, the worker must apply each week in order to continue to receive weekly benefits. For many people the process is degrading. Wes Little had been laid off once before in his life, for two weeks during the 1975 recession. "I just couldn't stand the thought of going down there then. It made me feel cheap. I didn't even bother signing up." To my knowledge, none of the Seiberling workers failed to register for benefits following the shutdown.

There are two registry offices in Summit County, one in downtown Akron and the other in Norton. The Norton office is in a shopping center near Barberton and is popular with many residents of the area because it has ample free parking and is closer than the Akron office. Most of the former Seiberling workers registered for unemployment benefits in Norton. The office is large and plain, a model of bureaucratic efficiency. The manager of the office hoped to avoid unpleasant lines by scheduling appointments. The office is run efficiently but lines form nevertheless.

Waiting in line at the employment office is a common necessity for the unemployed, and most of them regard it stoically. In the lines they see friends and others they know from work. The wait appears casual except when the lines are long. Occasionally some become impatient and irritable, and the monotony of the routine is punctuated by infuriated applicants venting their rage on a hapless clerk.

During periods of high unemployment, the federal government extends the number of weeks during which benefits may be paid. The trigger mechanism, a formula based on the monthly unemployment index, prompts the federal government to pay an additional six or ten weeks beyond the fifty-two paid by the State of Ohio (Murray 1974,

[47]

Padilla 1981). Filing for this benefit is a separate process; the line for the federal extensions flows into an entirely different room at the Norton office. The mood of this line is tense because the applicants have come to the end of their unemployment benefits and still have not been able to find work.

Because it was determined that the Seiberling jobs were lost because of importation of foreign automobile tires, the former workers qualified for benefits under the Trade Readjustment Act of 1975 (TRA). This act provided for an increased level of benefits and automatic extension of the benefit period beyond that furnished by the state. It gave the Seiberling workers an extra six months of income and raised their benefit payments from 50 percent to 70 percent of their former weekly income. It also provided for some retraining and relocation.

People talk about "riding it out" or "riding it to the end." One bitter woman said, "I drew out every penny—they owed it to me." This kind of sentiment was common. It might be easy to conclude that such recipients do not want to work and are abusing the provision. The argument stems from the old notion that unemployment benefits act as a disincentive to work. Though this assumption seems superficially plausible, the weight of the evidence suggests that the system does not increase unemployment levels (Pierson 1980, Munts and Garfinkel 1979). Aggressive job seeking when jobs are not available can hardly decrease the jobless rate; this fact makes the principle of incentive a moot point. The effects of the umemployment-insurance system on job seeking behavior are more complex than they appear on the surface.

If we put aside for a moment what some workers say about unemployment insurance and look at what they actually do while they are unemployed, a different picture emerges. The work histories of the Seiberling workers demonstrate that these people were eager to earn a wage, and they responded positively to any opportunity to work. Barberton has until recent times offered ample opportunities for workers. Those who had been laid off from a good job typically waited a couple of months to see if they would be called back to their favored place of employment, then took a job elsewhere. It was common to hear of a worker having had a series of jobs before he "got in at Seiberling," the final goal of those trying to better themselves. Many of the Seiberling workers had experienced brief periods of unemployment and even other shutdowns, but all had found work shortly afterward. There is little in their histories to suggest that they had ever been discouraged from looking for work by the unemployment-insurance system.

The work history of Bill Lexan, a third-generation rubber worker, is typical. His father and grandfather had worked at Firestone, and each had retired after more than thirty years of service. When Bill graduated from high school, an older friend got him a job at Barefoot Sole, a local factory. He worked there for two years, until he was laid off, and a week later was hired at Ohio Brass. Bill had an aunt in the bead room at the Seiberling plant who was "looking for him," waiting for a job to become available. When production at Ohio Brass slowed down in 1965, he was laid off, and a month later a man retired from Seiberling. With a recommendation from his aunt, Bill "got in at Seiberling." He was married soon after he obtained this good factory job; this is a common pattern among young blue-collar workers.

After 1979, the situation in Barberton was quite different. Even jobs in small shops offering low wages became difficult to find. Some of the former Seiberling workers who had special skills or a little good luck found jobs in the few remaining rubber factories in Akron, but most early job searches proved discouraging. The unemployment figure for Ohio at the time was 10.2 percent; Seiberling was only one in a wave of shutdowns in the Akron area. Some workers spent a lot of time looking for jobs immediately after the Seiberling shutdown, while others chose to wait and see what would happen. Their experience with past recessions made them believe that the present one would pass and the jobs would reappear. A few even imagined that the plant would reopen.

Tom Simeko made little initial effort to look for work. The woman with whom he lived, Maureen Manning, who had been refused both Social Security payments for her disability and unemployment-insurance benefits, was less complacent. She was not so caught up in the popular illusion of a short recession and pleaded with Tom to go out and look for work. Instead, he and some of his friends went out bird hunting for three to four days at a time for four months and spent only a few days looking for work. They were required to apply for two jobs a week to keep the unemployment check coming. Tom did that much, but suspected his friends of just writing down the names of places and not really going to look. Tom even reported the couple of dollars that he had made doing yard work, which were then deducted from his check. Time passed and nothing opened up.

[49]

Tom has not worked in three years and has not received benefits for over a year and a half. As our interview turned to casual conversation, Tom talked about his hunting. When he went into the kitchen to make some sandwiches for lunch, Maureen told me, "I'm not going to cook that stuff. He really thinks I'm going to eat squirrel." Tom seemed to harbor a fantasy about being able to live off the land. He told me in an ironic tone, "Well, I didn't have to file income tax this year." Denial of this sort protects his pride.

Maureen nagged Tom about looking for work as they shared their grilled cheese sandwiches with me. Tom had an application in at Goodyear Aerospace and was certain that he would get the job. Maureen was not so sure. He had been told that it could be eight weeks before he heard from them; seven weeks had already gone by. We talked about the job situation as Tom glanced through the want ads in the newspaper. He said, "If the damn interest rates would just come down, people would go out and buy, and things would open up again." Maureen retorted, "You know anyone with money to go out and buy?"

Two weeks later I visited Tom and Maureen again. Goodyear Aerospace had not called, and Tom was on his way out the door to apply for a job at Monarch Rubber. "I want to just send him back to his mother," Maureen complained. That night I read on the front page of the *Akron Beacon Journal* that 1,200 people had applied for 75 jobs at Monarch.

Wes Little had had two jobs since the closing. "With those two kids I just couldn't be thinking about passing up a job even though the pay was lousy." After looking for work for three months, he was hired to work in the stockroom of a paint store; the job lasted only one month. In Ohio, benefits can be drawn at any time during the benefit year, a calendar year following job loss. Wes had not worked long enough at the paint store to qualify for benefits, but he was able to draw the remaining income from the benefit year that had begun when he lost his job at Seiberling. Because of the flexible nature of the program in Ohio, the worker can take a chance on a job that might not work out and not have to fear the loss of his benefits. Wes drew unemployment insurance for the next five months until he got a job with a garbage-recycling plant.

Unemployment insurance gives the recipients a great deal of power over their own lives. The choices that it offers are significant; the unemployed have the option of waiting to be called back to a desirable job, waiting to find a comparable or better job instead of taking inferior work out of immediate necessity, or simply taking the time to sort out personal matters and attend to their health needs or family for a while. It is important to remember that this measure of power was a political victory for the labor movement in this country (Piven and Cloward 1977).

Unemployment insurance embodies the social philosophy that has informed much of the legislation of the last half-century. The program is designed to sustain workers at a financial level not too much lower than the one to which they became accustomed while they were working. Income should be high enough to pay for basic needs but low enough to encourage the worker to look for a job. This humane policy reflects basic realities we have come to accept about our society. The economy is constantly changing and forcing individuals into difficult situations through no fault of their own. Intrinsic to many pieces of legislation, union constitutions, and social policy is the notion that it is the responsibility of government to protect the individual from the cruelest aspects of what is generally considered to be a successful economic system, industrial capitalism.

These are noble social principles. The reality falls short of the ideal, however. Not all of the unemployed receive unemployment benefits. Many exhaust their benefits before finding a job. First-time job seekers (recent high school and college graduates) unable to find work are not entitled to benefits. Nor are workers who grow discontented at work and quit or who are fired in Ohio.

When demands for benefits are great, states tend to create restrictions on unemployment-insurance payments (Runner 1982). The State of Ohio tightened eligibility requirements in 1982. Full-time workers were required to have worked twenty-six weeks rather than twenty weeks, as previously. Part-time workers must have earned at least $90 a week rather than the $20 that was required before. The first week of benefit payments was eliminated, and striking workers no longer had the right to draw unemployment insurance (Padilla 1981).

It is the duty of the state to distribute tax money in a judicious fashion. Unemployment insurance is funded by direct taxation of the employer and thus acts as a disincentive to arbitrary layoffs. Consequently it is under constant attack by the powerful lobby of the National Association of Manufacturers.

[51]

Maureen Manning saw the state draw the line. When the plant closed, she was disqualified for unemployment insurance because the state claimed that she had not worked long enough before the shutdown. When the shutdown was first announced, she was on sick leave, pregnant, and two weeks after the closing she gave birth. Her doctor had ordered her off the job when it was learned she was pregnant. Maureen had lost her first baby, and her doctor suspected that the miscarriage was due to exposure to benzene in the shop. The union had wanted her to pursue the exposure case, but she refused because she feared she would lose her job. Although she had worked at Seiberling for a total of six years, she could not receive benefits because she had not worked the required number of weeks immediately before she was laid off. After two years of litigation, she was awarded $4,900 by the state in back benefits, a quarter of which went for legal fees.

Becky Koegel was not so fortunate. She received no benefits except a severance pay of $1,200 and the extended health insurance from Firestone. She too had been "out on a medical," as the result of a serious auto accident. She had asked her doctor to let her return to work so she could accumulate her required number of weeks, but he said it was impossible. Becky was finally allowed to return to work two weeks before the shutdown. The state calculated that she was short by one week of the twenty consecutive workweeks required to qualify for benefits. She begged Firestone to let her work one more week. Firestone and the union both assured her that the state would concede, but when she filed for unemployment insurance she was disqualified. After letters to her congressman and some pleas from the union, it became clear that nothing more could be done.

Three years later she remained bitter. "God damn, I shouldn't even talk about it, I get so mad. I resent it because I paid my taxes and plenty. We paid thirty percent of what we were making. I paid since I was thirteen years old and drew out of it one month in my life. I used to be proud to be able to pay that tax. Not now. The first time I ever needed it and I got nothing."

Among workers it is a commonsensical assumption that unemployment insurance is a disincentive to looking for work. Dennis Harper, who had been a tire builder for fifteen years, put it this way: "Hell, we were making good money with TRA and everything. So why work?" This statement cannot be taken at face value. The behavior of this man and many other former Seiberling workers prove them to be aggressive job seekers and reliable workers. Further probing into these sentiments yields a more complicated understanding of what people mean by statements that seem to reflect disincentive. On further questioning, Dennis admitted that after a month of playing golf and watching TV, he did begin to look for work; idleness had not agreed with him. He soon learned that good jobs were hard to come by.

The unemployed may make this sort of statement for a variety of reasons. One's work is a matter of pride, and confessing to abuse of the system conceals an even greater disgrace—that of being unable to find a job. Shame is thereby deflected, and the system is made to look foolish, not oneself. A few of the people whom I spoke with clearly felt that they had the right to be able to sort out their lives and find a job that could permit them to maintain their previous standard of living. That was their interpretation of the intention of the laws that provide for the unemployed.

Careful examination of statements by former workers about disincentives suggests more complicated interpretations. Many of those bits of conversation have led me to believe that such statements disguise a deeper, more troubled understanding of unemployment. Workers have ambivalent feelings about unemployment insurance. While most feel entitled to it, there is guilt associated with the closing of the plant and subsequent unemployment.

The right to unemployment insurance is not questioned by the working classes. The responsibility of the state to provide for basic human needs is accepted in principle by most workers, although many apply this understanding exclusively to their own personal circumstances. When I systematically asked unemployed workers in Barberton how they felt about receiving unemployment insurance, the overwhelming majority agreed that "it was something they had a right to." Large-scale attitudinal research confirms this observation (Schlozman and Verba 1979:47). Frances Fox Piven and Richard Cloward (1982) have described the belief that the society as a whole should take responsibility for certain needs, as part of the emergence of a "moral economy" in which the state is responsible for maintaining a minimum standard of living. Social justice is to some extent defined with reference to the state. Simple acceptance of one's fate in the labor market is no longer considered fair or adequate by most workers.

[53]

Many admitted to a feeling of entitlement with some embarrassment. Some workers even apologized to me about it. Mark Kelley, now working as a garbageman, expressed it in this way: "I used to think that people on unemployment were lazy, but when I got out there and saw what it was like, I changed." All the same, workers do feel some sense of guilt regarding unemployment. The sense of guilt surrounding contemporary unemployment must be distinguished from the sort that is described as being prevalent during the thirties. Many workers then felt personally responsible for unemployment, although it was obvious to most observers that they were innocent victims (Orwell 1937, Bakke 1933). This sense of personal guilt has given way to a more shared sense of guilt.

While I agree with Piven and Cloward that many people share a concept of a moral economy, I do not think that the implication of this change is as simple as they tend to suggest. They predict that cutbacks in public relief will lead to mass protest and perhaps progessive reform. However, the buffering effects of economic relief benefits are not the only forces that blunt the reactions of the unemployed.

The following exchange took place when I asked Jerry Staruch what he thought had caused the Seiberling closing; it is an example of collective guilt:

"Maybe we were living too high. Maybe we asked for too much. More money, more benefits. That's what the company kept saying."

"But the company continued to make a large profit, and does today."

"Yeah, and we was barely keeping up with inflation, and now look at us. I don't know. Was it the union's fault?"

If a sense of individual responsibility for basic human needs has given way to the belief in a more collective one, then so has personal guilt been transformed into a sense of collective culpability. The nagging question in the minds of many workers is: Are we in some way responsible for all this? Has the agent of collective bargaining, the union, asked for too much? They wonder if the union and their high standard of living did not have something to do with the closing. This sort of analysis is common enough among conservative economists, but I was surprised to hear it voiced so often by former union men and women. This is not merely a reflexive adoption of ideas purveyed by the powerful. The fact is that working-class people have always been aware of visible inequalities among themselves. This is the basis for guilt about the closing.

There are large differences in wages and benefits among industrial workers, depending on the industry in which they work. The wage differential between factories in Barberton created a status hierarchy in the community. The rubber workers, long the most highly paid workers in Barberton, had been looked upon as leaders who were breaking ground in the movement toward improved conditions for industrial workers in general. But with the economy no longer growing and the situation of other workers obviously failing to improve, many industrial workers began to feel that some were living too high.

Those who believe that the closing was in some way their fault now feel that, having joined the ranks of the less advantaged, they are getting what they deserve. These emotions and understandings defuse much of the resentment that Piven and Cloward anticipate. A war of ideas regarding the failure of the economy and factory closings has confused the understanding of workers on their position and makes it difficult for them to defend what they once fought for.

Retraining

Returning to the want ads, one might also have the impression that jobs are available for those with high-tech skills. There are openings for men and women with new skills, many in jobs that potential workers have never even heard of: "SYSTEMS DESIGNER: Contribute to software development and maintenance DEC, VAX, and PDP11 systems"; "COOLING GROUP LEADER should have 2–3 years laboratory experience" (*Cleveland Plain Dealer* 10 July 1983).

Computers and all sorts of modern technology are revolutionizing our workplaces and homes. The gap between the jobs and the skills of workers is widely discussed in the media (*New York Times* 28 March 1982, Ehrbar 1983). It is sometimes implied that the unemployed are afraid of the new jobs and the new machines. Factory workers have been made obsolete by computers. The solution seems obvious: train and retrain.

This message is heard frequently and illustrated by our daily experiences. Exotic new cash registers are installed in grocery stores. Children's toys are computerized. Sitting with Danny Lawson, I watched a dull image on a television set that should have been replaced years ago. A special science program, the kind Danny loves, explained the use of

[55]

a new kind of computer-operated X-ray machine that shows blood vessels in the brain. Danny was fascinated. "Man, I got to get into something like that." Public service announcements repeat the message. One such announcement depicts the unchanging figure of a woman over whom different occupational settings and uniforms are superimposed; she is shown as a hospital worker, an industrial worker, an office worker, and so on. The caption reads, "Train for the future."

Failure to retrain and lack of flexibility is not typical of the former Seiberling workers. Approximately two-thirds of the Seiberling workers took advantage of the TRA retraining option. For most of them it was a last option at the end of their benefit period, one that allowed them to extend the period of income maintenance for as long as six additional months.

However, the program was not successful in getting people back to work. I spoke to forty-five workers who had received some kind of retraining; of these, only one was working in the area in which he had trained. Nationally, the TRA training program was judged unsuccessful in helping displaced workers regain entry into the work force. The trainees I spoke with were usually pleased with the training they received, and they seem to have done well as students. The private trade schools they attended were approved by the state, but they were not able to place their students in jobs. Graduates of programs had no better luck on their own.

Katie Miller had always wanted to be a nurse. When she was counseled for retraining, she was urged to go to school for training as a medical assistant; TRA would not pay for nurse's training. She was advised to build on her high school secretarial training, and chose a training program in "allied medical professions." Impressed by the promotional material she received from the school, Katie had high expectations of finding work. "Look at this stuff they gave us. There's a whole list of jobs we were supposed to be able to get: medical secretary, medical technologist, laboratory worker, doctor's assistant."

She enjoyed the training, "except for one teacher that always came late. I figured, hell, I got two kids to take care of, and I'm paying money out of my pocket, and I can get here on time. Why can't the teacher?" This dissatisfaction with the school became deeper when the school failed to place her. "They didn't even call me, and I know they called some of the other girls that took the class. I wonder if it has anything to do with that lady that I had words with." The students' belief that the school had misrepresented itself led to an attempt by a group of her classmates to take legal action against the school. "They told us . . . I got the brochures right here . . . that we was qualified to do medical technology and all that stuff. Now I find out you got to have special diplomas to do that. I had a friend of mine write for that brochure, and see how they changed all that now!"

Katie was hired by a podiatrist to work as a receptionist one afternoon a week at $3.25 an hour. Her husband, Dick, complains about the job. He figures that she spends more time and money to get fixed up for work and to drive there than she makes on the job. She insisted, however, that she enjoyed getting out of the house, and she hoped that her hours would be increased as business picked up for the doctor.

Tom Simeko had been eager to retrain. He was enrolled under TRA for a course in general maintenance which was approved by OBES. At the time Tom was told that janitorial positions were available and that he should be able to get a job. The school had a good placement record, and Tom enjoyed the training. "I learned a lot, and I liked the teachers all right. They did their job, but I couldn't find a job when I was done. They sent us out on a couple of interviews, but none of us in the class got the job. Then I started looking around on my own. They wanted you to be a millwright [maintenance person trained in welding and other specialized skills] to do janitor work. And you know what? They are getting them."

Tom had finished his training over a year earlier and felt that the knowledge and skills that he had learned had grown rusty. He is not sure that he could handle a building-maintenance job now. "You have to stay with something like that."

Tom has in fact been retrained twice. After six months of unemployment he was called for a job under the Comprehensive Employment and Training Act of 1973 (CETA). This time it was on-the-job training as a tree trimmer for the city. When the money ran out and CETA could no longer pay the salary, the job was terminated. He talks cynically about retraining now. "I'm looking around for a training program now. Training, a job, welfare—it's all the same as long as you get the check." Again, it is not the quality of the training program or the motivation of the worker that is crucial but the availability of suitable jobs.

TRA training is a bitter memory for some people. Jeff Carey was resentful when I asked him about it. He said, "Rotten Ronny [Reagan] cut us off." In the spring of 1982 TRA funds were cut and the benefits of a large number of Seiberling workers were terminated. Many Seiberling workers had applied for training, expecting to be reimbursed for what they paid in tuition, but when the fund was terminated, nothing was paid out for training costs. Jeff was unable to continue to pay for his schooling in welding, and so dropped out of the class and was saddled with a $3,000 tuition bill. When I met him he was facing bankruptcy and the loss of his house. The tuition went unpaid, despite threats from bill collectors.

The program was also abused by some workers. John Damiani chose training at the Rand Loren School of Beauty. He really had no intention of cutting hair; however, TRA required a worker to enroll in an approved training program in order to receive the last six months of income maintenance, and his enrollment at the barber college qualified him. It was the cheapest training program in town, and he paid the $500 out of his weekly checks from the government. When the checks stopped coming, he dropped out of the program. When John was cut from TRA, he had no outstanding debt. In view of the results of Jeff Carey's and others' honest attempts, we may wonder whether John's action actually constituted an abuse.

Some people were denied retraining. Wes Little had worked as an instrument man calibrating hydraulic machinery, a highly skilled technical job for which he had received training in the army. He looked everywhere for work in his field without luck, and because he already had had a great deal of training, he was denied TRA funding for welding school.

Other workers were not retrainable—those who lacked sufficient intelligence, those with emotional or motivational problems. I met George Henning in the course of an interview with another Seiberling man. They had worked together, and George, who had become very involved with his church, had dropped in to try to sell his old friend some religious books. George had never considered the option of retraining. At the time of the Seiberling shutdown, Firestone had hired a firm to give seminars on job-hunting skills to the former employees. The program included the administration of tests to assess the workers' skills so that they could better understand what career choices were open to them. George had walked out in discouragement. He told me, "I just don't have the smarts for that kind of thing. Those guys that stayed with it, all of them got jobs, I imagine." I noticed that four fingers were missing from his left hand. He had lost them years ago in a press at a factory in nearby Orrville, where he had worked a second job. With a lifetime of hard work behind him, he was too modest to say that he had been a good worker and could still be productive, even if his capacity for classroom work was limited.

Not all attempts at retraining ended badly. Joe Mirovic now works as a traveling repairman for a firm that manufactures and services high-voltage transformers. He was the one person I interviewed who had found work in the area for which he had trained under TRA. Joe's brother-in-law, an engineer, had strongly suggested that Joe get training in a computer-related field. Joe's wife took the lead and insisted on it. He enrolled at Stark Technical Institute for training in computerized testing of machinery, and TRA covered 80 percent of his tuition. Joe and his wife paid the remaining $3,200 themselves, consuming nearly all of their savings. Joe found it painful to go to school with kids twenty years younger than he was. He believes that he could not have succeeded had it not been for a kindly teacher who took a personal interest in his situation. This teacher also made a special effort to place him by arranging an interview with an employer. He started work one week after graduating from the program.

Joe now travels around the country repairing and testing transformers owned by utility companies and large industries. He enjoys the work but finds it difficult to be on the road so much of the time. Both he and his wife consider the job inferior to the one he had at Seiberling: the pay is lower, the benefits do not compare well with those won by the URW, and the health-insurance policy is less comprehensive. The worst change is having to work on a year-to-year contract without much security. Joe is forty-five; he sees what happens to older management workers and worries. "When I'm on the road, I don't worry, but in the office you really have to watch and be political. You have to be real careful what you say to people."

While TRA did not help Frank Bush find a job, it did give him the opportunity to achieve a lifelong ambition. Frank took advantage of the retraining option to complete his high school education. When he was sixteen, he had dropped out of high school to work. It had been a source of embarrassment for many years. Under TRA, he took a preparatory course and passed the high school equivalency test. Frank took great pride in his accomplishment and saw it as a kind of luxury that the unfortunate turn of events had made possible, but he did not think it improved his chances of finding a job. He does industrial cleaning with machinery he bought with his severance pay. Business is very slow and he is constantly looking for a regular job.

Emphasizing the growth of new technology, critics of TRA charge that the program failed because people were trained in the wrong areas (Cetron 1984). Too much is made, however, of the discrepancies between workers' skills and those demanded by existing jobs. The kinds of jobs that are being generated by the economy increasingly require low levels of skill. The dominant trend of this century is the "deskilling" of labor (Braverman 1974:465). Technological innovation has had dual consequences: the introduction of machines that simplify work and break it into many discrete steps has increased productivity but taken the control of work out of the hands of workers. The use of computers and robots is popularly thought to constitute a new industrial revolution, but the introduction of this technology to the workplace represents only an incremental advance in an ongoing process (Levitan and Johnson 1982). Like earlier innovations, computerization and robotics tend to deskill work. The vast majority of present and future jobs are highly routinized and require only minimal training.

Projections made by the Department of Labor bear this point out (Carey 1981). Jobs involving new technologies will be in great demand but few will be available (Rich et al. 1983). For example, while a 157 percent increase in the number of data-processor mechanics is foreseen for the year 1990, the total number of new positions created will be only 162,000 (Fullerton 1980). Compare this figure with the future demand for two million cashiers. A 106 percent increase in the number of computer-systems analysts will create 392,000 jobs, but it is estimated that by 1990 there will be a need for three million more janitors. All of the areas (restaurant, clerical, custodial) in which a large increase in the number of jobs is predicted require little skill.

The prospect for the present blue-collar work force is made clearer by the glut of college graduates in many fields (Rumberger 1981). Already one of every four people in the work force has a college education. Many will be unable to find jobs commensurate with their education. A degree no longer ensures success in the job market. These facts are not lost on former Seiberling workers contemplating a college education. Bill Lexan began to consider college after he was unable to find a job as a typesetter, for which he had been trained under TRA on the most modern equipment. His wife, Gloria, encouraged him to go to college in order to get into a field where he might have better luck finding a job. She has a nursing job and supports them both while taking one course each semester toward a master's degree, which will qualify her to become a head nurse. Bill is now taking one course at a time at the University of Akron, a large state institution, and he is looking for a job. Ideally, he would like to work and go to school part-time.

Bill is interested in industrial relations. "We have been in the rubber industry all our lives in this family. It's something I know about." One of the first courses he took was an introductory class in developmental psychology, which he enjoyed. Bill was one of the men in Barberton I became friends with, and knowing that I had had many years in school, he was curious to see if I could help him get a grant. I gave him some ideas on how to go about looking but suggested he apply for a guaranteed student loan, thinking he might then be able to go to school full-time; he seemed to be quite capable. Bill shyly answered that he did not think that would be an option for him—he and Gloria feared going into debt. They were having trouble coming up with the monthly mortgage payment. "What if I got out of school and couldn't get a job? What would happen then?"

While displaced workers may continue to desire retraining, the hope that it will improve their prospects remains illusory. The more important problem is that the slow-growing economy does not provide enough jobs for those who want to work. When the issue of retraining is raised, we must ask, "For what jobs?"

Relocation

There are jobs elsewhere; unemployment is not so high in other areas of the country as it is in Ohio. During the past several years employment opportunities expanded in the southern and western states while jobs and people left the Northeast and Midwest (Rones

1980). In all kinds of employment, the South and West have gained over the Northeast and Midwest. Unemployment in Ohio, Michigan, and Pennsylvania remained extremely high, while Texas and Arizona enjoyed low rates of joblessness.

Why are there sustained high levels of unemployment in some places? People are free to move, but most seem to stay put. They seem to be imperfect actors who do not follow the rules of classical economics. Economic pundits celebrate the notion of free labor and see something irrational in displaced workers who do not move to an economically expanding area (Gilder 1981).

Business leaders in Barberton discuss this question as if it were a bizarre paradox. A local businessman reminisced about the Pennsylvania mining town in which he was raised and the unemployment created by the closing of the coal fields a generation ago. He recalled the image of an unemployed man shuffling along the streets after years of joblessness and asked, "Why do they stay?" He was fascinated by my research because he thought that I might discover some strange psychological inflexibility or cultural barrier that could explain the failure of the idled workers to relocate. Indeed, few middle-aged factory workers with families relocated. Studies of migration reveal that people who relocate tend to be young, unmarried, and college educated (Da Vanzo 1977).

Even though few actually take the step, moving away from Barberton is a popular topic of local conversation. Very few men and women I spoke with said that they had never considered moving to find a job. I participated in many such conversations about relocation. Danny and Marian Lawson frequently talked about selling everything and moving to a boom area. They would spread out a road map and wonder aloud what places like Corpus Christi and Laredo were like. Their schemes shifted as they heard stories or acquired some new bit of information.

What do workers consider when they think about leaving Barberton? What are the barriers to relocation? The factors my informants most often mentioned were their inability to sell their houses, the cost of moving, and their family responsibilities in Barberton. Another consideration, implicit in what was said, was the importance of family and other networks on which people depended, especially in connection with finding work. Those facing unemployment consider relocation in terms of risks and benefits, yet this calculation is often made without full knowledge of what those risks and benefits are.

[62]

Home and family responsibilities keep many of the unemployed in Barberton

Arlene Sheldon was one person who said flatly that she would not leave. "Barberton could dry up and blow away and me and Mom would still be in this house." The house is owned by her mother, and the mortgage is paid off. They feel that this, at least, cannot be taken from them. Arlene and her nine brothers and sisters were raised in this rather small house, now badly in need of repair. Arlene has lived with her seventy-year-old mother for most of her adult life. They have been through hardship before; Arlene has been on welfare, as has her mother, and they have gone without and been hungry. But they will not move.

Many families in Barberton have tried to sell their homes but few have succeeded. Local retailers estimate that between 15 and 20 percent of the houses in Barberton were for sale in 1982. The market price of the average house dropped by $10,000 but interest rates have climbed and buyers are scarce. Many people now feel trapped by their houses.

Mark Kelley's wife has relatives in Tennessee, so they investigated jobs at the new Nissan plant there. "We liked the Japanese ideas about management: 'Come let us reason together.' In this country they don't give a damn about the workers." The Nissan boom looked good.

The obstacle to relocation is their large, suburban-style house. They have invested a lot of energy and savings in it. Mark worked as a carpenter and built much of the house himself. The Kelleys proudly gave me a tour of the place. "There are doctors who live on this block," Mark's wife told me. Mark pointed out the deluxe carpentry he had installed: fancy woodwork, energy-saving design, special fixtures. His wife, a secretary for a real estate agency, told me, "We could never get out of this house what he has in it, not now, not for a while."

However, they have not given up the idea of relocating, because they realize that their situation is precarious. "Security is a big thing to us. This job I got now [garbage-removal service] is just not too secure. Those old guys that are real loyal to the company are being fooled. They would do anything for that company, but the management tells me they want to unload them and get some young guys. The foreman watches us with binoculars from a car to see if we ride the clutch. What's going to happen to me in five years?"

Ron Small and his wife had thought about moving to Florida. "Carole has a brother there who is in real estate. I went down and checked around. He could get us a house, but jobs are tight. The main problem is this house. We put it on the market as soon as the shop went down, and we went through a bunch of agents, but it didn't sell. We were asking what we had in it, that's all."

Their ideas about relocation are strongly colored by the stories they have heard from friends who have tried to move. A good friend of Carole's had gone to live in Texas for eighteen months. "She says she'll never say anything bad about Ohio again." The wages there were low and the work was unpleasant; the friend returned when her husband was laid off. Ron had his own tale. "One of the guys from Seiberling bought an old bread truck and left for Oregon. He packed his family and all their things in it and they left." Carole added, "They must have had some pioneer blood in them. No one's heard of them since." The few stories about people moving away and then returning circulated widely among the former Seiberling workers. Stories of failure discouraged others from taking the risk.

Moving costs are another consideration. Don Walker has a brother in California who encouraged him to relocate there so that he could help Don find a job. "Even if I could have sold the house I couldn't have made it. To rent a truck and move my stuff would have cost a couple thousand, even if I did it all myself. I didn't have that kind of bread. Moving came up when it was too late for me to get the TRA money." Don would find it difficult to move from Barberton under any circumstances. He is divorced and lives alone but remains close to his daughter and his grandchildren. Their visits are his greatest pleasure, one that he would hate to give up.

Family responsibilities weigh heavily on some couples. The Leslers have thought about moving. "I wouldn't mind getting away from these winters. But Agnes has her mother. She's all alone now; Dad died last year. She is getting up in age and needs help. We do her yardwork and house cleaning. She can't get out by herself any more. We owe her a lot over the years, and until she is gone, we've got to stay."

All of these factors—houses, moving expenses, family obligations, the uncertainty about opportunities in other places—were carefully weighed by Wes and Rita Little. After some consideration, they decided to dig in where they were. They own two acres of land littered with Wes's unfinished projects: a solar collector, a garden, a cement mixer for a future patio. They hope to be "self-sufficient" in five years,

[65]

by which they mean free from the need for cash. Wes sees himself as being different from his peers; he says that he has always "followed a different beat," that he belongs to a "counterculture."

Relocation would be very difficult for them. First of all, their house, which is conspicuous for its run-down appearance, would be almost impossible to sell. They live in a working-class suburb where residential neighborhoods are interspersed among industrial dumps, small factories, and junkyards, beyond the "lime lakes" (chemical dumps) of Pittsburgh Plate Glass, just outside of Barberton. Wes thinks of the area as rural. The Littles' two children were running around in the backyard as we sat at the kitchen table watching them through a steamy glass door.

Rita is a nurse and has a secure job. The prospect of moving and losing the job is frightening. "Right now my job is all we have. We are trying to hang on here." Family support also strongly influenced their decision to stay in Barberton. Both Wes and Rita were raised nearby. Their fathers were both raised on farms and moved into industrial occupations after World War II. The families retain a strong tradition of mutual support. If things get worse, they imagine they could move in with his or her parents. Relatives continue to try to help Wes find a job, as they have done in the past. Wes's uncle helped him get his job at Seiberling when Wes returned from the military. "Man, I thought I had it made in life. A job at Seiberling, a trade . . . *wrong!*" he said, imitating a radio announcer.

Wes no longer thinks of himself as unemployed. The week before he had done a little painting. The family helps him pick up odd jobs. This week he helped to install a carburetor in someone's car. He is a highly trained mechanic, and he bragged a bit about his talent. "See that Corvair? It's fifteen years old. My cars never die." Although Wes is able to keep himself busy, he has not had steady work for over a year. Smiling, he referred to his work as "freelancing." Rita interrupted politely but in an earnest tone: "So far you haven't made enough to cover gas money." He quietly conceded the point, and I moved to another question. He repeated his motto about his following a different beat in a variety of contexts. It became apparent that this self-description was his way of expressing his profound withdrawal from the larger world, in which he saw himself failing.

I do not want to suggest that economic considerations alone determined the feelings about home and community expressed by the workers. The values that bind people to people and places are created over many years. Relationships grow in an atmosphere of mutual assistance and obligation. Three generations of family and work life have created deeply emotional attachments to Barberton as a home, not merely as a convenient place in which to reside. The meaning of "home" became even clearer when I spoke with people who did relocate.

Migration was a long adventure for the families who undertook it. I traveled to Texas in 1983 and spoke with four families formerly of Barberton. The drive from Ohio to Houston takes twenty-four hours; most people looking for work make the drive in one stretch. Making the drive myself, I felt I shared some of the adventure with those families.

Migrants usually go first to Houston. The city is famous for its recent growth; it attracted 1,554,992 new residents between 1970 and 1980. The population of Texas grew 27.1 percent during the same period, while the population of Ohio increased by a mere 1.6 percent and the North Central states lost three million residents overall, over 90 percent of whom went to the South and West (Hacker 1983). Most were young and looking for their first jobs. A young construction worker from Ohio, Mike Lang, called Houston a "workingman's paradise," because it was so easy to get a job there. If you didn't like the boss on one job, you could walk out and find another job that day. Or at least it used to be so. In the previous year unemployment had climbed to 10 percent in the area, making the job market tight, especially in manufacturing.

Houston is not to everyone's liking. The conspicuous problems of rapid expansion besiege the city; its traffic troubles and pollution rival those of Los Angeles. Social services are underdeveloped, and many migrants complain about the quality of life. During my stay in Houston, I stayed with Mike and some friends of his who had also gone there looking for work. He told me, "All of us hate it down here. Everyone is here to hustle a buck and that's it. I'm trying to save some money and get out."

Glenn Meden, his wife, Tammy, and their two children from her previous marriage relocated to Houston from Barberton and were going to "make the most of it." Tammy did most of the talking. "The first thing I did when I got down here was to buy a cowboy hat. You have to come down here with the idea that you are going to stay. You

[67]

can't just be in a holding pattern, waiting for things to get better at home so you can go back, because they're not going to. I decided we were going to become Texans."

At the time of the Seiberling closing, Tammy had been working at the welfare department in Akron helping Asian refugees relocate. When she saw Glenn going through the predictable reactions to unemployment—disbelief, withdrawal, and finally depression—she began to worry. "He got to the point where he would joke about not being able to go out and look for work until his soaps were over. The problem was that it was true! Then he got frantic. He was giving up."

She was much criticized when she proposed relocation. "Everyone told me I was crazy. 'You'll be back' is what they all said." The Medens left the children with relatives and traveled to Houston to investigate the possibilities; TRA paid some of their expenses, since this was a job-search trip. "We joked about it and went on a lark. We had never had a honeymoon and said that this would be it. I was dead serious, though. It was a terrible trip. We fought all the way, the most horrible week of my life. The places we stayed all had roaches. I was scared to death by it all: Tent City, all the trailers. By the end of the week Glenn was convinced he could find a job down here."

Glenn returned to Houston immediately and got a job in construction at $4.50 an hour. He rented a small apartment with another former Seiberling worker. He signed the necessary papers to receive reimbursement from TRA for the moving expenses, which covered 80 percent of the $3,000 cost. The Medens had married only recently and did not have a house to sell. "We sent him down with his care package, and I kept sending him money while I packed up and got the kids ready." Glenn continued to look for a better-paying job and eventually got one as a driver for UPS, at $10 an hour.

The move has worked out well for the Medens. They live in a new house in one of Houston's huge new subdivisions. There is a swimming pool at the end of each street for the residents. Tammy abruptly dropped the southern drawl she had been affecting for me: "I love the house. We could never have afforded this house at home. They're cheap down here. No insulation costs, I guess. We paid fifty thousand."

Her daughter, Kim, is in high school, and it had been hard for her to leave her friends in Ohio. Tammy admitted that Kim is still unhappy about that but added that there are some things that the kids should be pleased with. "Kim got a summer job making three-sixty at an ice cream place. Glenn's sister is trying to raise a daughter on less than that working as a salesclerk at O'Neil's [a department store in Akron]! Mat [Tammy's son] is doing yard work and delivering papers, and he makes a hundred dollars a week."

Since arriving in Houston, Tammy has worked at three jobs, which she found through temporary employment agencies. Like many Houstonians, she and Glenn each spend two hours daily commuting to and from work. Tammy takes pride in her new city and gave me old copies of *Houston Magazine,* a color glossy that celebrates the mystique of the Sunbelt. She is irritated by the reports of northerners who have left Houston. "My mother cuts stories out of the newspaper and sends them to me. One steelworker from Youngstown was on the news down here and said he would rather starve in Youngstown than live in Houston."

I found other former Seiberling workers living in Waco, which is halfway between Houston and Dallas. Waco, like most of the rest of Texas, is a low-income area, consisting of rude, sun-bleached houses set up on cinder blocks, with galvanized metal roofs. While driving in Waco I was filled with emotion, which I then connected with the smell in the air. The odor was from a rubber factory. I remembered it from my years at the University of Akron when the plants were blooming and perfumed the campus. The smell in Waco came from the General Tire plant, which had attracted some of the workers who left Barberton.

In Waco I stayed in the rented apartment of Ben Wood, an acquaintance from Barberton who was in the process of relocation and had gone back to Ohio to visit his wife. Ben warned me, "It's not much." The apartments were cheaply made, a long single-story structure with the parking lot abutting the front of the building, like a motel. In back of the building were scattered metal trash cans and empty clotheslines. The inside walls were covered with dark simulated wood paneling; the ceilings were waterstained. Tiny cockroaches crawled across the clean sheets that had been put out for me. In the closet were clean workshirts that Ben's wife had packed for him. Her picture was propped up on the dresser. Places like this are usually the first stop for contemporary working-class migrants.

Another former Seiberling worker, Paul Whitman, lived in a new community of modern ranchhouses with well-manicured lawns. Paul had come to Waco to work at the General Tire plant but was laid off after only four months. He quickly found a job in a frozen-meat warehouse and did well: he proudly told me he had received a series of raises sooner than some of the longtime workers. At the time of our interview he was making $7 an hour. Kathy, his wife, said, "He's embarrassed to tell you . . . should I tell him? . . . He started at four-fifty an hour." The cost of living in Waco is roughly the same as that in Ohio, but wages are lower. Paul works a second job, nights, at Sears to supplement his income. "We just can't seem to get caught up even with Paul working the two jobs. We will never get to where we were at Seiberling. Paul wants to get a business degree and get into management or something. It might help."

The Whitmans had definite ideas about what constitutes an acceptable standard of living for a couple in their forties, which included a yearly vacation trip, a new car, and a bit of savings for emergencies. These are the things they had had to give up after the Seiberling closing. When I mentioned that some of their friends in Ohio might envy Paul's wages, he felt better about their sacrifices.

In Barberton Kathy had preached gloom and doom, predicting the closing of the Seiberling plant several years before the fact. "I read a lot and kept hearing about the plants moving south to the Sunbelt years ago. I knew it could happen to us. I kept nagging Paul to look for a new job even then. I'd do things like put drawings of tombstones on the refrigerator: 'R.I.P. Barberton.'"

Paul had investigated several relocation opportunities within the rubber industry during the years before the closing. "I interviewed with tire companies in Tennessee and Omaha. When I saw those automated, air-conditioned plants, then came home to old Seiberling, it made me believe her all the more. I thought I had the Omaha job. I was one of the first applicants for a brand-new plant and had plenty of experience as a tire builder. They asked me how I felt about the union and I said what I thought they wanted: that the union had overstepped their bounds. Well, I guess they figured I had been in the union at home. They hired all people without experience and opened as a nonunion shop."

A year before the shutdown announcement, Kathy had the house up for sale. "No matter what we said about leaving, really, we would never have left if the plant hadn't closed. But then it happened!" It took the Whitmans two years to sell the house. Meanwhile Paul looked for work in Barberton and unsuccessfully tried to start a lawn-care business. During the spring of 1981, before his benefits ended, Paul and a friend traveled to Houston to look for work. After several disappointments, they stopped in Waco, where they found one of their former supervisors from Seiberling. He was able to help them get jobs at the General Tire plant. Paul immediately returned home to prepare for the move to Waco, and TRA helped pay the expenses. "We took a real beating on the house, but we had to sell. We had put a lot of money in it and had it just like we wanted, but it was overbuilt for Barberton. It was appraised at a hundred thousand dollars but went for fifty thousand. We had to get out."

The move took its toll, despite their advance preparations for the change. Kathy told me, "I love my family and spent a lot of time with them. We always got all together at the holidays. Cars would be parked all down the block. I have a grown daughter, a grandchild, my mom, sisters, brothers. The thought of not seeing that baby grow up and of her not knowing her grandmother hurts."

Kathy tried to encourage her family to join them in Texas, with little success. "Mom had a stroke this spring, and the doctor said it was because she can't adjust to me being gone." Kathy arranged for one of her sisters to come to Waco and found her a job. "My sister Debra came down and left a job at Acme to live with us for a couple months. She hated it. They treat the workers terrible down here. She finally quit when her boss threw something at her. A boss can hit you down here, and there is nothing you can do except call the sheriff."

Kathy became depressed and is now seeing a psychiatrist. She has developed colitis and gynecological problems during the year she has been in Texas, which her doctor says are due to her emotional upset. Christmas was particularly hard for her this year. "On the TV from Dallas they showed people from the North lined up at the Salvation Army for food and toys, free bedding. I cried and cried. Those are our people. What is happening to us?"

The Mitchells are another Barberton family that moved to Waco. Greg Mitchell now drives a delivery truck for 7-Up. He and his father had both been at Seiberling. "Dad just couldn't take bagging groceries at fifty any more." Greg's father came to Waco first to work at the

General Tire plant but was laid off after several months. The father quickly got another factory job and offered his son a loan to help him move his family down.

Greg eventually got a job in Barberton after the shutdown. "I just kept looking and hoping. I figured I had as good a chance as the next guy. I'm a good worker. I'll do any damn job. I ran that filthy banberry [mixes resins for rubber] at Seiberling." The job lasted only a few months. When the unemployment insurance ran out, he and his wife were no longer able to pay the rent and had to move in with his grandmother. He was quick to take up his father's offer.

Greg is now a salaried employee but figures that he makes $7 an hour, including his work on Sunday mornings, when he makes deliveries to a nearby Air Force base. Virginia, his wife, works as a beautician. They rent a modern apartment, which she has decorated. Virginia, however, is unhappy—she hates Texas and finds it difficult to be so far from her family. Greg finds Texas tolerable, even though working conditions are not pleasant. "I don't understand it, but they just don't let you *be* down here. They need a union down here, but you talk union and you're out. But I'm not going back for less money, no way."

Some workers went to Texas and then came back to Barberton. Jake and Regina Ryder left for Texas to start a new life after losing their home and declaring bankruptcy. Jake went first, with friends, and found work in Pasadena, Texas. He then sent for Regina and the babies. They spent $600 a month on rent, struggling to get by the first year. "And that was not a very good neighborhood." During their second year in Texas, Jake got a better job in a chemical plant but was then laid off. New at the plant, he had no idea if he would be called back. Unemployment benefits are meager in Texas and did not even cover their rent. With no job in sight and the unemployment level higher than 10 percent in the Houston area, the Ryders began to worry.

Jake's mother still lives in a large house in Barberton. He knew that his family would at least have a place to stay and some food to eat with his mother. The Ryders put their few possessions in storage and left for Ohio. After a month of searching, Jake got a job at a local rubber-reclaiming plant with the help of old friends. Coming home seemed the right decision, at least for the time being.

George Bastic had gone to Texas temporarily to make some quick money after the bank began foreclosure proceedings on his house. He and his girlfriend, Sue, left her two children with a sister and lived for four months in Tent City, a state park outside of Houston where migrants had congregated on inexpensive campsites. I asked how they had liked it. Sue said, "Well, we were never there. Working twelve hours a day at least, then just going to the tent to crash. It was a real good deal, and then the camp screwed up and didn't charge us for the last month." George and Sue worked as a team installing television cables in private homes, spending most of the day in attics and crawl spaces. Temperatures ran over 100° on many days.

Their plan was to save enough money to catch up on the mortgage and have a little left over for security. Because they were happy to be working again, they considered staying permanently in Texas. George wanted to be sure the children would be happy with the move. For the last month of the summer the children stayed with them in the eight-by-ten tent. "They just loved it. The campground had a pool and they swam all day and messed around with the other kids." The camaraderie of the camp gave them the spirit to go on. "Most of the people there were from the North and come to look for work. Lots of them had kids, and some of the mothers had their kids doing schoolwork every day right in the camp." Camp life was not without its difficulties. Feeding the family became a major problem without the convenience of a refrigerator. "Then there was the guy in the tent across from us. He kept flashing Sue. Well, I made sure he saw my gun, and he cut it out."

By the end of the summer they had saved $6,000, and they planned to go back to Texas to install cable again once they settled their affairs in Ohio. When George and Sue returned to Barberton they learned that penalties had been assessed for the overdue mortgage payments. Their savings barely covered what they owed the bank. There were still no buyers for the house and no jobs, and George quickly found himself in arrears on his mortgage again.

Some of the former Seiberling workers have done better than others. Individuals differ in their resources, abilities, and energy, and the qualities that make a dependable factory worker are perhaps not the same as the qualities that help people survive unemployment. Underlying the diverse responses and problems is a persistent fact: there are fewer jobs to go around than before, and fewer jobs that pay well. Put

[73]

simply, the reason that so many people remain unemployed is that there are not enough jobs for all who want to work. Retraining policies are often misguided, promising much but delivering little. Relocation is a serious risk with questionable benefits. The individual differences in the reemployment experiences of the Seiberling workers I interviewed seem to have been due in part to the luck of the draw.

[4]

Not by Bread Alone

Work is the major organizing principle around which the working class, and almost everyone else, structures life. When work is gone, so is much of the order in our lives. It initially appears paradoxical that work, which causes so much human misery, is also essential to individual psychological well-being. While the content of various occupations may be unpleasant, the absence of a usual occupation is perhaps even more distressing. Work confers on a person a status, a place in the human community; and though the occupant of that place may think his status too lowly, it is preferable to the isolation and meaninglessness of unemployment. Similarly, the sense of personal identity, which is profoundly experienced through occupation, is disturbed by unemployment. Moreover, the experience of time is rooted in work. When the structure and support provided by the routine of work is lost, people find themselves unable to keep track of time and unable to use it efficiently. Freud recognized the difficulty:

> Laying stress upon the importance of work has a greater effect than any other technique of living in the direction of binding the individual more closely to reality; in his work he is at least securely attached to a part of the human community. Work is no less valuable for the opportunity it and the human relations connected with it provide for a very considerable discharge of libidinal component impulses, narcissistic, aggressive

and even erotic, than because it is indispensible for subsistence and justifies existence in a society.   [Freud 1930:34]

The psychological suffering of the unemployed has been well described in a number of studies (Leventman 1981, Rubin 1976, Ferman and Gordus 1979).[1] However, these studies fail to appreciate the extent to which this suffering results from the loss of the psychological benefits of employment. Psychological well-being is grounded in work, and unemployment can be understood as a deprivation of the benefits of that experience (Jahoda 1984).

Unemployment is more than lost income; it causes deprivation and disruption of some of the most fundamental categories of human experience through which we come to know ourselves, others, and the world. The sense of time, social status, personal identity, and participation in the collectivity are part of a cultural system that gives a certain shape to the experience of the unemployed. This cultural system, which could also be called a set of values, works as a structure in ways similar to the rules and opportunities of the labor market or governmental agencies, constraining and enabling people to go on with their lives.

Time

Unemployment often entails a lot of free time. For the jobless, time is more a burden than a luxury, since many are disturbed by the disappearance of the order that work imparts to life.[2] In places like

---

[1]M. Harvey Brenner has done a large amount of research that strongly suggests a causal relationship between unemployment and a number of diseases, in particular mental illness. For his most extended treatment of the subject see his *Mental Illness and the Economy* (1973). For a critique of Brenner's work, see Cobb and Kasl (1977), Eyer (1977), and Liem (1983).

[2]Marx made this point in *Grundrisse*: " 'Thou shalt labour by the sweat of thy brow!' was Jehovah's curse that he bestowed on Adam. A. Smith conceived of labour as such a curse. 'Rest' appears to him to be the fitting state of things, and identical with 'liberty' and 'happiness'. It seems to be far from A. Smith's thoughts that the individual, 'in his normal state of health, strength, activity, skill and efficiency', might also require a normal portion of work, and cessation from rest. It is true that the quantity of labour to be provided seems to be conditioned by external circumstances, by the purpose to be achieved, and the obstacles to its achievement that have to be overcome by labour. But

Barberton the experience of time conforms to the contours of the industrial workday. Whistles announcing the end of a shift shape the daily routines of the men and women at the plant; their coming and going, mealtimes, and leisure time are determined by that schedule. Work defines a major category of experience—time—and the absence of that category is psychologically disorienting (Applebaum 1982). The unemployed are often unable to use time efficiently or to keep track of it. Katie Miller reported that she was stunned by the loss of her job and sat staring out the window most of the day for a month after the shutdown. John Damiani found that he arrived late wherever he went, though he had usually been known for promptness. He had trouble keeping track of the time without the workday to refer to.

The use of time was frequently a bone of contention between Danny and Marian Lawson, with whom I boarded while I was in Barberton. Danny found it difficult to get out of bed in the morning when he had no place to go. He often stayed in bed until 4:30 in the afternoon, then quickly dressed and left before Marian arrived home from work. He thus avoided being faced with the question "Have you been in bed all day?" Marian began calling home in the morning at 8:30 to awaken Danny, but her calls did not alter his sleeping pattern. Despite the fact that Marian worked forty hours a week, she continued to do all of the cleaning, the laundry, and what cooking she could manage. Danny rarely found time to pick up his clothes from around the house or to wash the dishes, although he had regularly done his share of the housework before.

Marian did not often complain, but she found it difficult to hide her irritation at Danny's failure to get organized. Much of their household bickering concerned Danny's seeming inability to get anything done. On a few occasions Marian's anger surfaced. Danny had begun several home-improvement projects but had left them unfinished. He had done major renovations in the past, while he was working full-time; now in 1983, however, the kitchen cabinets, woodwork refinishing, new screen windows, and other projects were uncompleted. He stepped

---

neither does it occur to A. Smith that the overcoming of such obstacles may itself constitute an exercise in liberty, and that these external purposes lose their character of mere natural necessities and are established as purposes which the individual himself fixes. The result is the self-realization and objectification of the subject, therefore real freedom, whose activity is precisely labour" (1971:123–24).

into the kitchen one evening and announced, "I'm gonna put a screen on the back door." Marian retorted with some bitterness, "Yeah, in 1986." Later, when Danny planned a trip to visit his mother, Marian blurted out to me in his absence, "At least it will get him out of the house."

Marian knew that Danny was a hard worker and never accused him of laziness. Her walnut dining-room furniture stood as a reminder of the eight months of twelve- and sixteen-hour shifts he had worked to pay for it. They had managed the house efficiently then, Danny arriving home to cooked meals, then going immediately to bed, and off to work again in the morning. Marian knew that his efforts to find work were no less conscientious, having spent months helping him conduct a job search and typing his résumés.

The unemployed do not perceive their free time as leisure. Leisure is in fact created by work and is its complement; without work there is no leisure. Danny complained that he didn't have money for entertainment, yet the problem was deeper. When he found me on the porch reading or drinking a beer, he would predictably comment, "Rough life, eh, Greg?" Not once during that very hot summer did he enjoy a cool evening out-of-doors. Many of his neighbors cleaned and decorated their porches for the season and spent pleasant evenings with family and friends. Danny could not create leisure out of his free time—he clearly felt guilty about entertaining himself in public while he was unemployed.

To blame the unemployed for their failure to use time well is to miss the point. "It would amount to asking that they single-handedly overthrow the compelling social norms under which we all live and which provide a supportive framework which shapes our lives" (Jahoda 1984: 26). Three generations of family experience and support enabled Danny to clock in at a factory daily, something many people would find difficult to do. The traditions of their families and the community had enabled working-class people in Barberton to do boring, routinized work and to dream on their own time. These adaptations are not easy to unlearn. Professionals have a different sense of time which demands personal responsibility for the structure of the workday. Although creative use of time is their habit, a complete lack of structure can pose difficulties even for people accustomed to the absence of a regular schedule.

[78]

Social Status

The sidewalks of Barberton were often deserted during the day. I frequently enjoyed walking down the quiet streets on my way to interviews or meetings, getting a closer look at the neighborhoods. An incident that occurred during one of these walks illustrates one way in which unemployment becomes more than just a loss of income. It is also deprivation of social status.

Going through an alley on my way home from a morning interview, I was noticed by a middle-aged man parking his car; he was wearing a red-and-white welder's cap. Emerging from his car, he addressed me: "Well, what are you doing?" Surprised, I turned and responded, "Just walking." He shot back in an aggressive tone, "Why don't you get a job?" Later it was clear to me that the man's hostility toward my seeming lack of employment was representative of the traditional system of values, which has no place for people who do not work. These values led to anxiety among my informants concerning their status; to be unemployed is to have no place in the community.

Work creates a place in the world for workers and a set of relationships with their families, friends, and the larger community. A shutdown not only destroys a source of income but also radically cuts off workers from their social status (Buss and Redburn 1983b). Reemployment, while it restores one's identity as a worker, frequently entails a lowering of status. Former Seiberling workers had once been at the top of the status hierarchy among factory workers in Barberton. Their good wages, job security, and strong union made them enviable. After the shutdown, few found jobs that permitted them to regain their former status.

Curtis Hill was forty-eight years old and was never able to find work after the Seiberling closing. He thought that he and his wife, Esther, were lucky because she was still working at the county welfare office. She had decided to go to work in 1975 when they felt the pinch of inflation strongly; he had objected at first, but afterward they both enjoyed the extra income. Esther is now the sole wage earner in the family. Curtis stays at home and tries to pick up his share of the relationship by working around the house. "She would come home and laugh and laugh. I never did housework before and I dusted around the things on the table. She had to teach me to pick up the stuff and dust."

[79]

Curtis also began to do the shopping and some cooking. He said, "She's still the cook. I learned some recipes, but she's real good." In time, though, his new role troubled Curtis.

A year after I interviewed Curtis in his home, he spent three weeks in the psychiatric ward of an Akron hospital. Esther explained the circumstances that had led to his hospitalization. The Hills had been well established in a black neighborhood, had raised their children well, supported their church, and participated in the block club. In their social circles a good union job conferred high status. The loss of his job at Seiberling and his inability to find another had undermined Curtis's position in the community and in his own eyes. He began to think of himself as a "lazy nigger that lays around while a woman supports him." It hurt him deeply to become what racists allege black men to be; it was a stereotype he had devoted his life to refuting. His situation eventually led to a suicidal depression.

Many women disdain dependence as much as most men do. Becky Koegel began working in a glass factory in West Virginia when she was thirteen and ever since had worked at various jobs continuously, except for the three years she spent at home with her children while they were small. During her seven years at Seiberling, Becky made better wages than her husband did. "Hal has been at PPG for twenty-four years. When I was able to hold the job at Seiberling and bring home that kind of money, I was so proud. We were working together, just like partners, to get something better for our kids." She found her new status obnoxious. "I have to ask him for money just to go bowling. He don't mind, but I do. I feel like I'm not pulling my own weight."

The position of wage earner is, of course, an important aspect of an individual's status within a domestic relationship (Ehrenreich 1983). Unemployment denies one the autonomy, highly prized by most Americans, associated with making one's own money. When a family member is not working, new forms of relations emerge. The status of the person not working may come under attack, with the resultant erosion of the balance and accommodations that make relationships possible. The expectations on which marriages are based can be undermined. It is no exaggeration to say that decisions made in boardrooms affect what goes on in the bedrooms of Barberton.

When the status of a family member is lost, disruption of the marriage is likely (Leventman 1981). Bob Younger was divorced three years after the Seiberling shutdown and believes the divorce was due to the closing. He was one of the highest-paid tire builders in the plant, drawing a salary that allowed his family to live very comfortably. During our first meeting he was still married, and his wife, Linda, was quick to point out and lament their downward slide. As a tire builder Bob had made approximately $30,000 a year, frequently working overtime. A high standard of living was an inherent part of his relationship with his wife. They enjoyed going to nice restaurants on weekends and throwing parties. Leaving Seiberling meant a dramatic decline in their standard of living. Though Bob remained a loving husband and father, their relationship began to sour.

Soon after he had found a job working for the state Workman's Compensation Board for $12,000 a year, Linda "ran off with another guy," as Bob put it, leaving their two sons behind. I vividly remember her complaints on an evening I spent with them. She hated hearing their old friends talking about "scrounging" and telling each other about where they could get a free bag of groceries or free medical care. Linda had been raised on welfare during the fifties and had bitter memories of her mother's struggles. She feared a slide down the social ladder and turned against her husband. When it was over he said, "She left me because I couldn't give her what she wanted any more."

On the other hand, the wounded pride of the unemployed worker can be healed by a supportive family. When the self-esteem of the wage earner is damaged, some families are drawn together. Glenn Meden was shaken by the shutdown and his inability to find work. "I began to think that I was a loser. No job, running out of money, sitting around all day. I got scared." His wife, a social worker, became alarmed when Glenn became apathetic. Tammy told me, "I did everything I could to let him know I'd stick with him. He began hearing about his friends whose wives were running out on them. I tried to pull the family together and sat the kids down and told them to be understanding about money being tight and to help them understand that their dad needed support through this."

In a few cases unemployment led to the formation of a new family. Katie Miller had worked in factories for twelve years to support her mother and two children. She and her steady boyfriend, Dick, were married two years after the closing of the Seiberling plant. They had met shortly after Katie's divorce from her first husband, who beat her.

Katie, then eighteen years old, decided to move back in with her mother. Dick, a friend of the family, had bought a much-needed crib when Katie was expecting her second child. "I guess he had more plans for us then than I knew." Katie grew to love Dick and spent a great deal of time with him during the next ten years, but insisted on remaining single and working.

Katie spoke enthusiastically about her recent marriage and was glad that they could now go to church together as a family. The wedding had taken place several months after her benefits had run out and she still had not found work. She did not say that the shutdown had led directly to her decision to marry Dick; she did say that she was happy to be married because she did not want to have to go back to living on welfare, which had been a bitter experience for her after her divorce.

Both women and men experience the pain of losing status and esteem through unemployment. Some have connected the rise of unemployment with the increased numbers of women in the work force. If fewer women worked, they reason, jobs would be available for men. Such thinking assumes that a family wage system still exists in our society. The family wage system, in which only one member of each household, traditionally the man, earns a wage and supports the rest of the family, has for a long time been supported by the efforts of political parties and unions. The system has for many reasons largely broken down. The consequences of this change have evolved slowly (Levinson 1980); women still work for less money and still shoulder most household responsibilities, but more and more families need two wages. Women have entered the work force in increasing numbers, especially since 1970, when inflation made it impossible to maintain a high standard of living on one income (Brand 1981). Under present economic conditions, it is futile to propose that society revert to the family wage system.

Personal Identity

Unemployment undermines personal identity as one's sense of competence and stability is supplanted by feelings of incompetence and instability. Aspirations are abandoned and the unemployed worker is left with broken spirits and doubts about his or her identity. Loss of identity is, perhaps, less of an issue for professionals who lose their jobs. As educational attainment is not dependent on place of employment, professional identity is more portable (Buss and Redburn 1983b; Leventman 1981). For factory workers the place of employment is crucial; their identities are bound up in a particular place, and plant shutdowns compromise their ability to understand themselves.

Personal identification with industry was important to the displaced workers in Barberton. Gene Bendycki began working in heavy industry when he graduated from high school, first at PPG until the layoff in 1972, then at Seiberling. His brother, father, and grandfather had been rubber workers. Gene and his family took great pride in being associated with an internationally known company and an essential commodity, tires. They were also strong supporters of the URW.

Gene was hired by the local hospital as an orderly in 1980. The job is not demanding—he had done strenuous work as a tire sorter—but he found hospital work repugnant, for it gave him none of the personal fulfillment he had felt in the rubber factory. "I used to get kind of psyched to go to work at the plant, but how psyched can you get about emptying a bedpan?" His identity as a rubber worker could not be easily replaced.

The question "Who am I?" remained unanswered by Artie Simpson for a long time after the closing. Artie attempted a number of ventures, including a lawn-care service and a pizza-supply business. None of them worked out, and he then took a big step, using his severance pay from Seiberling to buy a small neighborhood bar. His wife, Ellen, knew the business well, her father having managed a bar for thirty years. Although the income from the bar paid the bills, Artie was restless and unable to think of himself as a bartender and bar owner. He began to socialize with the customers, drank too much, and eventually began an affair with one of the women who frequented the place. Ellen was shocked and humiliated in front of the many people she knew through her work at the bar. When she confronted Artie, all he could say was "I don't know who I am any more. I need some space." Ellen divorced Artie, took over the bar, and now supports herself and her two children. Artie has found work stocking shelves at a store. The cycle of disruption begun by the closing of the Seiberling plant left Artie unable to resolve the issue of his personal identity.

At thirty-three, Steve Tummonds lives with his retired father and

[83]

mother. The Seiberling shutdown blighted his romance and has deprived him of the sense of personal competence that his job had given him. After finishing high school, Steve had served in the army and then worked at a small tool factory until his father helped him get a job at Seiberling. "Getting in at Seiberling was my dream." Steve worked there for six years, saving money for a house, and was engaged to be married at the time of the shutdown.

Young men in Barberton commonly married after finding work in one of the larger factories. Steve postponed the wedding in order to give him time to find a new job. As time passed and no job was found, he and his fiancée drifted apart, and she finally married another man. Steve said that he did not like to talk about her much now. Unemployment had given him a sense of his own inadequacies and left him without the resources to develop his adult identity. He was a thin, nervous man. Sitting next to his fleshy father, who had retired at the time of the closing, he joked, "I need a little hillbilly woman to cook and put some meat on these bones, isn't that right, Dad?"

Steve is also unhappy that he can't afford to move out of his parents' house. Unable to find work, he remains in the family's small bungalow filled with boxes of old records, large stuffed animals won at forgotten carnivals, stacks of old magazines, and model airplanes, all piled around several large chairs and a couch. We sat at the dining-room table, which was covered with pieces of a model airplane. Steve mentioned that he had hoped to have a place of his own by this time, but the shutdown prevented him from moving out. His sister interjected naively, "You could go on welfare like cousin Jim." Steve blushed and pretended to ignore her, but his embarrassment and distress about his failure to establish himself as an independent adult were obvious.

Hopes and aspirations are based on one's sense of identity, what one feels one can become, what one thinks one can achieve. Nothing seems more characteristic of working-class Americans than the hope of giving "something better" to their children. The ability to realize this hope is one way in which they judge their success in life. Something better for the children was a dream the Seiberling workers shared with their parents' generation, and a job in a rubber factory both defined the standard and provided the means of realizing the dream.

The dreams of something better were modest. Becky Koegel wanted to be able to leave her house to her children. Mark Kelley had hoped to send his children to a private Christian academy. Bob Younger wanted to help his son go to the University of Akron or to welding school. The closing of the Seiberling plant and the difficulties of displaced workers in finding good jobs have rendered these dreams impossible. A sense of personal failure has set in as the hopes of achieving something better have begun to fade.

Eddie Wechenbacker found that he was no longer able to think of himself as a good provider. He needed that identity in order to distance himself from the failures of his father. Eddie had worked since the age of fifteen in order to have the things his father could not give him. His father drifted from job to job. Eddie had been "raised poor" and bitterly remembered the charity his family had received when he was a child, the government-surplus milk that formed lumps at the bottom of his glass.

Eddie worries that he may be poor again. He sighed when I asked him if the closing of the Seiberling plant had changed any of his long-term plans. He said, "I wanted something better for my girls." At that point he was unable even to pay child support. "My ex-wife dragged me into court and they wanted to know why I wasn't paying. They thought I was still working at Seiberling and making big money." He now earns $5.35 an hour (and negligible benefits), enough only to cover basic living expenses. Eddie got up at this point in the conversation to make another pot of coffee. While he was out of the room his girlfriend, Valerie, told me, "He cries about not being able to pay that support."

Many of the unemployed in Barberton felt they had failed not only their children but their parents as well. The role of good son or good daughter has become more difficult to realize. Many of the former rubber workers found themselves unable to do as well as their parents, let alone to excel them. I dropped by Mark Burke's apartment frequently. Once he invited me to go to his father's house with him. Mark's children were visiting from California, where they live with his ex-wife. Because Mark lived in a one-bedroom apartment with his girlfriend, the children spent the month at his parents' house. His father, now retired from Firestone, had lent him the money to fly the children to Ohio for the visit, but Mark had no idea how he could pay him back.

When we arrived, Mark's two children rushed into the kitchen to show him the new digital watches their grandfather had bought them. Mark blushed. He had been unable to give his children anything, and his shame showed on his face and made him irritable with them that evening. On our way home, I asked Mark about his relationship with his father. He began with a complaint, then retracted it. "My dad's been great to me. He's bailed me out more times than I care to mention. Only he's kind of hard. He worked two jobs most of his life and can't understand why me and Jack [his brother] can't even get one." Mark feels that he is a failure in his father's eyes, denying the man the pleasure of seeing his son having something better.

Participation in the Collectivity

Job loss has important consequences for the way in which people encounter the wider world; such encounters provide pleasant social interchange and also give people a sense of purpose in the human community (Jahoda 1984). Friendships and social networks often depend on work relations, and loss of work diminishes social contact. The shrinking of social experience puts a strain on domestic relations. Casual social contacts are a relief when highly charged family relations become difficult (Barrett and McIntosh 1982). The diminution of social interaction caused by joblessness narrows the psychic space in which the unemployed maneuver. Being cut off from work also makes many of the jobless feel useless, since they view themselves as failing to contribute to the general welfare.

The isolation of unemployment involves withdrawal from many kinds of social activity. Bob Younger told me, "I never knew how bad TV was before I started watching it like I do now." Jeff Carey said, "We used to go out for a drink with this or that friend almost every weekend. Can't do that any more. I drink my beer at home now." Richard Calvino commented that it was hard to go shopping and bump into an old workmate. "It's kind of embarrassing. Nobody wants to talk 'cause they're afraid to ask what you're doing. So I just stay home and avoid people." Sally Baines has stopped going to the local shopping mall because she found it difficult to go merely to look and not buy. "I used to go just to walk around and look. I can't now 'cause it makes me feel so cheap. Just sitting around not buying anything." Bob Younger and his wife stopped going to church. "That bunch was only interested in what you put in the tray. When you needed something they didn't care if you came around much. What kind of church is that?"

[86]

A stable job provides a stable network of friends. Seiberling workers repeated over and over again that they missed the people at work, that Seiberling was like a family to them. Keith Hagen was particularly sentimental about these memories. On two occasions he had organized a reunion for the formerly working members of URW Local 18. The first drew fifty people. The second year he planned for a larger group but fewer than thirty came. He was eager for me to interview him because he enjoyed reminiscing about the plant and hearing news of his former workmates. I was twenty minutes late for my visit with him. After I apologized, Keith excused me with a polite comment about a project that he had been busy with. His little girl interjected, "Yeah, he sat by the window for an hour saying, 'I bet he doesn't come.'" He showed me photographs taken at the plant and walked me to my car after the interview, obviously reluctant to end the conversation.

Changes in social networks and social patterns put strain on a marriage. Working-class couples have classically been described as belonging to distinct male and female networks (Komarovsky 1964). Husbands and wives tend to have separate spheres of friends and contacts. They meet to share meals, time with children, and sex—a pattern that seemed characteristic of many of the couples I knew in Barberton. Unemployment changes the situation by throwing the couple together more often and for longer periods. Katie and Dick Miller's recent marriage had not been without its problems. Dick was laid off for nine consecutive months. He spent most of his time at home, working in the yard, cleaning his rifles, or sitting in an easy chair reading the daily newspaper over several times. One afternoon in late 1982 I stopped for coffee, as I often did, and Katie began to complain to me about Dick. "Is my old man a grouch! I can't do nothing without him yelling. Now I go over to Donna's next door and talk and he comes over to yell and tells me, 'What's she got so hot over there?' Then me and Donna wanted to do that Fifties Night at the Varsity [a local club] and he just shit. I told him, just because we're Christians now don't mean we can't have fun." Having Dick around the house irritated her, and she was eager for him to go back to work. "We got to do something about this if we are going to stay together." Fortunately, he was called back to his job in a small tool factory for a while during the summer in 1983, and the tension was eased.

Problems with social relations have another dimension. The unem-

[87]

ployed are deprived of the sense of purpose they once derived from work. While individualism is often emphasized as a primary value in our society, a sense of collective purpose is nonetheless present. Reba Brown put it rather directly, saying that being in a high tax bracket was, in a way, a matter of some pride. She had felt that she was thereby helping those less fortunate than herself. Being workers in an essential industry gave many of my informants a sense of usefulness. The unemployed find themselves cut off from the sense of being useful members of society, contributing to the collective good. Unemployed workers expressed to Jahoda (1984) their feelings of "being on the scrap heap" during the thirties. Former Seiberling workers say that they feel "good for nothing" and "no good any more." Jeff Carey expressed this sense of deprivation in his reaction to the closing. "It was like an execution. Chop! They don't need you any more."

This lack of a sense of purpose was evident in many statements I heard and was symbolized in unexpected ways. Like many other men, Orville Baker took great pride in being involved with the production of tires at Seiberling. Even after the plant closing he carefully followed the trade journals to learn about technological changes and new products in the rubber industry. Despite the emotional support given to him by his family, he found much of his life meaningless during his long period of unemployment, cut off from the things he had been involved with for so long.

Orville enjoyed the solitary sport of the woodsman, exploring the forests and streams of the nearby countryside. He took great pleasure in catching baby bluegills in springtime and stocking his fish tank with them. He would feed and care for them until they had become too large for the tank; then he would return the fish to the pond from which they had come.

During the evening I spent with him in his home he watched the fish with great enjoyment as they darted in and out of their rock caverns, their scales shining in the red light behind the tank. He thought about his condition in life, comparing his own lack of purpose and his isolation with that of the fish. He looked forward to the spring, "When I leave them go, that's the best part. They go back where they belong." He shared this bit of homespun symbolism with mild embarrassment.

The mention of the positive psychological value of work would have brought smiles to the faces of many of the Seiberling workers before

March 1980. Oppressive work, work that is highly routinized, work that affords little control, is the source of much of the dissatisfaction in industrialized society today. It is not surprising, then, that work is not perceived by industrial workers as a path toward personal fulfillment.

The relationship of unemployment to mental illness is a complicated one. The epidemiological association between unemployment and mental illness has been well established.[3] Rises in the unemployment rate are associated with increases in first-time psychiatric hospitalizations, suicide, homicide, and alcoholism (Brenner 1973). These conclusions are reached from a study of data from large regions. No such epidemiological studies of data from Akron or Barberton have been done, but there are indications that a similar pattern exists there. Crime, particularly rape, has increased in the county during the period of increasing unemployment (Criminal Justice Commission 1980). Mental health professionals have noted a rise in the demand for services although the population has decreased.[4] The number of phone calls to the centralized social-services information number for all problems, including mental health problems, rose after 1980.[5] Among the former Seiberling workers there were two suicides in the three years following the closing. Drinking and divorce were commonly mentioned by the people in Barberton as problems they saw among the unemployed they knew. The anecdotes in this chapter add to the impression that plant closings in Barberton, as elsewhere, have had a significant negative impact on mental health.

[3]Some studies (Buss and Redburn 1983b) suggest that job losers themselves may not be most vulnerable to the mental health problems associated with unemployment. It may be that it is the general effect of a tight labor market and declining resources in the community that puts pressure on those more vulnerable to mental illness. The "healthy worker" effect—that is, the hypothesis that workers with good jobs are a selected group of especially fit individuals—may hold for mental health. More research must be done in this area to answer these questions.

[4]Interview with Nancy Fouche, director, Portage Path Mental Health Center, Barberton, 23 August 1982.

[5]Presentation by Gary Cook, executive director, Info-Line (a telephone service to provide information about regional social services), Akron, before the Barberton Area United Way Agency Review and Allocation Committee, site visit, 14 July 1983.

[5]

Providential Ancestors

Barberton grew up along three arteries of commerce: the Tuscarawas River, the Ohio Canal, and the railroad lines. The industrial base of the city depended on access to raw materials and outside markets; the location of the city and much of its physical arrangements are bound up with the requirements of its industries. The development of roads, sewers, communication systems, and many other aspects of the city were determined by the history of those industries. The story of Barberton's industries involves economic circuits of investments and profits, the rise and fall of industrial empires, and the development of technologies for increasing production and controlling people.

The history of Barberton is also a story of the men and women who made their homes there, worked in its mills, and created a life among the factories. A working-class community developed out of the struggles of these people over issues that affected them as a group.[1] Commu-

[1]The word *community* is used in this chapter to refer to a unified group of people with common interests, people organized around particular issues and goals, rather than a group simply defined by residence in a geographic location (cf. Raines et al. 1982). The term *working-class communities* has other implications. First, it excludes the interests and organizations of corporations. Working-class community is not, however, synonymous with class. The position taken here is that, despite the gravity and reality of class in our society, a class should not be visualized as a concrete entity, group, or institution. Community does refer to people in their capacity as members of social

nal interests historically found expression through such organizations as political parties, unions, and protest movements. Fundamental contradictions exist between the interests of the corporations and the communities that grew up with them. Economic transformations have often caused distress for the people in those communities, and they have attempted to challenge the power of the industries that impinge on their lives.[2]

Origins of Capital and Community

Barberton is situated on an ancient portage first used by the Indians traveling between the Ohio River and Lake Erie. An eight-mile stretch of land separates the southward-flowing Tuscarawas from the Cuyahoga River, which flows north. Along this portage path grew the city of Akron and a later expansion that became Barberton.

Less than two hundred years ago the entire region was a virgin wilderness, the home of hunting and gathering peoples. After the Revolutionary War, Indians were gradually driven from the territory. Connecticut laid claim to what is now northeastern Ohio and designated the area its "western reserve." Land companies bought the territory from the state government and then eagerly surveyed it and sold it as farmland to people who wanted to escape the tyranny of factories and the ten-hour workday in eastern cities. The earliest settlers of the Western Reserve came from Connecticut, Pennsylvania, and New York to carve homesteads and farms out of the wilderness after 1800.

The wilderness was gradually transformed into rich farmland, worked by independent farmers on small holdings that produced grains for flour, cornmeal, and whiskey. When the local economy stagnated in the 1820s, the State of Ohio built a system of canals, an inland waterway that made it possible to export the abundant agricultural produce. Port towns grew up along the locks that connected the Tuscarawas and the Cuyahoga, including Akron, Cascade, New Portage, and Port Clinton.

---

groups and institutions. Anthony Giddens has discussed this distinction in terms of group and structure (1979:76).

[2]To explain the rise of unemployment in Barberton I have adopted the analysis in *Beyond the Waste Land* (Bowles, Gordon, and Weisskopf 1983).

The Tuscarawas River (left) and the Ohio Canal flank the railroad in Barberton

The first commercial concerns were stores and small production firms: grain mills, tanneries, ceramic factories. As the industries grew, the economy of the region was transformed from a system of small independent farmers into one based on capital investment and factory production. Industrial capitalism took hold of the erstwhile agrarian society.

Ohio became the center of the biggest industrial region in the world. By 1820 Ohio was ranked third among the states in industrial output. There was an eightfold growth in industrial output between 1860 and 1908, and the population increased fourfold (Ohio Chamber of Commerce 1975). Shrewd businessmen built economic empires by choking off competition and garnering government subsidies. The first industrial fortunes made in Summit County were in milled grains, coal, ceramic products, matches, and farm machinery.

A man who rejoiced in the name Ohio Columbus Barber took over an Akron match factory from his father in 1863 and built it into an international cartel. At its zenith the cartel included stands of timber in California, coal mines, and match factories in several countries. Barber, whose firm was the largest producer of strike matches in the world, was an entrepreneur of international stature and was Akron's leading industrialist, involving himself in many major economic undertakings in the area.

In his later years Barber spent a sizable fortune building a 3,000-acre fantasy farm adjacent to Barberton. It was landscaped with plants brought from all parts of the globe and supplied with exotic livestock housed in magnificent barns resembling palaces. The farm was complete with a baronial mansion staffed by English servants. Barber had intended that the farm be taken over by Western Reserve College as a research center for scientific farming, but the dream was never realized because he was unwilling to relinquish his control over the property and allow the transformation to take place before he died. After his death in 1920, the empire was quickly dismantled and the farm abandoned.

O. C. Barber is known as the founder of Barberton because a series of his economic ventures led to the development of the new city. In 1880, Barber acquired a 550-acre farm along the Ohio Canal near New Portage, seven miles southwest of Akron. His original plan to develop a soda-ash plant feeding off the nearby limestone mines turned out to be

Two of O. C. Barber's abandoned barns loom over the Little League Field

impractical and was abandoned. When in 1890 it was discovered that Barber was delinquent in paying $100,000 in property taxes owed to Summit County, he became involved in a bitter public dispute with the county auditor and the leadership of the Akron-based government. During this period Barber began a flurry of new enterprises on the land near New Portage. His grudge against the Akron leadership stimulated his interest in creating a separate town not ten miles away. The usual pattern of development at the time was the incorporation of industrial expansion into existing cities (Grismer 1952, Fleming 1981).[3]

Barber enlisted the help of M. J. Alexander, a Pittsburgh investor who had already successfully promoted the building of two new towns, Charleroi and Jeannette, in Pennsylvania. Alexander's plan was to attract industry to an area and then sell land to people who came to work in the factories. The Barberton Land Company was formed to lay out the town and sell the private plots for housing and shops. The properties went on sale in 1891; a few factories were already being built. The first workers lived in tents.

Barber himself established eight industries in the town, including the National Sewer Pipe Company and the Sterling Boiler Company, later Babcock and Wilcox. Alexander invested in a valve plant and a ceramic insulator factory, while W. A. Johnston, the surveyor for the land company, attracted the Pittsburgh Plate Glass Company to the area to build a soda-ash plant (Grismer 1952:281). The Portage Rubber Company was also founded at this time and was built on the banks of the Ohio Canal, which ran through Barber's town. Shortly after this initial growth period, the panic of 1893 rocked the new town and many of its factories were forced out of business. The ensuing economic stagnation lasted until the end of World War I. In 1899 Barber built what was at the time the world's largest match factory in Barberton and moved his Diamond Match Company there (Fleming 1981:23). By 1920, the industrial base of Barberton had been solidly established.

[3]The factors that led to the founding of Barberton are disputed. Fleming (1981) argues, unconvincingly, that the disagreement over taxes had nothing to do with the development. Grismer (1952) reported that it was common knowledge at the time that Barber's grudge precipitated the creation of a new town. Whatever Barber's intentions, and they were no doubt complex, this belief animated the community that defined itself in opposition to the control of industrialists.

The basic infrastructure of the economy remained much the same for the next fifty years.

Industrial capitalism quickly established itself in the Midwest, and by 1850 individual advancement to higher economic status had become much rarer and more difficult than before (Zinn 1980). Rapid industrialization led to serious problems: working conditions were harsh; jobs were insecure and unemployment was a constant threat; cities did not provide the necessary services to support the needs of a population of urban factory workers. A social movement emerged to address the problems in the workplace and neighborhood. Working-class communities began to define themselves in opposition to the corporations that dominated them. Protests were organized by trade unions, unemployment councils, and political parties. The creation of a community that could effectively pursue its interests was not without difficulties, as rapid growth, ethnic and racial differences, and the persistence of small farms created internal divisions (Davis 1980b).

The condition of the industrial working class in Ohio led to much protest and eventual reform. The workdays were very long, often more than ten hours; low wages barely covered the necessities of life. Barber's match factory was one of Summit County's worst plants, employing mostly women and children at the lowest wages in the region. Many workers died of "phosphorus necrosis," brought on by exposure to phosphorus in the workplace. Neither medical bills nor compensation were paid by the employer or the state.[4]

Strikes, disruptions, and protests led to a reform movement in government. Progressive legislation instituted the eight-hour workday, child-labor laws, and compensation for industrial accidents. Labor Day was created in response to the demands of workers for a holiday between Memorial Day and Thanksgiving. The creation of Labor Day

[4]Fleming in his biography of O. C. Barber (1981) goes to some lengths to place Barber in the progressive tradition of the late nineteenth century. I think this effort is quite inappropriate. O. C. Barber was not a progressive in any sense of the word. He was an ardent member of the Republican party; he never supported the Progressive party. He opposed most major reforms both in his practices and in his public statements. He defied child-labor laws and work safety laws; he made public pronouncements to justify his position. His one progressive stance was his support of the nationalization of the railroads, which was clearly motivated by an incident in which a railroad company cheated Barber out of a large sum of money.

was also supported by industrialists as an alternative to May Day, which had become associated with radical worker movements.

Unemployment was one of the worst hardships faced by factory workers during the nineteenth century. The instability of the economy led to repeated waves of slowdowns and closings, resulting in dramatic increases in unemployment. As early as the 1870s, jobless workers began to organize unemployment councils in efforts to secure jobs and relief. In 1893, unemployed workers in Akron demanded that the city council create jobs by passing a bond issue to sponsor public works. A riot ensued when the jobs were given to lower-paid Italian immigrants (Grismer 1952:280). In 1894, James Coxey of nearby Massillon organized a march to Washington, D.C., a living petition demanding the creation of jobs by the federal government. Coxey's Army, as it came to be called, was dispersed by federal troops (Boryczka and Cary 1982: 147). Problems of neighborhoods and homes also brought together the working-class community in political actions. Rapid growth in Barberton and Akron created crowding, inadequate water and sewerage facilities, and a lack of social services, including schools. In Akron rooming houses for workers slept two consecutive shifts in the same beds.

In Barberton, controversy arose over the operation of the Barberton Land Company, which was by then commonly known as the Syndicate. In 1893 the company mounted a large advertising campaign to draw workers to the factories and sell them land for homes. Newspaper advertisements in the Akron paper and an elaborate brochure described Barberton as the "Garden Spot of the Western Reserve," "far from the squalor of the big city," a place offering maximum wages and minimum taxes. The brochure promised "improved" water and sewers, landscaped parks, and schools (Wales 1893).

It soon became clear to the new residents that the land company would spend no money for those improvements. Frustrations over the conditions of the roads, sewers, and schools led a group of community leaders to apply to the state to incorporate the region as a town. This move was understood by the townspeople as an act of defiance toward the company.[5] It is no exaggeration to say that the first expression of community sentiment in Barberton reflected the fundamental conflict

[5]W. A. Johnston, surveyor for the land company and historian of Barberton, wrote (Johnston and Olin 1976) that the land company was secretly pleased when the citizens incorporated the town. The move lifted some of the responsibilities from the company.

between capital and community. In 1893 the people voted on an official name for the new town. Despite widespread criticism of the land company, Barberton, the name then in use, won over New Portage, but only by one vote (American Legion 1922).

The development of a cohesive community was difficult because of the many differences among the early residents. Internal divisions limited the effectiveness of movements to improve conditions in the town and were often exploited by the opponents of reform. Barberton, unlike older cities, had no groups of skilled artisans who could lead the popular resistance. The notion of the "industrial frontier" fostered hopes of individual mobility and impeded collective action (Gordon, Edwards, and Reich 1984).

Rapid growth inhibited effective community formation because newcomers from divergent backgrounds did not automatically cooperate with one another. In 1890, the area around Davis Lake (later named Lake Anna, after Barber's daughter) owned by the land company contained only a single farmhouse. By 1891, the area contained several factories and several houses, a hotel, and more than 2,000 people. The population grew to 4,354 in 1900 and to 18,811 in 1920. While native-born Americans were always in the majority (never less than 93 percent of the population), European immigrants made an important mark on the community. Barberton received immigrants from thirty-one foreign nations, the greatest numbers coming from Italy, Yugoslavia (Slovenes), and Czechoslovakia (Slovaks) (Renninger 1932:21).

The American-born workers, eager to protect their jobs, objected to the influx of immigrants. Employers, on the other hand, were keen on attracting new residents in order to keep the labor pool as large as possible and to use one ethnic group to undercut the demands of the others. It was a common practice for companies to advertise for workers in newspapers in many parts of the United States and Europe. The employers' strategy was clear from the earliest days in Barberton. When workers building the first roads went on strike, sixty black men were brought in from Virginia to finish the work (Johnston and Olin 1976:51).

Despite rapid industrial growth, the labor supply always outstripped the availability of jobs. Workers were almost powerless because of their constant fear of being replaced. By 1916 a local movement had developed to keep new immigrants out of Barberton. Italians in particular were held in low esteem because they worked for very little; they were perhaps the poorest of the immigrants. This desire to protect their position in the labor market also led to a movement to block the building of a streetcar between Barberton and Akron. Barberton workers saw no need to encourage "barnacles," people who worked in Barberton and lived in Akron, and thus posed another threat to their job security (Fleming 1981:260).

The native-born workers were relatively slow to identify themselves with the city and factory life. For many years workers moved back and forth between agricultural employment and industrial work. Small farms to the south of Barberton provided a constant source of new workers and also a place that could reabsorb them during economic lulls. Turnover in the early factories was very high; many men worked there for short periods and then returned to the land. During the crash of 1921, 50,000 people left the Akron area, most of them young men returning to the countryside (Grismer 1952:414). Because of this long-standing association with farm life, self-identification as a landless urban working class developed very late among these people. The process was not completed until recently, and many of the ideals and attitudes of the small farmer have persisted. The romanticization of rural life, with its individual freedoms and independence, has for a long time stood in sharp contrast to the constraints of urban life and the economic vulnerability experienced by factory workers. The slow development of Barberton workers' identity as industrial laborers weakened their potential to recognize their shared interests and to undertake collective action.

Rubber and People

The Akron rubber industry began as a small, uncertain enterprise, like the many other businesses floated by local investors during the nineteenth century. The location of the rubber industry in Akron occurred to a large extent by chance. B. F. Goodrich, a physician and speculator, was searching for a place in which to establish an industrial enterprise. The rubber industry on the East Coast was highly competitive and the Midwest offered an attractive new market. Promotional material published by a group of Akron businessmen brought Goodrich

[99]

to Akron. The low wages in the region attracted his interest. Substantial capital was also offered by local investors. These attractions led to the founding in 1870 of Goodrich, Tew, and Company, which produced rubber hoses, waterproof cloth, and rubber boots (Allen 1979: 116).

Dr. Goodrich's company, with its slow but steady growth, survived the series of economic downturns that caused many other concerns to fail in the 1890s. High profits attracted others to the rubber industry and to Akron. By 1919 there were no fewer than 477 rubber companies in the United States (Roberts 1944:4). It was no surprise that John A. Seiberling, one of Akron's leading industrialists, invested in a rubber factory. Seiberling's factory was lost in the panic of 1893 along with the rest of his fortune. His sons, Frank and Charles, were by that time themselves established in the rubber business, and in 1898 Frank Seiberling founded the Goodyear Tire and Rubber Company. By the eve of World War I, the two brothers had built it into the largest rubber company in the world.

The Firestone Company was founded in 1902. Harvey Firestone, son of a prosperous Ohio farmer, returned to the region after several ventures in the rubber industry in Chicago and Detroit. While in Detroit, Firestone met Henry Ford, with whom he shared ideas about mass production, low prices, and defiance of patent laws. The relationship established then between the two companies has continued to the present day (Lief 1951:15).

The period between 1870 and World War I was marked by cutthroat competition as more and more producers entered the field; prices and wages were slashed to drive competitors out of the market. Every form of cartel was created to gain a competitive edge. The Akron rubber companies repeatedly broke patent laws and defied court rulings in order to gain an advantage.

Ford began mass production of automobiles in 1907. The national appetite for automobiles created a demand for tires. The Firestone Company received the order for the original tires on the Model T, the first automobile produced for mass consumption. From these early days the fates of Detroit and Akron were connected. A local saw, "When Detroit gets a cold, Akron sneezes," dates from that period. By 1928 the auto industry bought 85 percent of the rubber produced in the United States (Roberts 1944:6).

[100]

Technological change in the rubber industry proceeded rapidly in Akron. Rubber had become commercially important after Charles Goodyear developed vulcanization, a process of making rubber heat resistant. The pneumatic tire was developed after the bicycle had become popular. Air-filled tires gave a more comfortable ride than the solid tires that preceded them and were quickly adopted for carriages and then for automobiles. The changes in the technology of production were no less stunning. The application of Taylorism (assembly-line production) in the rubber industry led to the replacement of the skilled craftsmen who had previously built tires and resulted in a net loss of 7,155 jobs between 1921 and 1931, despite a dramatic increase in production (Roberts 1944:11). These changes also led to the construction of huge factories, where hundreds of workers came together.

Vertical and horizontal monopolies also developed as profits continued to attract competitors into the field. Tire companies acquired latex plantations in Africa, Asia, and South America. Cotton acreage and cotton mills under their control ensured a steady supply of tire cord. Rubber firms bought coal mines and railroads to supply inexpensive energy for their factories. Gradually competitors were driven out or absorbed and empires were formed. By 1920, the Big Four companies—Goodyear, Firestone, Goodrich, and U.S. Rubber—shared 80 percent of the nation's rubber business (Roberts 1944:15). All but one had headquarters in Akron (U.S. Rubber was located in Michigan). This dual process of technological innovation and corporate consolidation, which has been called homogenization (Gordon, Edwards, and Reich 1984), helped to give form to the protest that followed.

The period between World War I and 1929 saw spectacular, albeit erratic, economic growth. The U.S. automobile and tire markets expanded rapidly: 1.6 million vehicles in 1914 to 8.2 million in 1920. Growth was interrupted by a slump after the war and again in 1921. The crash of 1921 proved devastating for the Seiberling brothers. Financially overextended, they lost control of the Goodyear Company to a brokerage firm on Wall Street. The brothers, then both over sixty, raised local capital to purchase the defunct Portage Rubber Company in Barberton. They renamed it, opened it as the Seiberling Tire Company in 1921, and concentrated on producing high-quality replacement tires. The company proved very profitable but never grew to the size of any of the Big Four.

[101]

The decades of growth were followed by a long period of economic stagnation, linked to an instability in world prices, a regressive income structure, and wild speculation (Bowles, Gordon, and Weisskopf 1983: 249). Demand collapsed, companies vanished, and the billion-dollar rubber industry was reduced by half. Capitalists and government leaders alike were at a loss to cope with the crisis, and stagnation lingered.

The depression hit the Akron area in 1930, when the rubber companies began costly price wars and production decreased. The Akron Chamber of Commerce estimated that 14,200 factory workers were dismissed that year, over 21 percent of the city's work force. Goodyear cut production and instituted a six-hour workday. The value of common stock fell dramatically: Seiberling from 29 to 1¼, Goodyear from 106 to 10, Goodrich from 69 to 3½, and Firestone from 271 to 10 between 19 October 1929 and 1 March 1933.[6] Average weekly wages dropped from over $29 to less than $19 in 1933 (Grismer 1952:477).

After the 1932 election, the Roosevelt administration attempted to stabilize the economy by dramatically expanding the role of the government. Responding partly to popular protest and partly to the needs of industry, the New Deal fundamentally restructured the relationship between labor and capital through the institutionalization of collective bargaining. Redistribution of income, in the form of relief work, created a demand for products and reduced the threat of political destabilization. The rubber industry vigorously opposed the New Deal and sought to undermine many of its reforms.

The rubber mills brought people of diverse backgrounds together in the struggle against capitalism. The socialist movement developed in response to the problems of the working-class communities, to which factory issues were crucial. In the years before World War I, the Socialist party under the leadership of Eugene Debs gained widespread support and some electoral power. Cleveland elected a Socialist mayor, Tom Johnson, and Socialists held city council seats in Akron and Barberton.[7] While the Democratic party remained in control of

[6]Firestone stock split three for one in 1929. Its decline was comparable to that of other major tire companies during the Depression.

[7]Fleming (1981:261) is mistaken in his claim that Barberton elected a Socialist mayor in 1912. A Democrat won in that year, but the Socialist party had a full slate of candidates and had significant support in Barberton.

Barberton and the country, the Socialists shifted the political climate of the era decidedly to the left.

The first major labor confrontation in the Akron area came in 1913, when workers at Firestone walked out to protest a speedup. Other issues raised by the strikers were crowding in the shop, poor drinking water, benzene fumes, company espionage, blacklisting, and the practice of advertising for workers in many states, which kept a steady stream of migrants—and an oversupply of labor—coming to Akron.

Bill Haywood, organizer for the International Workers of the World (IWW), came to Akron to help in the strike, and a bitter public battle ensued. The company branded the union organizers as agitators and the IWW as outsiders. They argued that the claims of the workers were unfounded and their demands arbitrary. Firestone organized a "citizens' group," vigilantes who physically harassed the strikers—the "mob of the rich," Haywood called them when he was accused of supporting violence and driven from town. Organizers for the American Federation of Labor (AFL) were latecomers to the scene and weakened the strike by dividing the workers (Roberts 1944:38).

Workers in other plants gave the strike strong support. A sense of community had grown out of the common experience in the shops and the struggle for improvements. Across the city of Akron, more than 15,000 rubber workers refused to work at the height of the strike. In Barberton, workers at Pittsburgh Plate Glass staged a sympathy strike, and the women at the Diamond Match factory walked out in protest. The local newspaper, the *Barberton Leader*, reported, "Barberton strikers paraded every day this week, some days morning, noon, and evening. The men and women have numbered about a hundred, rain or shine they parade" (28 February 1913). Saloons in Barberton were closed by the sheriff.

The 1913 strike was the last major labor dispute in Akron until the 1930s. After World War I, wages improved slightly, but the distribution of income became increasingly regressive. Between 1923 and 1929 productivity increased 31 percent, while wages rose only 5 percent (Keyserling 1979:22). Companies followed an aggressive antiunion policy, introducing "company unions," publishing newsletters to persuade workers to oppose unions, and harassing workers who supported unions (Roberts 1944:133).

Reformers in industry called for "welfare capitalism" to improve the lot of the workers. Some companies and individuals embarked on philanthropic projects, but reforms in the 1920s had little effect on the general welfare of the population of the United States, of which as much as one-third lived in poverty (Keyserling 1979:23). Repression of the Socialist party and the IWW partly explains the low ebb of working-class power at the time. During World War I the Socialists were attacked for their refusal to support the war. Eugene Debs, who as a presidential candidate in 1912 won nearly 6 percent of the votes (compared to Woodrow Wilson's 42 percent), spent four years in prison for expressing in public his ambivalence about a war that, in his eyes, brought no benefit to the working class of America. Violence and repression silenced the opposition (Zinn 1980:359).

Whatever expectations or illusions the American people might have had about peace and prosperity came to an end after 1929. The response of Akron's leaders and industrialists was feeble; editorialists urged the unemployed to go back to the farm and claimed that men could find jobs if they really wanted to work. The city of Barberton offered fifteen permits to unemployed men to sell apples on street corners, and hundreds applied. Unemployment councils sprang up in both Akron and Barberton. They organized marches and demanded that the city create public works and relief. An angry crowd of demonstrators was dispersed with tear gas in Barberton after protesting the mysterious disappearance of a member of the Unemployment Council (Davis 1962).[8]

Speedups, wage cuts, and threats to job security led to renewed militancy among people who still had jobs. Roosevelt, struggling for a way to stabilize industry and labor, had enacted the National Industrial Recovery Act (NIRA), intended to institutionalize labor–management relations through collective bargaining. Section 7(a) of the NIRA provided that "employees shall have the right to organize and bargain collectively through representatives of their own choosing and shall be free from interference, or coercion of employers in designation of such representatives." Unions were recognized by federal law for the first time, and a wave of union organizing spread across the rubber industry and the nation.

---

[8]The *Barberton Herald* reported the incident on 9 June 1931, claiming that the disappearance of C. Louis Alexander was a "flight of fancy." One of my informants who participated in the events surrounding the incident reported that the police abducted and murdered the man. The mystery of the disappearance has never been solved.

Organizing the Seiberling workers was a risk even after the passage of the NIRA. They feared the loss of their jobs during the terrible depression. Still, a few workers defied the threats, meeting secretly in alleys and taverns and posting signs around town and in the shop. A meeting was called in 1934 at the Opera House (a boxing ring) in Barberton, and Local 18 of the URW was formed.[9]

In accord with its policies in other industries, the AFL had initially organized the rubber workers into sixteen craft unions, creating conflict inside the union movement through the decade; progressive labor leaders understood that real power lay in industrywide organization. Conflict over this issue eventually led to the creation of an organization within the AFL, the Committee for Industrial Organization (CIO), which in 1938 became the Congress of Industrial Organizations and went its own way. The URW became a strong supporter of the CIO.

While these divisions caused some problems for the new unions, the biggest impediment was the opposition of employers who refused to recognize the unions. In 1935 the Supreme Court ruled the NIRA unconstitutional, and the unions faltered. The National Labor Relations Act (the Wagner Act) was passed to replace it, but companies again defied the laws, hoping to prevail through yet another court action (Roberts 1944:255).

Throughout this period, shop-floor militancy remained high. The first sitdown strike arose spontaneously among rubber workers in Akron and the tactic was widely adopted by other unions (Lens 1973: 285). Organizers frequently met with police brutality, company espionage, and violence. Some of the worst conflict, which led to virtual street warfare, occurred in Barberton.

The workers at Ohio Brass went on strike for recognition of the Union of Electrical Workers in 1935 (Boyer and Morais 1972). The employers brought strikebreakers into the plant and provided them with food and water so they could hold out against the strikers. Picketers were dispersed twice by the police with tear gas and clubs. The workers, with the community behind them, rallied to build street blockades, hurl rocks through factory windows with catapults improvised out of inner tubes, and throw tear-gas bombs back at the police.[10]

[9]Interview with Victor Flayerty, former president, URW Local 18, Barberton, 30 July 1981.

[10]Interview with Dick Niebur, organizer, International Brotherhood of Electrical Workers, Cleveland, 25 January 1982.

[105]

After fourteen weeks the company bowed to the workers' demands. During the coldest weeks of January 1936, a strike at Goodyear drew a picket line eleven miles long encircling the plant, the longest picket line in history.

In 1937 Firestone workers went on strike for a union contract. Firestone refused to negotiate until the Supreme Court handed down a ruling upholding the Wagner Act. The company signed a contract recognizing the URW fourteen days after the announcement of the Court's decision. It was the first of the Big Four to do so. Other companies followed, but not without much dispute and some bloodshed. The Goodyear strike of 1938 resulted in brutal attacks on workers by police and company thugs. In 1939, URW Local 18 signed its first contract with the Seiberling company. Strife continued until the declaration of World War II, and it was not until 1941, under pressure from the War Labor Board, that Goodyear signed its first labor contract (Roberts 1944:252).

The unions fought many other political battles. In addition to union contracts, they pressed for the enactment of unemployment-insurance legislation, the Social Security Act, and the federal minimum wage. Their hopes for national health insurance, fought for at the time, were never realized. Unions supported the Works Progress Administration (WPA), which in 1938 provided jobs for more than 20,000 workers in Summit County (Grismer 1952:458). The contribution of the WPA to the public welfare was substantial, and its accomplishments should not be underestimated. The WPA built 600 miles of road and 55 bridges in Summit County. It constructed a sewage-treatment plant in Barberton. Lake Anna saw its first major improvements: cattails and industrial refuse were removed from the banks, stone walls were built, and a beach was created. WPA workers built a large addition to the Barberton High School, still in use today. All told, the WPA spent $51 million in Summit County and assisted perhaps one-sixth of the population during the hard times. Critics charged the WPA with boondoggling when unemployed men were hired to turn over the paving bricks on Barberton's Second Street to give it a renewed appearance.[11]

The city did not soon forget the desperation, loss of homes, and

[11]Interview with John McNamara, former member of Barberton City Council, 29 January 1983.

hunger of those years. Out of the struggle for survival developed a sense of common purpose that pervaded Barberton for thirty years. It was a community that understood its own interests as distinct from those of the companies and the government. The unionists became leaders in the community, unions being the strongest institutions in a social movement that fundamentally changed life in Barberton.

The events of 1936 were pivotal in the direction the working-class community would take. The URW held its first convention in Akron that year, breaking away from the AFL and establishing an independent and capable leadership. Within the URW there were two tendencies: a conservative one encouraged the bureaucratization of the union and conformity with the needs of industry; a leftward one strove for changes at the national level which would affect the working class as a whole.

This schism became apparent during the URW's 1936 convention, when factions formed over the issue of Roosevelt's reelection. The left wing, made up of union militants and Communists, pushed for the formation of a third party (Shrake 1974). The conservative faction prevailed by a narrow margin, setting the precedent for an alliance with the Democratic party and locking the union within the limitations of collective bargaining. With the coming of World War II the politics of the union and of the community took a distinct turn in this more conservative direction.

Boom Time: Boomtown

American industry emerged from the war as the undisputed victor over labor, its power consolidated on all fronts. War production had brought soaring profits, and labor militancy had been subdued as industry learned to manipulate unions to discipline the work force. The U.S. military presence secured and expanded American capitalist interests in most parts of the world. The priorities of industry superseded all others, including concerns about shop-floor issues, pollution of the environment, and the welfare of factory-based communities (Bowles, Gordon, and Weisskopf 1983:70).

The war created a huge demand for rubber products. Akron and Barberton rubber factories made barrage balloons, dirigibles, the Mae

West life preserver, and tank tracks. Seiberling made rubber rafts and tires for military trucks, jeeps, earthmovers, and airplanes (Grismer 1952:500).

Latex, the raw material for commercial rubber, was produced on the plantations of the Big Four in Southeast Asia; Japanese expansion during World War II had threatened the supply of raw materials. The U.S. government therefore made a major effort to develop synthetic rubber, which led to the invention of substances known as GR-S and GR-N (government rubber). The government spent millions of dollars to build factories to produce synthetic rubber, which was then sold cheaply to companies making essential war matériel. After the war ended, Harvey Firestone, who was eager to preserve "free enterprise," spoke out strongly and successfully against government operation of these plants (Lief 1951:354).

During the war, the unemployment of the thirties had given way to local labor shortages. Women streamed into the factories to build tires. The War Labor Board imposed a wage freeze and thereby cut off much of the leverage that a tight labor market had created for workers. Shop-floor militancy had been forestalled in the name of "winning the war through industrial cooperation." A postwar consensus emerged in which unions ensured steady production for a guaranteed part of the profit (Bowles, Gordon, and Weisskopf 1983). An outbreak of wildcat strikes immediately after the war notwithstanding, the labor struggles of the thirties had ended. Union demands were regarded as legitimate only as long as they were restricted to the narrow issues of wages and benefits.

During the period between the end of World War II and the Vietnam War (roughly from 1945 to 1965), the U.S. economy expanded at an unprecedented rate. Profits grew steadily, and investments followed suit. Growth in the rubber industry was splendid, with dividends increasing and reliable. Sales broke records year after year, and American companies gained increasing control of the world market. Goodrich announced a stock split and record profits in 1959; Firestone sales increased from $1 billion in 1953 to a record $2 billion fifteen years later. Technological innovations and steady increases in productivity continued throughout this period, which saw the introduction of the automatic tire machine, automatic extruder, and computerized banberry to mix plastic resins. The total number of workers in the rubber industry declined by 20 percent while output increased by 30 percent between 1947 and 1959 (Abbott and Glazer 1961). Workers who were displaced by automation found other jobs waiting as the American economy continued to expand.

The expansion of the market led to the building of rubber factories in many parts of the country and the world, but Akron remained a primary site for tire production; its rubber factories consumed a large fraction of the world's crude rubber and were responsible for a hefty proportion of the total American tire production. Akron was still the Rubber Capital of the World.

Barberton's economy grew and diversified. The thriving Seiberling, Pittsburgh Plate Glass, and Babcock and Wilcox were joined by new plastics, metal fabrication, and electronics plants. Economic dips in 1955 and 1959 were quickly forgotten as America continued on an upswing. Employment opportunities grew in Barberton; there were 17,600 jobs in 1964, over 55 percent of them in heavy industry. In 1959, the match industry with its 265 jobs moved to nearby Wadsworth, but the effect on the local economy was slight.

The federal government played an important role in smoothing out the effects of the business cycles. Growth periods of the past had tended to be chaotic, punctuated by panics. Keynesian economic policy, which industry had bitterly opposed in the thirties, subsequently became a welcome alternative to the crashes and panics of the nineteenth century. Recessions, thought to be the result of high wages, were seen as cooling-off phases during which wage pressures from workers were reduced to levels consistent with a healthy economy.

The height of the boom came during the mid-sixties. The rubber companies shared in the tax break given to large companies in the form of rapid depreciation of property. The government fueled demand by waging war on two fronts—Lyndon Johnson declared war on poverty and enacted social legislation reminiscent of the New Deal, and the war in Vietnam created a demand that kept the factories of Barberton humming. Corporate profits soared from 1961 to 1966; a 30 percent increase in wealth outstripped the growth in the adult population by 350 percent (Bowles, Gordon, and Weisskopf 1983).

One of the results of the growth was a dramatic increase in the demand for labor. In 1965 unemployment dropped to a postwar low of 4.6 percent in the nation and 2.8 percent in Summit County. American commentators began to look upon the 1 percent unemployment rate in European countries as a realizable goal (Ginzberg 1968:52). In Barberton, the experience of full employment led to the belief that anyone who really wanted to work could find a job. These high levels of employment and sustained growth had profound effects on the industry and people of Barberton.

World War II and its aftermath changed the nature of the working class in Barberton. Once a community that understood its interests as opposed to those of capital, it became a community whose members identified their interests with continued economic growth and cooperation with their employers. Union power continued, but labor's relationship to capital was now circumscribed. The companies began to use the unions to enforce discipline on the shop floor, and legislative changes made union officials responsible for guaranteeing compliance with the terms of union contracts.

A sign of this new era in labor relations was the fact that some of the rubber companies invited unions to organize their newly built plants. The unions were able to promise and obtain increases in wages and benefits for their members, but they also sacrificed much of their ability to meet the needs of their members on the shop floor as grievances were put aside to ensure production. Strikes were few after the war: agreements between the URW and the companies in 1952 ended wildcat walkouts, and between 1954 and 1967 there was only one major strike in the entire rubber industry.

The trend toward institutionalizing class conflict through contract talks continued in the direction taken during the pivotal events in 1936. During the postwar period, companies were able to exploit internal differences within unions because of the atmosphere of fear and suspicion concerning communism. The left wing of the URW remained strong, however, and a majority of the members of its executive board refused to endorse the Marshall Plan and supported Henry Wallace, the Progressive party's candidate against Truman in 1948. Anticommunist sentiment grew after 1950, fired by Senator Joseph McCarthy's repeated allegations that Communists had infiltrated unions and the federal government. The position of the URW's executive board drew suspicions of subversiveness, which damaged the unity of the institution. After a series of confrontations (including one that resulted in a fistfight, known as the Pottstown Affair) the left-wing leaders were expelled by the conservative faction (URW 1975).

The Taft-Hartley Act of 1947, which limited the ability of unions to organize new locals and made sympathy strikes illegal, codified the transformation of labor unions. By making cooperation between unions increasingly difficult, the act dealt a crucial blow to working-class solidarity.

Unionists in Barberton were outraged, and the Barberton Joint Labor Committee sponsored its first Labor Day parade as a rally to protest the attack on the union movement. Congressman Walter Huber (D-Ohio) came to Barberton for the event and declared that the act "turned the clock back a hundred years. . . . We know that labor has made some mistakes but so have the bankers and other groups. Why a punitive law like the Taft-Hartley Bill?" (*Barberton Herald* 5 September 1947). Despite the objections, events had changed the labor movement, and the militant political marches of the thirties were giving way to parades with floats and baton twirlers.

A subtle change had taken place in the basis of union power. Originally the strength of unions rested on broad support from the larger community. Strikes were possible during the Depression because the picket line was an effective barrier then, for two reasons: most people were afraid to cross them and community morality condemned those who did. Scabs were anathema, the most despicable of human beings, people who would take away your job and your chance to better yourself. Unemployed men and women often joined picket lines in a show of solidarity.

The economic growth and stability of the postwar economy led to a different basis of union power and community. High levels of employment gave workers security in their jobs. Workers could strike then without having to fear that others would try to take their jobs. The apogee of this power was expressed in the strikes of the sixties, when near-full employment prevailed. The picket line became more a symbol than an enforcement of the strike.

The community developed a belief in progress and followed the lead of the stronger unions. Contracts with the rubber companies improved, with increased wages, company-paid pensions granted in 1949, hospitalization coverage in 1952, joint safety committees in 1959. The average wage of the rubber workers increased from $1.15 an hour in 1942 to

$4.11 an hour in 1968. The members of URW Local 18 were at the forefront of Barberton labor with strength of organization and a record of success. The community rallied around the URW during contract talks and strikes: merchants extended credit to workers and banks deferred payments on home mortgage loans. Other workers in Barberton saw the URW contract as a model and a standard for their own contract negotiations.

With the improvements in union contracts came an improvement in the standard of living. Median annual family income in Barberton rose from $3,213 in 1950 to $8,359 in 1970, representing a rise in the standard of living during a period of modest inflation. The town's substandard housing, reported as late as 1948, began to disappear (Fang Li 1948:83) as a portion of the workers' increased earnings went into household improvements. The proportion of houses with full plumbing increased from 79 percent to 99 percent between 1950 and 1980. Many workers moved to suburban real estate developments, which older residents sometimes referred to as High Mortgage Heights. A flood of consumer products became accessible—appliances, new cars—as well as affordable college education at the nearby state university.

Progress could be observed even in Snydertown as the shacks there began to disappear. The south end of Barberton, originally farmland belonging to a German family by the name of Snyder, had long been the poorest section of town. Shacks that had been built to house the boys and men who constructed the Ohio Canal remained to house the subsequent waves of people who moved to Barberton. Blacks were among the last to occupy Snydertown. Some of the most shockingly primitive housing was torn down only in the 1960s.

The rise in the standard of living and the buoyancy of the economy brought forth an efflorescence of community spirit and development. Catherine Dobbs led the city as mayor between 1956 and 1961, the longest term ever held by a mayor in Barberton. A remarkable person, Dobbs was the first woman mayor of a large town in America. The communitarian values she brought from her original home in Zoar, Ohio, inspired the city to reform and action. For many years Barberton had been notorious as a center for illegal gambling, until Mayor Dobbs mounted a successful offensive against organized gambling and vice. Major public works undertaken during her term in office included the building of a large viaduct spanning the railroad and canal that divided the city. The city's library was built and a major improvement in the schools was financed. The Planning Commission, established under Dobbs, prepared studies for future development (Davis 1962).

A sense of birthright and belonging developed out of the affluence that came to Barberton. The link with the farm had been severed; by 1960 only 4.4 percent of the Ohio work force were in agriculture. People had developed a strong allegiance to the city and its blue-collar identity. High school sports and the school colors were taken seriously; Barberton's basketball and football teams won many state championships. Grandmothers proudly wore their purple-and-white nylon team jackets in the supermarkets.

A sense of ownership in the factories themselves had developed. Former Seiberling workers often talked about the shutdown in terms of lost investment. "All those years invested, gone, *lost*," one of them said to me, reflecting on his twenty years as a tire builder. Seiberling workers had looked forward to lifetime employment and good pensions. Workers who had been able to help their children and relatives get jobs in the plant felt proprietary toward it. Their sons in college could often earn enough money in a summer factory job to pay for tuition.

For the generation that had been nurtured on hopes of a bright future, the illusion of ownership was a part of the belief in progress. The sufferings of the past had ended, and they began to express long-suppressed needs. Complaints about health issues and the quality of work were raised, along with continued demands for better wages and benefits. Conflict over these concerns erupted on the shop floor in the sixties, when near-full employment gave labor a sense of security.

Traditional authoritarian practices on the shop floor and rapid changes in technology led to ever-mounting complaints. Workers became less passive and began to express discontent over the quality of work life. Change itself was feared less than changes that decreased income or the workers' ability to control the conditions of work. Grievances accumulated over changes, then were used as bargaining chips by union representatives during contract negotiation talks.

Workers were no longer willing to overlook dangers in the workplace. Exposure to dangerous chemicals, such as benzene in the rubber industry, became a growing topic of concern. Nationally, industrial accidents doubled between 1960 and 1979 because of speedups (Gor-

[113]

don, Bowles, and Weisskopf 1983). A new consciousness about health issues spread among workers, and union committees for health and safety took on new importance. Protest and concern over health and safety issues in the workplace led to the enactment of the Occupational Safety and Health Act of 1970. Two workers were fired from Seiberling because they refused to work after nearly being killed when a machine threw a piece of metal through a wall. The unions suggested that heavy screens be installed to protect the workers. The company fought the request for two years. Finally the union prevailed and the workers were reinstated and the screens installed.

Discontent on the shop floor had important consequences for industry: a fall in productivity and a modest decline in profit margins. The dissolution of the postwar labor-capital consensus was taking an economic toll. Instead of meeting the new demands by broadening the locus of control, corporate executives redoubled their efforts to control workers and suppress their demands. Had they been willing to further the democratization of the workplace during this period, they might have maintained their profits.

The course of events led the economy in other directions. Corporate efforts to hold together the original terms of the postwar consensus failed and led to a decline in reinvestment in many American plants, the next step in the evolving strategy. The result of these policies was to choke off economic growth.

Postindustrial Barberton

Profit margins slipped at both Goodyear and Firestone in 1965. Despite upturns after the recessions in 1970 and 1974–75, recoveries were limited in duration and magnitude and did not stem the decline of the rubber industry or the general economy.

With the decline in profit margins, the rubber companies took a new direction in labor relations: increased supervision, refusal to rectify grievances, attacks on unions, and renewed legislative initiatives to limit collective bargaining. Adversarial relations between the URW and the rubber companies reemerged after 1967, when the major companies provoked a strike. Problems during contract negotiations were compounded when it was learned that the major rubber companies had made a secret mutual-aid pact to defeat the union. The newly elected president of the URW, Peter Bommarito, led the union through an industrywide strike involving 75,000 workers and lasting fourteen weeks. The strike won the membership its best contract to date.

There were several reasons for the new aggressive stance of industry. The tremendous growth of wealth during the first half of the postwar period had transformed the world economy. As a consequence of that change, challenges to corporate power arose on many fronts. Undeveloped nations grew into struggling economic powers that no longer accepted domination by American economic interests. Citizens' groups in the United States demanded a cleaner environment and more corporate responsibility for faulty products. Security and affluence led labor to make new demands for improvements in the quality of work life. Corporate leaders responded to these new demands by increased investments in control and repression of labor. The unintended result of these policies was a decline in profits, investments, and productivity, causing the stagnation and unemployment of the contemporary economy (Gordon, Bowles, and Weisskopf 1983). Investment in control occurred in two areas: control of work itself and control over the larger economy.

Industry responded to new shop-floor demands by introducing innovations that increased control over workers and permitted speedups in production. An early example of the strategy could be seen at the Vega plant built by General Motors in Lordstown, Ohio, which was later imitated by the rubber industry. Methods of observation and control, some sophisticated, some ancient—industrial psychologists, intensification of supervision, watchtowers—created a space-age version of Taylorism. Industrial psychology was one of the fastest-growing occupational categories in the seventies. In essence, professionals attempted to persuade workers that the new style of work was bearable. The discontent of workers with the widespread implementation of these new techniques made quality of work a national issue (U.S. Department of Health, Education, and Welfare 1973).

Supervision was stepped up at Seiberling, the number of supervisors for the forty-five tire builders increasing from five to twenty-one between 1967 and 1979.[12] Industrial psychologists at Seiberling offered

---

[12]Interview with Joseph Albanese, president, URW Local 18, Barberton, 6 October 1982.

small groups of workers a three-day seminar in labor–management problems, consisting of lectures, films, and role-playing. The purpose was to train workers to be passive in the face of speedups and other changes. Officially titled "Seiberling and You," the program (for which participating workers received three full days' pay) came to be called "the ordeal" and "propaganda," and it proved futile. Dissatisfaction was exacerbated, not diminished.

The failure of cooperation led to tragic waste. Antagonism over incentive rates escalated. Many workers at Seiberling received bonuses for meeting certain production quotas. The managerial staff conducted time studies with the intention of setting new machinery at the highest possible pace, making bonuses hard to earn. In one attempt to set production records on a new machine, a manager at Seiberling was killed when he was accidentally caught in a press.

Sagging profits and declining productivity were followed by faltering rates of investment. Goodyear stock values dropped by 50 percent between 1971 and 1981. Firestone had a similar decline in 1970; although sales were at a record high, profits actually fell (*Wall Street Journal* 27 August 1970). These failures led to declining investments in existing facilities, a strategy recently termed "disinvestment" (Bluestone and Harrison 1982). Older tire plants were milked for short-term profits and left to grow obsolete while profits were invested elsewhere (*Washington Post* 9 February 1979). The Seiberling plant is a good example of this practice. From 1965 to 1980 the management reinvested an average of $2 million a year. Given the inflation rate at the time, this figure constitutes declining investment in a facility that was already more than forty years old in 1965. Most of the investments were made in movable equipment, which represents less commitment to a particular factory. Firestone spent $50 million to put up a new tire-building facility of similar capacity in Oklahoma, a right-to-work state where laws impede unionization (*Wall Street Journal* 20 March 1969).

The next step in the corporate offensive was another decisive break with the past. Corporate leaders no longer considered unions to be a necessary or inevitable part of industrial life; unions had outlived their usefulness, they said. Corporate strategists embarked on systematic efforts—decertification campaigns, public education, plant relocations—to weaken and destroy unions (Gordon, Edwards, and Reich 1984:219). They spent millions of dollars on consulting firms that offered programs designed to decertify unions (Brody 1980). Goodyear built a new plant in Tennessee, another right-to-work state. The companies waged antiunion campaigns among the new rubber workers in order to block the URW's efforts. They carefully screened job applicants for attitudes toward unions, and chose workers without experience over those who had worked as tire builders for years.

The strike at Sun Rubber in 1972 signaled the trend for Barberton. During this dispute, the company announced that it would close, move to Georgia, and open there with a nonunion work force. This was Barberton's first so-called runaway shop. At the federal level the Labor Reform Bill of 1978 created new constraints on union organizing and strikes (Gordon, Bowles, and Weisskopf 1983:109). The Ohio Manufacturers' Association pushed for drastic changes in the Workman's Compensation Bureau.

The rate of mergers was very high during this period (Bluestone and Harrison 1982). The drive toward conglomeration was a wasteful activity, another huge corporate effort that resulted in no improvement in productivity. By 1983 mergers led to a situation in which the 200 largest corporations made 80 percent of all profits (Stone 1983). In 1921, when Seiberling was founded, 367 firms were producing rubber products in the United States. Today there are 16. Among the firms that have disappeared is Seiberling, which Firestone purchased in 1965 for $31 million.[13]

Goodrich invested in industrial supplies, Goodyear in petrochemicals; General Tire bought television and radio stations and the RKO motion picture studio. Firestone took steps toward several mergers outside of the rubber and chemical industries; none materialized, but the attempts cost time and money. The rubber companies showed less interest in the production of rubber than in financial intrigue. In 1982 John J. Nevin, Firestone's chief executive officer, announced, "Our object is not to remain among the top three tire manufactures in the world; our objective is to make money" (*Akron Beacon Journal* 12 September 1982). Mergers are an indication of the extent of financiers' power in the wider economy and the distance at which they stand from the productive process (Bowles, Gordon, and Weisskopf 1983:255).

[13]The Seiberling family sold the factory to Charles Lamb, founder of the Seilion company, which subsequently was sold to Firestone.

As corporate leaders became preoccupied by financial intrigue and speculation, they lost interest in engineering problems and technological progress. Firestone's top executives involved the company in an international scandal. Through Firestone Bank, a bogus company was created to carry on an illegal trade in millions of dollars in gold beginning in 1974. In 1976 it was discovered that Firestone executives had also been involved in a political slush fund that had been used to bribe government officials all over the world between 1960 and 1973. A Firestone executive was eventually found guilty of bribery and sentenced to prison. These activities led to suits and countersuits among the executives concerning the money that had been hidden or misused in the gold deal.

At the same time, Firestone developed and produced a new line of radial tires, the Firestone 500. The Firestone radials were poorly designed, however; the tire ply tended to separate from the steel belt. In 1976 the National Highway Safety Administration demanded that Firestone recall the product. During an investigation it was learned that Firestone's executives had been aware of the tire's defect during the very first months of its production. When consumer complaints began, they attempted to deny the company's responsibility.

Corporations also tried to influence government economic policy in their struggle to suppress the demands of workers. Industry had come to rely on occasional recessions to temper the demands of workers, but there had not been one between 1961 and 1968. President Nixon engineered a minor recession simply by restricting federal spending (Bowles, Gordon, and Weisskopf 1983:104). In Summit County, unemployment jumped from 3.4 percent in 1970 to 4.7 percent in 1971, and more than a hundred Seiberling workers were temporarily laid off. In time for Nixon's reelection, the economy was fueled by an increase in spending. Unemployment—a major domestic issue for George Mc-Govern, the Democratic hopeful, disappeared. While the URW and the Ohio AFL-CIO supported McGovern, Ohio voted for the "recovery" and for Nixon.

The character of the postwar economic decline had now been determined. Rising prices followed by wage hikes led to inflation. After the 1971 recession, the trade-off of inflation for unemployment was firmly established as a political alternative. Stagflation had been born. During a cooling phase, decreased productivity was the cost paid for the slump designed to suppress workers' demands.

Breaking with previous economic policy, President Ford cut federal spending as the nation began to slip into a recession in 1974. Postwar economic wisdom dictated the opposite strategy: fuel the economy to soften the downturn and buffer the business cycle. With this tightening of spending in addition to rising oil prices, the nation went into the deepest recession since the 1930s. The 1974–75 recession led to the temporary unemployment of 20 percent of the rubber workers; 260 at Seiberling were on layoff (URW 1975). National industrial production dropped by 10 percent and unemployment rose to 8.2 percent in 1975.

The recession did depress demands for wage increases somewhat; investment had not, however, been invigorated. Disinvestment continued and productivity continued to fall in the aging facilities. The corporate offensive of the seventies did not have the overall effect of sustaining economic growth. This strategy has been called the Great Repression. The costs of maintaining corporate power created a huge drag on the economy.

> By encouraging the Great Repression, however, corporations were cutting off their noses to spite their faces. With idle capacity spreading as a result of restrictive monetary and fiscal policy, the incentive to build new plants and equipment vanished; corporations had enough capacity to produce what was demanded. And with the utilization levels so low, the stock market recorded the immense costliness of the protracted assault on labor.   [Bowles, Gordon, and Weisskopf 1983:112]

Disinvestment intensified, and the obsolescence of the production facilities in the Midwest and Northeast became conspicuous. The stage was set for the disastrous events that began in 1980, a deluge of plant shutdowns.

Before the 1980 recession began, the unemployment rate was 5.8 percent, only partly recovered from the 1974–75 recession. In northern Ohio the national recession became a regional depression distinct from the six preceding postwar recessions in that it was characterized by plant closings rather than by slowdowns and temporary layoffs. In 1982 alone, 619 plants closed in the country and 215,000 jobs were eliminated (Bureau of National Affairs 1982). Fifty of those plants were in Ohio. Additional jobs were permanently lost because of partial shutdowns. In Barberton, jobs were lost at all major employers: 1,100 jobs were lost at Seiberling, 900 at Pittsburgh Plate Glass, 250 at Rockwell, 200 at Electromelt, 250 at Babcock and Wilcox, 300 at Ohio

Brass. In hospitals and other service industries jobs were also lost as demand and purchasing power declined. Barberton's industrial base had been fundamentally destroyed. In adjacent Akron, the tire-production industry was almost totally dismantled as 7,000 jobs were lost after 1975 (Stone 1983). On 20 March 1983 the last automobile tire was made in Akron, the Rubber Capital of the World.

In October 1979 the contract between URW Local 18 and Firestone expired. The union began negotiations fully aware that the country was going into another recession. It was prepared to make concessions to avert a strike. Contract talks were stalled by company negotiators, whose decisions had to be approved by top company executives, an unusual arrangement. Strangely, Firestone was not interested in the union's offer to extend the previous contract, a major concession on the part of the union. The union reacted by sending its members to work in the plant when the contract expired. This move forced the company either to lock out the workers or to operate on a day-to-day basis without a contract. In other times the union would have gone on strike if the company had not settled before a contract expired. Contract talks dragged on for many months with no apparent movement toward an agreement.

The unusual events of the negotiation made Joe Albanese, president of Local 18, suspect that a shutdown was imminent, and he filed an application with the Department of Labor for benefits provided to displaced workers under the Trade Readjustment Act. A month later the closing was announced. The management negotiating team claimed to have been unaware of the company's plans; they had been bargaining in good faith, they said, right up to the day the shutdown was announced.

The announcement of the closing on 19 March 1980 came as a shock to the workers. At a meeting of representatives of the union and the company, the union members voiced their objections but the company representatives remained resolute. The workers at Local 18 were in a precarious position, since the contract, which had provided many benefits in the event of a shutdown, had now expired; the company was no longer legally obligated to honor that agreement. Firestone planned to continue production for four months and asked for full cooperation from the union during that time. The URW agreed to continue production and promised an orderly closing in return for the benefits that had been provided in the previous contract: retirement benefits, severance pay, extended health-insurance benefits, and some special arrangements for individuals who found themselves short of retirement by a matter of weeks. In this way the company protected itself from the threat of sabotage inherent in a disorderly closing.

During the subsequent months, departments of the Seiberling plant were slowly phased out, the workers with least seniority going first. The slow, painful process gradually emptied the plant. Movable machinery was crated and hauled away. Some men cried as they clocked out for the last time. A few went into a rage in the locker room, putting their fists through metal cabinets and breaking wooden benches. Others left whistling, as if they had in some way had the last laugh. By June 1980 production had ceased.

In a symbolic gesture, a group of union activists picketed the plant to protest the closing. Most were the wives of Seiberling workers; their husbands looked on in bewilderment from the bar across the street from the plant gates. The protest was met with indifference: the community failed to rally round the rubber workers. Most distressing was the booing from a few of the cars that passed. One positive gesture came from the mayor of Barberton, who attempted to locate a buyer for the plant but failed.

The company hired a consulting firm to handle the closing. A job placement service was provided, offering tests to assess work skills, lectures on job-seeking techniques, and a session on résumé writing. In retrospect, most workers felt that the service had been a waste of time and money. One of them said, "They wanted to grease the tubes, that's all. They didn't want us to get the idea right away that there was nothing out there for us."

The union held a series of meetings to assist its members to obtain benefits through unemployment insurance and the TRA. There was also the matter of $20,000 in Local 18's treasury. Federal law prohibits the turning over of such money directly to members. The union decided to spend the money on a huge party for its members.

In November 1980, Local 18 met for the last time. Its members feasted, drank, and walked away with expensive door prizes, televisions, stereos. Later some members complained that the money had been wasted; it should have been used to assist those faced with bankruptcy and mortgage foreclosure. The local union hall across from the silenced plant became the property of the URW International and was sold to a dance studio.

The period of economic decline leading up to the plant closings had slowly eroded the working-class solidarity that had been built by the union movement (Edsall 1984). While the economic problems of the community had been worsening for quite some time, it was the closing of the Seiberling plant that made the workers and their families finally understand that times had changed. In the years leading up to the closing of the Seiberling plant, the workers had lived through the gradual stagnation of the national economy, disinvestment of local industry, and increasing unemployment rates. Their standard of living declined as wages failed to keep pace with inflation. Stable union jobs with high wages became increasingly rare (Sawhill and Stone 1986).

The economic problems of Barberton deepened as the resources to meet them dwindled. The failure of an attempt at urban renewal in 1968 brought the initial faltering in community confidence. The commercial district of Barberton had been in decline since the suburban shopping centers grew in the 1960s. Physical deterioration ensued. Federal grant money could have provided over $5 million for major renovations, but local merchants waged a campaign to reject the money in order to protect their businesses. The merchants feared that in the process of renewal they would be driven out of business by stores of national retail chains. The voters turned down the federal money: chain stores were built in a nearby shopping mall, outside of Barberton and beyond its tax base. Local commerce continued to deteriorate.

The unemployment rate crept upward. Between 1967 and 1979 Seiberling phased out 400 jobs. In 1972 Pittsburgh Plate Glass closed its limestone mines in Barberton, eliminating almost 1,000 jobs. The number of manufacturing jobs declined while the total number of new jobs failed to keep up with demand for work. The unemployment level rose in Summit County from 4.7 percent in 1971 to 8.2 percent in 1975 to 14.3 percent in 1983. Women entered the work force in increasing numbers as inflation continued to eat away at incomes and families found it impossible to maintain their former standard of living or to fulfill hopes of improvement (Brand 1981). Indeed, a family with only one wage earner was increasingly likely to live in poverty. New jobs were mainly in the service sector and were characterized by low wages, insecurity, and lack of unions.[14] The new employers in Barberton were Taco Bell, K-mart, Kroger's, Burger King, and the chain stores at the Rolling Acres Mall. The local hospital also grew, offering more jobs but also low wages and few benefits.

A dual labor market began to dominate the economic life of Barberton. Widening discrepancies in wages and benefits led to jealousy between workers in different sectors. Rubber workers were now regarded as a privileged group, and no longer as the leaders of a movement toward a general improvement in the standard of living. The union movement no longer seemed to pursue actively the interests of the community as a whole. While the wages of rubber workers had kept pace with inflation after 1976, the wages of other workers had not. Thus the community did not rush to the assistance of the victims of the Seiberling shutdown, but instead seemed to begrudge them even the little help they received from TRA. This segmentation of the work force fundamentally weakened unions (Gordon, Edwards, and Reich 1984: 226)

Daniel Bell (1960) forecast a postindustrial society as a clean, comfortable, computerized future in which work will be primarily mental and differences of social class will be insignificant. Postindustrial Barberton suggests another image for the future: detritus, decay, a social garbage heap. The postindustrial landscape of Barberton is a ravaged environment. The marshland and forests of the early Western Reserve, once a refuge for exotic birds and rare orchids, are now industrial sewers. PPG alone has left behind it 1,000 acres of chemical dumps, the picturesquely named "lime lakes." Barberton residents will continue to wake up with the taste of chlorides on their tongues for many years as fetid odors drift into town from the surfaces of those chemical lakes.

The signs of deterioration are clearest in Barberton's neighborhoods. A drive down the quiet streets of the city reveals overgrown shrubs, broken-down porches, falling gutters, and peeling paint. The once-proud owners of the modest bungalows can no longer maintain their homes. Some of the housing has become hazardous, infested with

[14]Those who look to the service sector to stabilize employment are mistaken. The exportation of service-sector work is already under way in the communications and information industry.

roaches, endangered by faulty wiring, and plagued by plumbing too old to repair. The percentage of dwellings rented in Barberton rose from 32 percent in 1964 to 40 percent in 1980 as the possibility of home-ownership declined.

The downtown commercial district is full of vacant buildings with plywood nailed over the windows. The city has purchased and torn down many of the most dilapidated structures, leaving gaping wounds on the face of the city. In 1982 there were fifty-two empty commercial sites in the downtown district.[15] The city has avoided fiscal crises only by cutting services and holding down the wages of city workers.

The skyline of the city is haunted by the carcasses of the old plants, many of them built before the turn of the century. Like shells of dead sea creatures, some of the old buildings house fierce new occupants: factories in which workers have returned to sweatshop conditions, ten-hour days, forced overtime, and seven-day workweeks. Talk of a union ensures dismissal.

The physical changes are mirrored in the new social landscape of unemployment, poverty, and despair. Unemployment remained above 14 percent in Ohio through 1984; no recovery or new industry is predicted for Barberton (Brooks 1983). Unions have been destroyed and wage concessions have been dramatic. Twenty percent of the children in the Barberton school system are now supported by welfare. Many older workers will never be able to find work again and are forced to live in poverty, many dependent on public assistance. The number of people on general relief in Summit County rose dramatically, from 1,100 in 1975 to over 10,000 in 1984. These changes parallel the national picture, in which the number of people living in poverty rose by 25 percent from 1979 to 1984 (Harrington 1984b).

Crime, especially homicide and rape, has been on the increase in the county (Criminal Justice Commission 1980). Unemployment does not produce good citizens. Police report an increase in shoplifting. Many offenders appear to be unemployed adults who are driven to theft by necessity and anger. At a free-food distribution center I heard a recipient express a common sentiment: "I know what to do if I'm hungry."

Symbolic of the decline is the transformation of Barberton's Columbia Café, which until the closing of the local PPG plant was a tavern

[15]Interview with Michael Gavin, Planning Office, City of Barberton, 19 October 1982.

long patronized by workers on their way home. Today it is Cherries Lounge, a go-go bar where young women dance and strip until three o'clock in the morning. The atmosphere is somber, despite the "exotic" dancers; in better times, these same women might have married and sat alongside the young men who now pass their idle time watching their gyrations on stage.

Another sign of faltering public spirit is the failure of Barberton's residents to pass a single school levy during the last thirteen years. In the fall of 1983 a proposed emergency levy failed, and major cuts in the school system were implemented. Local politicians made a scapegoat of the school superintendent, ignoring the fact that too many people had suffered economically to be able to support increased taxes.

For the young people of Barberton the future is uncertain. Their fathers and mothers had their pick of local factories in which to work. Recent high school graduates find themselves in difficult situations. Many leave the state in search of opportunities in the Sunbelt. In years past, one or two graduates of Barberton High School joined the military directly after school. In 1982 the number jumped to 30 out of the 317 graduating seniors.[16]

Illegal drug use among teenagers surfaced as a major problem in 1983, and some students were arrested in the high school building. Teenage pregnancies increased precipitously. Many parents still had an image of Barberton as a small town free of such problems. Some of those arrested in the drug raid were described by the high school guidance counselor as "OK kids who feel like there's nothing better to do." A traditional threat used by parents to temper teenagers' behavior has been lost; parents could once remind them that misbehavior would limit their choices of occupation in the future and claim that employers looked for students with proven records of good attendance. The disappearance of employment prospects weakens parental sanctions. Indeed, the goals for which the children of Barberton had been raised to strive now seem out of their reach.

Barberton has never been far removed from the main currents of American history during the past hundred years. Ohio was a focal point of rapid industrialization, the emergence of labor unions, wartime

[16]Interview with Sonny Paleya, guidance counselor, Barberton High School, 18 November 1982.

production, and the postwar boom. The decline of Barberton is not the problem of an isolated group, a city, or a region, but a reflection of the troubles of a stagnating national system.

The decline was precipitated by the decisions of corporate leaders who attempted to tighten their control over the economy through increased supervision, attacks on unions, mergers, and other wasteful practices. In the Akron area, a failure to reinvest in local plants allowed them to become less productive than plants elsewhere. However, disinvestment is but a local manifestation of a national problem.

The failure of economic growth must be directly addressed if the everyday life of the people of Barberton is to improve. What role these people will play in the future and what form of community will emerge out of the contemporary crisis is uncertain. Increases in unemployment have precipitated action by many local groups, and they are establishing new alliances that may be the beginning of the re-creation of the community.

[6]

Mark and Danny: Two Case Studies

Anthropologists, chroniclers of the disruption of societies, have contributed a sophisticated literature on the adaptation of individuals to societal disintegration. Styles of suffering have been observed to vary widely among individual personalities. What seems universal is the manner in which members of a society lose self-respect and a sense of well-being when their usual modes of attaining satisfaction are disrupted. Cultural disillusionment results, a vision of an unpredictable and barren world (Wallace 1970:191). In Barberton, failure in the customary ways of pursuing an acceptable way of life—stable work, economic stability, homeownership—has forced individuals into confrontation with their former set of expectations. As reality in Barberton becomes less stable and predictable according to old norms, the levels of stress and disorder increase for many people.

Let us observe the struggles of two individuals and their adaptation to plant closings in Barberton. These two cases are not intended to represent typical response or an ideal typology of character; they reveal two unique individual responses to social change. None of the styles of adaptation to unemployment or the cycles and stages I observed could be singled out as a most common response.

All the same, a thread connects the adaptations of these two individuals, and it can be seen in most of the responses to unemployment that

I observed in Barberton. The unemployed tend to personalize their difficulties; that is, they deal with and understand their experiences in personal rather than public terms (Brittan 1977). They did not readily think of their problems in finding work or paying bills as social or political issues. While interest in politics among working-class men and women in general has waned, the unemployed tend to withdraw from public affairs to an even greater extent (Schlozman and Verba 1979). Yet not everyone who loses a job responds in this way, as we shall see in Chapter 7.

To emphasize action is not to imply success. People respond to the exigencies of their lives and often fail. We can actively perpetuate the conditions of our own domination and exploitation by our acceptance of them. The lives described here may seem disturbing because of the disappointments and difficulties these men faced. Yet they were actively making decisions, sometimes defiant, often resigned in their day-to-day struggles. People function not as automatons playing out a script but as knowledgeable actors, though often with a good share of disappointment. To suffer the consequences of unemployment is to construct life anew.

The two men described here were both experienced factory workers in the Akron area. They were quite similar in outward circumstances but responded to their predicament in very different ways. They struck me as very typical or ordinary men. Mark Burke and Danny Lawson appear to be rather idiosyncratic, as must anyone examined in much detail, but they were considered quite normal by their neighbors, friends, and family; they are not people with significant psychopathology. They are experiencing difficult circumstances, however, and in this way differ from some of their neighbors, but they are not unusual for this community, given the great number of people adversely affected by the regional depression.

Mark Burke

A bare-breasted woman stepped up onto the small, three-sided stage of Cherries Lounge and began to dance. The dancer who would succeed her was at the jukebox putting in quarters for her numbers. She wore nothing but a pair of sheer lace panties. "God, what a mule,"

Mark said. He and I had stopped in for a beer after having spent most of the day looking for work. The woman was quite heavy, most conspicuously around the belly. When her music started she climbed onto the stage in her spiked heels and began to dance. During the second song she stood on her head, balancing herself against the wall mirror behind her, and spread her legs, almost in time with the music. "I want a drink. Want one?" I said to Mark. "No, I've had enough. Chris wouldn't like it if I came home drunk."

The significance of the change in this old neighborhood tavern in which we sat was not lost on Mark, with whom I spent a good deal of time throughout 1983 during his various jobs and bouts of unemployment. He compared the bar's transformation from a stopping-off place for men on their way home from work to his own downward spiral in life. Mark had attempted to uphold his values in the face of difficult circumstances. He had suffered through a long series of temporary and part-time jobs and had not had what he could call a real job since the Seiberling shutdown. During those years Mark had suffered resignedly. The closing had started him on a long skid from which he was not sure he would recover.

Mark remembered his ten years at the Seiberling plant as though it had been a pleasant dream. His father had been raised on a farm in West Virginia and came to Akron to work in the "gum mines," as the rubber factories were called then. Jack, Mark's older brother, worked at Seiberling and helped Mark get a job there when he graduated from high school. It was his first and only job before the shutdown and in many ways he had grown up there. Most of Mark's free time had been spent with other young men who worked at Seiberling. Mark became active in the local union and was regarded as one of the leaders among the younger men in the shop. He had helped his brother campaign for office in the local. Even after the closing, he thought of himself as a union man. Mark told me emphatically that "no decent man would cross a picket line and take another man's job." Commitment to decency characterized many of his actions. Mark thought of himself as belonging to "your working class of people," a class for which unions had an important place.

Following the common pattern, Mark had married soon after he got a job in the factory. His ex-wife, Carlinda, had been his high school sweetheart. "Yeah, I knocked her up. Did the right thing and married

[129]

her. It wasn't all bad. I got two great kids out of it." The marriage did not go well. They were both very young, and after seven years Carlinda was restless and Mark weary. The divorce came in 1978, two years before the shutdown. He was happy to be out of the marriage, and when his best friend from Seiberling started dating Carlinda he was not disturbed, until there was talk of marriage and a move to California. Mark was very close to his children and was furious about having them taken so far away.

After the Seiberling closing, Mark, like many of his friends, received training under the Trade Readjustment Act to be a mechanic. Proud to see his son take up his own trade, Mark's father had offered him the full set of precision tools that he had used as a mechanic at Firestone. The tools sat in the basement because Mark was never able to find a job as a mechanic.

In the fall of 1982, five months after his benefits had run out, Mark got a job in a used-tire yard throwing rain-filled tires into piles. He described the job as "under the table" and was paid $2 an hour, tax-free. His boss was flexible and allowed him to take time off when he was able to make a bit of money in some other way. Mark went to Florida once for two weeks to clear land on a construction site. A foreman hired a group of young men, drove them down to Florida, and gave them a trailer to sleep in. Mark came home with $400. He had also made money chopping wood, working with a friend who did home remodeling, and doing some yard work. In the late spring of 1983 Mark finally found a regular job in a labor gang, doing landscape work on a large new racetrack. The work was grueling, ten hours a day, forced overtime, in the worst heat of the summer. Toilets and drinking water were a mile from the work site. The wage was $5 an hour. Mark complained about the heat and the dust. He would spit phlegm, brown with dust, all through the evening as he tried to quench his thirst with can after can of beer.

Mr. Gillespie, the owner-foreman of the company, and his son drove the men cruelly. The gang hated them, especially the son, who was nearly their own age. In an accident at the work site, the son once cut his arm severely with a chain saw. Mark told the story. "The guys just stood around and looked at him. We all hated him so much they could have just stood there and let him die. The idea made me sick, so I took off my shirt and pressed it on him to stop the bleeding and started hollering for some of them to get someone quick. Well, the son-of-a-bitch didn't die." It was characteristic of Mark that his hardship did not distort his values or the way he viewed the world.

Despite the harsh conditions, he was proud to have a full-time job. His brother Jack was still not working, and Mark helped him get a job with Gillespie. Jack, although by no means a weak man, found the work too strenuous and quit after two days. Excusing himself, Jack told me privately that it hurt him to see his brother being treated like an animal at the job. Mark got a bit of subtle satisfaction out of the fact that he could endure the work. He valued work for its own sake and felt some shame when he was reminded that his father had worked at two jobs simultaneously for many years.

After the shutdown Mark had moved a number of times. His life had become chaotic, but he still thought that selling his house as soon as the plant closed "was probably the only thing I've done right in my life." He reduced his expenses by moving in with George Bastic, but "there were just too many of us in there." At one point four men, three women, and two children were living in Bastic's house. George did not deal well with the tension. "He just got kinda crazy and one time even pulled a gun on me."

When he could no longer stand life at George's, Mark's girlfriend Chris offered to let him move in with her. They had been dating since his divorce. Mark's sister-in-law Donna worked with Chris at the hospital and had introduced them. Although she had been a bright student, Chris had followed the secretarial curriculum in high school. No one in her family had a college education, and Chris was destined to work as a secretary, starting months after graduation.

Mark had impressed Chris when they first met. He was then working at Seiberling, earning a substantial income and working regularly. When he lost his job she did not lose faith in him. She understood the vagaries of factory work, having seen her father go through layoffs during her childhood. Mark was good to Chris and helped her brother, Tommy, get a job in the used-tire yard with him.

They had a modest one-bedroom apartment in a recently built complex in Barberton. The outside of the building was covered with stained plywood already beginning to show signs of wear. The living-dining room formed an L with a tiny galley for a kitchen. The cheaply made complex compared rather poorly even with the federal housing projects that could be seen from the doorway. The walls and ceilings were very thin, so that noise was a major problem. Mark had been in a fistfight with the man who had once lived above them. The man called Mark a "pussy" when Mark complained that the man had left his stereo blasting for two solid days. Though they had lived in the building over two years, they had no friends there.

Mark and Chris had been happy together and considered their relationship permanent. They had talked about marriage several times, but for a number of reasons they went on living together without formalizing the arrangement. Mark had had poor luck finding work and did not think himself in a position to marry. His future was uncertain. They had, in fact, planned a wedding once, but the night before they were to speak with the minister Mark and his brother went out drinking. Mark was so sick the next day that he missed the meeting. Chris canceled the wedding date in anger.

Chris believed that Mark was becoming an alcoholic. Several of her friends at work had husbands or boyfriends who had drinking problems. A woman she worked with frequently came in with black eyes inflicted by her drunken mate. Chris had protected more than one friend from a raging man by offering the women a place to stay overnight. Mark had never hit Chris, but he did come home drunk and rowdy too often. His drinking was worse when he was not working. After the incident that led to the cancellation of the wedding, Mark promised to stop drinking liquor, but he continued to drink beer. Chris complained that he still came home drunk every other weekend. Mark claimed that he couldn't get drunk on beer but admitted that he "had a bit too much once in a while."

Mark and I often talked about his drinking, and we traded drinking stories. He drank often to escape from the things that bothered him. He was quick to point out the differences between our stories. "You're different. You're going someplace with your life. Me and Tommy and the rest of us—where are we going? What do we got to respect in ourselves? We got nothing to look forward to, and after a while it kind of gets you down on yourself and you want to just bust loose sometimes." Mark saw himself in an undistorted light, but felt powerless to change the objective circumstances he faced.

His responsibilities weighed heavily on him. He was proud of the fact that he had sold the house and thus avoided bankruptcy. Even though he was working, he had never since the shutdown been able to pay off all his bills and get out of debt. Bill collectors added to his exasperation. A small doctor bill that Mark had left unpaid was turned over to a collection agency. "Man, that asshole Harrison called me today. It was a recording and said something like, 'In your heart you know it's the right thing.' Did you know that guy is the head of the Health Department?"

It was an unending source of shame to him to be without money so much of the time. He had become dependent on his family after the shutdown. His parents were happy to have him eat a meal with them. When it became apparent that those meals were his primary source of food while he was not working, he became embarrassed and stopped going so often. Mark complained bitterly when he was refused food stamps. "I went down there and ate humble pie, then didn't even get the damn things because I told them that I lived with Chris." He felt he should have qualified. "There's been times, too many to mention, that I've been so broke that I didn't even have money to buy a burger." Mark's pride was an obstacle to my relationship with him. Often I would order food in a restaurant and offer him some or try to buy him lunch, but he would refuse, claiming that his stomach was "just not quite right."

During that summer I saw Chris and Mark frequently. In the long evenings they played softball with Donna and Jack in a women's league. Mark and Jack coached the hospital's team. Chris and Mark became engaged again in August. For the occasion he gave her a gold-plated necklace, paid for by his mother.

The unstable nature of his job was one of the things that troubled him most. He counted the weeks going by, wondering whether he would accumulate enough workweeks to receive unemployment insurance. He hoped Gillespie would just keep him on long enough to allow him to work the requisite twenty-six weeks. With no money saved, bills unpaid, and the responsibility of paying support for his children unfulfilled, unemployment without benefits would lead to serious problems.

Softball and hard work made the summer pass quickly for Mark. He began to notice that, slowly, the work on the site was ending. They had begun to close up for the winter. Mark had tried hard to make a good impression on Mr. Gillespie in the hope that he would find something

[133]

for Mark to do with the winter crew, but the first week in October his hours were cut. "Damn it, he's just counting the days, I bet, keeping me up to the time he'll have to pay the unemployment insurance." Mark began to worry.

The next week he learned that his hours would be further cut to fifteen a week, and he began looking through the newspaper help-wanted ads. In reality he had been looking for another job ever since the shutdown: his mother or father would call with leads, a friend would give him a tip. I offered to help him look in a systematic way for a couple of weeks, to go through the ads with him, to drive him to interviews, and to help investigate possibilities. He appreciated the offer and accepted. We met for breakfast at a restaurant and carefully went through the newspaper want ads, discussing leads and the applications that he had already made.

Mark's frustration came to a head on Saturday of that week. He usually enjoyed his weekly telephone call to his children. This week, however, they were cool toward him. He had been late with his child-support checks, and Carlinda got on the phone first to ask about the money. As usual, she reminded him of the $3,000 in back support that he still owed. The rebuff from his children was the last in a series of problems from which he wanted to escape, at least for an evening. He came home very drunk that night, stumbling in noisily. Chris greeted him at the bedroom door with insults; worst of all, she told him that as long as she was paying the bills, he had better stay sober. In anger Mark put his fist through the dining-room wall, and Chris ordered him out of the apartment. He slept in his car and in the morning arranged to stay with a friend.

The next day he meekly returned to the apartment to collect his few things while Chris was at work. By chance I phoned while he was there, and he told me the story. We arranged to meet the following morning to talk. He was dejected, sure that Chris would never take him back. "She says I'm an alcoholic. Well, I ain't. What's she want me to do? Go to AA?" To persuade her to take him back, he had promised Chris that he would stop coming home drunk, but she insisted that he seek help to stop drinking altogether. "If I can't have a beer at home after work, I guess I'll just have to live without her." I encouraged him to continue to try to work things out. We agreed that I would drive him to investigate several factory jobs in the area the next day, and I arranged to pick him up at the place where he was staying.

Mark's friend lived in a part of Akron that he described as run-down. Mark was given an attic room that smelled of rotting wood and had paint peeling from the walls and woodwork. On the floor around the bed were his few possessions: a stereo, a clock-radio, an electric skillet, and a few shopping bags full of clothes. He was not yet dressed when I arrived. He said he had been disoriented during the last couple of days and couldn't seem to get himself organized.

We drove to three factories on the first day. He had been to two of them before and had applications in but now wanted to follow them up. The plants were in widely separated areas around Akron, and the traveling took up most of the day. Mark chose to go to the place where he most wanted to work. Screwing up his courage, he said, "I guess I have as good a chance as anybody." Teledyne in Hartville had announced months before that they might be hiring 200 workers. They had a large military contract to produce rubber extrusion-mold products. The wage was $10 an hour. So many people had responded to the advertisement that the applications had to be distributed from the back of a truck as job hunters drove through the factory gate. Some had come a great distance, from West Virginia and Tennessee, and put the names of their home states on the tents they pitched outside the gate. Mark sounded distressed when he told me about it.

The Teledyne factory consisted of several small buildings surrounded by a high wire fence. I sat in the car outside of the personnel office and had waited no more than five minutes when Mark returned. He had asked if they were still doing any hiring. He was told that they were still making selections and that they would call. With that he left. "You didn't even tell them your name?" I asked. Mark was surprised. It had never occurred to him to tell them his name. He joked about it later. "*Mark Burke* is the name. I want a *job. I need a job,*" he said, imitating the voice of a high-pressure salesman. After the incident we rehearsed what he should say when he went into an office.

On our way to the next plant, we talked about his brother and sister-in-law. Mark felt vaguely guilty that Jack was not with us. Jack had similar problems finding work, but his wife had a job as a nursing supervisor and had supported the couple adequately since the shutdown. Donna, his sister-in-law, had been quite skeptical about Mark's new burst of enthusiasm for looking for work, having seen Mark and Jack go through many rounds of job searches without success. Her husband was going to school but had not worked for three years. I had been present when she expressed her doubts that they would ever find good jobs again, with an implied skepticism regarding Mark's abilities. I asked Mark how her attitude made him feel. "I don't know. I used to think I was all right. I worked and brought home good money. But now it seems like I'm just a drifter, can't do nothing right anymore. Maybe I'm just a good-for-nothing." I tried to explain to him that he was internalizing a problem that was in reality external, pleading with him not to let himself see mass unemployment as his personal inadequacy. He was moved and glad for the encouragement, but said, "There's a big difference between what I could be and what I am."

Mark had heard from a friend who worked at Nabisco in Seville, Ohio, that the plant was hiring. Jack and Mark had both filled out applications there two weeks earlier. The woman at the desk did not have any information, and the personnel manager was out for the day. Mark left his name that time.

Next we headed for Cuyahoga Falls on the far northern side of the county. The job was in a rubber-reclaiming factory. "I hope I don't get that job. The place is a real sweatshop. You walk in and you can't see for the dust. The guy I know that works there always has that black crap on his face." Driving through Akron on the expressway we saw crews of young men picking up trash along the roadside. A van parked nearby proudly advertised "Project Akron—Keep Akron Working." These were men on general relief working for the county under the workfare program. Mark complained to me, "I can't even get one of those jobs." He had once been to the county welfare office to investigate going on relief. They told him that he had to have proof that he had not worked for six months. "Now how the hell do you prove a thing like that?" Mark asked me. He had little experience with the welfare system and did not know the proper way to answer the many questions that were asked before assistance could be granted. At the rubber-reclaiming factory, Mark filled out an application and was told that they would call if they had an opening.

The only thing left to do was to visit the OBES office and reregister with the job-placement service. Mark felt that he did not have the energy to face them that day. He hated the place. "They treat you like dirt." Once an employee at the Norton office had insinuated that he was not serious about looking for work and Mark was insulted. He promised me that he would go the next day to check out the listings at the office.

A couple of days later we returned to Teledyne. Mark politely requested that the woman in the personnel office check his file. She suggested that it would be to his advantage to have a recommendation from his former foreman at Seiberling. Firestone had been uncooperative about sending out work records. He was happy to have a chance to do something but angry about the failure of Firestone to send the information. After a series of phone calls to the union and to Firestone, he learned that the records had in fact already been sent and he concluded that the woman had lied in order to get him out of the office.

At his father's house that afternoon we discussed the pros and cons of bugging employers about jobs. We decided that persistence could not hurt. He would get the letter of recommendation that the woman asked for. We also discussed his beard. He was concerned that it might be hurting his chances and was willing to shave it off. His father thought that was unnecessary. Later he called his sister, who worked in personnel for an industrial firm in Vermont. She told him to keep the beard. Mark's foreman was working in a bar in Barberton. We stopped there for a drink that afternoon, and he agreed to write a letter.

Chris had by this time taken Mark back. Donna and Mark's mother had spoken with Chris, urging her to reconsider. When I visited them at the apartment, she was still tense about the decision but happy to have him back. Mark had promised that he would not come home drunk and that he would cut down on the drinking.

The next week Mark got the job at Teledyne. He had been persistent. He had returned there twice after we had last been to Hartville. During his last visit, the head of personnel called him into his office, interviewed him, and asked him if he could start the same day. The man emphasized that many people had applied for these jobs. He hoped Mark would "go along" with the way they ran their shop; they did things very differently from what Mark might have been used to at Seiberling. Mark joked: "I told him I'd have to check my calendar to see if I had any conflicts, but I thought I was free."

I asked Chris about her reaction. "Sure it's great. I'm real happy, but

[137]

on the same day I got all this other bad news. My dad went in the hospital. He had pneumonia, they thought, but now they think it's cancer. Why did it have to be on the same day? I got the call from Mark at work and then from my mom crying and everything." Chris had also learned that her brother had been arrested for arson at the tire yard. "I know he didn't do it. It was that creepy son of the owner's. They're doing it for the insurance money. The place was going broke. Tommy wasn't even in the place when it happened." Unfortunately for Tommy, he had a police record and recently had been arrested for drunk driving. "Anyways Tom had no beef with the owner, it was the only place he could get a job." Mark commented to me uncharacteristically, "Greg, it's a dog-eat-dog world out there."

It seemed that Mark's luck had turned. His father had decided to buy a farm in southern Ohio. It was possible that if he could not sell his house, Mark and Chris might be able to live in it and eventually buy it. "Dad has been kind of moody lately and thinking about his boyhood on the farm. He really wants to get back there. He says he's not too sure about a lot of things any more. He keeps talking about them taking away his pension and his social security and he wants to be in a place where he can grow his own food. Mom's real unhappy about it. She doesn't want to go nowhere. She keeps telling him that if he wants to be outdoors in the woods, it's OK with her. She doesn't want to leave her church friends."

Mark was now working second shift at Teledyne forty hours a week making rubber mounts for engines. "Hell, Greg, I'm back in the saddle again." Far from being happy that he was once again employed in industry, he was discontented and suspicious of both the company and the union. I asked him about his work. "The place is hotter than shit. We open those ovens and the vapors hit you in the face all the time. Then we put the pieces on the presses and that's real dangerous. Twelve guys were out on injuries when I hired in. You're always nicking your hands and stuff." Many of the men had lost fingers on the job.

After a pause he told me, "It's funny. It's like I've been there forever already." He was on probation status for the first thirty days, after which he would join the union. "Oh, yeah, it's the URW. They want nineteen dollars a month. It's OK, I guess. But when they come around at contract time I'll tell them where they can stick it. I'll pimp them if they try to do it to me again." I was stunned by Mark's change in attitude.

Mark's feelings about unions and their demands had changed. Corporate strategists had hoped to dampen the expectations of workers during periods of high unemployment. The strategy had worked, at least in Mark's case. Three years of financial instability and employment troubles had changed his expectations and attitudes toward work. It seemed to me that he would be a docile employee for a long while. The sense that he had in some ways pleaded for this job humbled him in the face of the employer.

Mark no longer saw that he could further his own needs and interests by cooperating with people in like circumstances. At that point he felt that unions had their own interests, which did not coincide with his own and indeed would drain his resources. His standard of behavior was now less contingent on a sense of community solidarity, and he was left with a Hobbesian view of the world. His solitary struggle to maintain personal decency had been difficult. His experiences had shaken his confidence in the union movement and eventually shifted his world view. He could no longer sustain a vision of the common good won through collective action.

Danny Lawson

Judy served a big country meal on a Sunday soon after I had moved into her house in Barberton as a boarder. We passed around the whipped potatoes, thick flat noodles with butter, green beans with bacon swimming in the juice, a pork roast, hard-boiled eggs pickled with beets, and instant iced tea. Everyone's favorite dish was the powdery biscuits and the thick, grease-laden gravy. The meal was abundant and filling. Judy Rhodes rented rooms on the second floor of her house. Taking in boarders constitutes a cottage industry for working-class women. She sat next to her second husband, Mat, who was weeks away from retirement as a welder at the Babcock and Wilcox boiler manufacturing plant in Barberton. I had been invited to dinner so that we could all get acquainted. Judy made it very clear that she wouldn't ordinarily cook for any of "her boys," as she called the men who rented from her, except Charlie because he couldn't take care of himself. Charlie was a chronic schizophrenic, managing on high doses of antipsychotic drugs and a disability check from Social Security. Next to Mat at the table was Little Judy, Margaret's daughter. Margaret, one of the foster children Judy had raised, had named her daughter after her foster mother. Judy's namesake was often in the house, especially when Margaret had trouble paying her bills, which recently had been often.

"Now, Greg, I don't cook like this all the time 'cause I got sugar [diabetes], you know," Judy told me with some anxiety. At fifty-five she was almost blind in one eye, gray-haired, and quite obese. Like many working-class people, she looked much older than she actually was. Both she and Mat had lost their first spouses. Judy was happy to tell me the story of how she and Mat first met and soon afterward became engaged. Unabashedly she told me that she had quickly ascertained that he was a fine man, but she had not known whether he was interested in having an intimate relationship. "Well, I just asked him *do* you or *don't* you? He said he did. And Greg, I'm so happy to have a man who is in the way of the Lord, too. Some of these guys . . . !"

This was a religious household and around the kitchen were various reminders: plastic praying hands to hold the napkins, metal trivets with the scriptural quotations "Praise the Lord" and "Great Is His Name" enameled on them, a framed colored print of a family at prayer. Judy had raised her children as Baptists and was proud to tell me that one of her sons-in-law was a minister. She made it clear that we were to have no liquor upstairs and no women, and went on to tell stories about the transgressions of former renters.

Judy told me not to be bashful as second helpings went around the table. She did most of the talking and began to tell us about her yard sale. She was cleaning out her closets and packing things away because they had put the house up for sale and planned to move to Tennessee as soon as possible. Mat's retirement was an opportunity to leave Barberton, which Judy was convinced was going to become a ghost town because of the factory closings.

The kitchen door opened and in walked her thirty-year-old son, Danny Lawson, who lived three doors away on the same block. I learned later that he often dropped by at dinnertime. Danny weighed 250 pounds and was under five feet six inches tall. He wore a long full beard, little round glasses that sat on his round cheeks, and bib overalls. During the summer of 1981 Danny was around his mother's house quite a bit because he was not working. He was "out on a medical" (a leave of absence) from McNeil, a machinery manufacturer, where he worked as a repairman. His hypertension had been out of control and he complained of headaches and dizziness. "Man, most of the time all I do is sleep." He recently had been in the hospital for two months. Danny made light of his rather serious disease and preferred to emphasize the fact that he was getting time off from work. This was my first clue regarding Danny's way of adapting to his personal situation and, later, to unemployment.

Judy brought out ice cream and began to make sundaes with chocolate syrup and whipped cream from a spray can. She spoke to Danny in an annoyed tone about his children, who were coming to visit from southern Ohio. She had invited them but expected Danny to spend some time with them. Danny and his mother had a tense relationship, particularly when the issue of his ex-wife and children came up. Now that he was divorced, Danny lived with another woman; Judy strongly disapproved. Marian Kessler, Danny's girlfriend, had not come to dinner and was rarely seen in the house although she lived on the same block. Danny said nothing throughout all of this and continued to fill his plate and eat with his head a bit too near the table. After eating, Danny lumbered out while the rest of us retired to the screened porch to enjoy the cool summer evening. Eager to explore the night in Barberton, I asked where Danny had gone. Judy said, "He goes up there to Jimbo's [an all-night diner] a lot. He's running all night, that boy."

I saw Danny at his mother's frequently during that first summer in Barberton. His daughters, ages ten and seven, visited for three weeks. Danny remained an elusive character; we talked sometimes, but never really got to know each other. I had hoped that Danny would introduce me to some of his friends and show me around town. The summer passed quickly and my overtures of friendship were not returned. That winter I did not live in Barberton but visited occasionally on weekends, dropping in on the Rhodes household to keep in touch.

The following spring I returned to the Rhodes's looking for lodging again. The situation in the house had changed. Judy's mother had moved in after selling her own house nearby. She could not be left behind if Judy moved to Tennessee, and so she had resigned herself to

[141]

selling the house for whatever she could get. Judy had changed realtors several times and was still looking for a buyer for her own home. Judy's sister, Virginia, had also moved into the house. Virginia, a chronic mental patient, had until recently lived by herself. Her children were not interested in assisting her so Judy took her in, using Virginia's welfare check to pay for her expenses. Little Judy had also come to live in the house because Margaret had left her husband, who was out of work and drinking. Judy now had no room available to rent.

Danny had taken in boarders in the past, and Judy asked him if he was interested in letting me rent a room on the second floor of his house. That week the McNeil Company, where Danny worked, announced the closing of their Akron plant. Several days later I moved into the house. Danny and Marian had been reluctant to take boarders again because past ones had often proved troublesome. In the face of the shutdown and the financial uncertainty it brought, however, it now seemed prudent to let me come.

Their house was similar to Judy's though a bit smaller, the second floor having no kitchen or bath. It was an example of the "improved housing" built in Barberton during the forties, on wider streets and more generous lots. For the factory workers of Danny's father's generation it represented the security and affluence they had sought. To those with roots in rural America, the plots, with their small gardens and yards, symbolized a little bit of the country. To own one's own home was to regain the freedom that had been lost by those who had migrated from farms, as Danny's father had done. Many dreamed of recapturing the freedom of rural life. The plots were jealously guarded, and city ordinances regulating the use of residential property were deeply resented.

For Danny, this fear of intrusion was part of a more general understanding of the world, one that was fundamentally antiurban. Danny had never completely identified himself with his position as an urban factory worker. Instead he thought of his home as a little estate and dreamed of owning a place in the country with some land around it, "where no one can tell you what to do." He resented the rules that prohibited the use of industrial production equipment in his basement and the restrictions against gambling operations in homes. He saw the city codes as impediments to his attempts to augment his income.

The house itself was a short bungalow with a brick-and-stucco facade, slowly falling into disrepair. The siding badly needed painting, and many of the gutters had fallen off or hung rusting. The hedge had lost all shape. The inside of the house reflected Marian's sensibilities. An air of propriety had been created by the substantial furniture: a mahogany Federal-style dining-room set complete with hutch and sideboard stood solidly at one end of the room. It was used twice during the year I lived in the house. The cut-velvet couch and chairs at the other end of the room near the fireplace were a bit less formal. The solidity and formality reflected Marian's upbringing on a small Ohio farm.

During the past three years Danny had worked irregularly because of layoffs and health problems. Danny had worked in factories since he graduated from high school in 1970, except for the three years he served in the navy during the Vietnam War. He had worked at the Seiberling plant for a year in 1971 but left because he was unable to break into the skilled trades there. With his father's help and encouragement he had become an apprentice machinist, learning to repair extrusion-mold machines, which had come into wide use in the plastics industries during the sixties. His skill gave him some mobility, allowing him to work at several local firms. He and Marian would often reassess the decisions they had made to move from one factory to another. One firm would pay more than another, but it would be more prone to layoffs, and so on. Those decisions were now reconsidered in the light of the McNeil closing. Had they been smart, Marian thought, Danny would have stayed at the plant he had worked in before, which was still in operation. But would his total earnings have been as much? They had no way to be sure.

Danny's moves from factory to factory were also to some extent motivated by his feeling that he could "do better." Marian pushed him in that direction. When McNeil announced the closing, she said it was for the best. "Danny can do better than punch in and out on a time card all his life." When he did eventually find work after six months of searching, it was on a part-time basis. A small plastics plant hired him as a subcontractor, which meant that he could not join the union and was ineligible for benefits. By calling it "freelancing," Danny and Marian endowed some of the prestige of a private business.

The number of hours Danny worked varied from week to week but was rarely more than twenty. He had to be cautious about displaying his attitude on the job. In the large union shops in which he had worked he had enjoyed a certain amount of freedom of expression with his foreman because of the protection afforded by the union. Working without a contract, he was subject to termination without notice for making an off-color remark, which Danny was quite prone to do.

He also did occasional electrical repairs on apartment buildings owned by a local landlord. This sort of change from full employment to sporadic work is a common result of the large structural changes in the economy (Scase 1982). It is Danny's unique view of his position that interests me here. The financial situation was clearly unsatisfactory, yet Danny was happy to think of himself as a small businessman rather than as unemployed. This understanding was more than a simple maneuver to protect his pride; it reflected something of his view of the world.

Danny considered himself superior to the average worker. His status as a skilled tradesman was a matter of pride and gave him an elevated position. His vision of the social world situated him somewhere between the "rich who run big business" and the masses of "lower people," and he was sensitive to what he interpreted as slights to his social status. He wanted to imitate the behavior of the big men of his world, but rebelled against the forces that he felt excluded him. His desire to emulate those above him led him to think of himself as a small businessman; his resentment of those above him led him to attack their propriety through unacceptable behavior.

A strange mixture of propriety and the grotesque characterized his behavior. Danny had certain expectations about how a meal was to be served, demanding attractive everyday china, a salad bowl, and a formal place setting. Marian happily accommodated him. During a meal, however, he would behave offensively, belching or calling attention to the fact that he had farted. His personal appearance was equally inconsistent. He bathed and groomed himself meticulously but wore patched jeans and threadbare shirts. He was acutely aware of moles on his body, which he thought of as ugly. Yet he used his excessive weight as an affront, as an attack on fashion. His grotesque appearance and behavior were a sort of reverse snobbery, calculated to protect him from insult. Danny did not object to the existence of social class or a hierarchical system, but protested his exclusion from its upper strata. His belief that he was being kept from his destined station in society escalated as he began to confront his failure to find work. His inability to find a regular job made him worry that he was descending into the ranks of the "common people."

His circumstances and his ideas about the world were in sharp contradiction much of the time. Despite his own suffering as an unemployed worker, he strongly defended President Reagan's cuts in social services. He said, "Greg, if this [poor employment prospects] keeps up, I'll be in the poorhouse." Yet he remained enthusiastic about restrictions on food stamps and welfare. In general he thought of people on welfare as lazy and having loose morals. But when his mother complained that he did not support his ex-wife and children by paying child support, he retorted, "Why the hell doesn't she go on welfare?"

Marian shared many of Danny's attitudes. His relationship with her was another clue to his character. Part of Danny's attraction to Marian was based on his feeling that she was above ordinary people. He was impressed with the fact that her family owned its own farm and was "independent." Their relationship was an assurance that he had not fallen into a lower social order, as his mother charged.

Marian was raised on a modest farm in western Ohio, where her parents still live. It was a life of discipline and reserved behavior. In a sort of revolt or escape she left college and came to Akron to work as a secretary in an office in the city. She found herself in a crowded rooming house, where she met Danny. He had recently left his wife. Marian was raised as a Catholic but then thought of herself as an atheist. His own religious convictions had kept him from divorcing his wife. Their relationship gave Danny strength to extricate himself from the influence of Judy, who insisted that he return to his wife and children.

Danny and Marian had lived together for six years. They would have married, but their families raised obstacles. Her mother demanded a Catholic wedding. They had looked into it and learned that the Catholic church would require an annulment of Danny's first marriage (and payment of $300) before a ceremony could be performed. Judy complained that an annulment would make Danny's children bastards. They opted to continue living together.

In Marian, Danny found the propriety he lacked. She was a "good woman"; she "didn't run around on him." The issue of fidelity was important in their relationship. Marian would frequently joke about Danny's old girlfriends, and Danny would joke that Marian kept him fat so no one would take him away from her. Her superior status also created problems. Her family did not approve of Danny. Trips to their home usually ended in some kind of unpleasant exchange stemming from insults directed at Danny by Marian's mother, who was particularly uncharitable about his lack of work. "They think I'm just a big hillbilly. Well, at least I was never in jail." His retorts, repeated many times when they returned home, emphasized his differences from the lower classes. Once at home, they would try to forget the attacks and console themselves with their propriety, pretending that life was going on as usual. But it was not.

As it became increasingly clear that Danny was failing in the labor market, his tendency to reject the rules of his world became accentuated. Unemployment made Danny less than a good citizen. He considered helping friends deliver marijuana to make extra money, but Marian objected. He considered opening an illegal gambling house, something he had once done during a previous period of unemployment. Instead he became involved with gambling machines, which he managed for the lodge he belonged to, taking his cut. Danny announced with malicious glee that he failed to report to the Internal Revenue Service the money he made doing electrical repairs for the local landlord.

Danny's increasing resentment and unwillingness to accept social convention was also manifest in the way he dealt with his health and with doctors. At the time of the shutdown, he was not working and was being treated for severe hypertension; his eligibility for unemployment insurance was therefore problematic. Although he had worked for McNeil for a total of five years, he had not accumulated the twenty workweeks in the current year needed to qualify him for unemployment insurance because he had been in the hospital and off work. The United Steelworkers' contract, however, permitted Danny to continue to collect disability payments and to have health-insurance coverage for six months. He had been granted these rights only after many months of contention between the union and the company. The company appealed three times to a labor-relations board to have Danny disqualified from disability status. Their evidence included a second opinion by a company doctor, who certified Danny as able to work after a fifteen-minute examination. Danny's own doctor, a cardiologist in Akron, had admitted Danny to the hospital three weeks earlier to control his blood pressure.

The company hired a private investigator, who appeared at Danny's house one morning to ask questions about his whereabouts and activities. Danny was, as usual, in bed, and I answered the door. Because of the strange nature of the questions and the overly friendly attitude of the woman, I denied any knowledge of him, telling her that I was only a boarder in the house. Later we learned that she had also made inquiries among the neighbors. Mrs. Wallenberger, who lived next door, had suspected that the woman was some kind of investigator. She vividly described their conversation for us. "I told her, 'He looks *terrible*. Walks around with his head down like some kind of zombie. Never says nothing.'" Danny was pleased by her loyalty and amused by the way she imitated him.

Eventually his status as temporarily disabled was confirmed by the company, and his health-insurance coverage was continued. This was fortunate because his health was actually quite poor, and he had to return to the hospital for three weeks that fall. Mrs. Wallenberger's caricature of him was in fact accurate. Danny slept over ten hours a day and was able to do little more than sit at the diner in the late hours of the night, his head pounding persistently. These are symptoms of severe hypertension.

Despite evidence to the contrary, Danny did not think of himself as ill and ignored his disease. He much preferred the identity of cheater to that of disabled. The struggle to maintain power over his life had led him to think that he had "put one over on everyone." He was thus able to think of himself as a normal young man instead of a victim of a chronic disease.

While Danny's obesity, hypertension, and enlarged heart were all closely associated, he did not make any connection between them himself. His concern with his weight was primarily cosmetic. It did not bother him except "socially," as he put it. He preferred to ignore the fact that his weight and high blood pressure significantly contributed to his difficulties in finding work. On one job application he had lied about his medical history, but the deception was discovered when the insurance company that covered the firm learned that he had had multiple hospitalizations. He was unaware until then that information was centralized to that extent.

He attributed his hypertension to stress and thought that a "better lifestyle," by which he meant a higher-paying job, would improve his health. He claimed to be able to tell when his pressure was up, associating it with times when he described himself as "hyper." This conceptualization had a direct effect on his behavior. After his insurance was terminated and money was short, Danny began to run out of some of his medications. He had been prescribed nitroglycerine pills for his chest pain. When he ran low he took Valium, a tranquilizer, for his pain. Valium, he reasoned, would have the same effect as the nitroglycerine: the pain was caused by being hyper, and Valium would calm him down. This potentially lethal misconception reflected his perception of his relations with others as a contest. Danny resented the exclusive control that doctors exercised over drugs. Self-medication was an act of power for Danny.

Danny enjoyed stocking his medicine cabinet with drugs he had obtained by buying prescriptions illegally from a notorious local doctor. In Danny's bathroom, large fishbowl beer mugs displayed his collection, which included Darvon, Valium, Tylenol with codeine, and several types of antibiotics. Danny did not ordinarily take any of these drugs. Indeed, he had to be prodded to take medicine that had actually been prescribed for him. His collection stood as a symbol of his measure of power in the world, where only doctors were allowed control over drugs.

There were other reasons for his resentment toward doctors and hospitals. His grandfather had died after a month in a local hospital, leaving his grandmother saddled with a huge bill. The hospital put a lien on her house and took it over when she died. Danny remained bitter about the family's loss of the house, blaming it on the greed of the doctors.

Danny had formulated his health problem as a power struggle, in accordance with his more general world view. An encounter with a doctor was not so much a way to reveal some truth about his condition as it was a contest between himself and the doctor. While working he was more willing to go along with usual standards of behavior. The disorientation and privation brought on by unemployment pushed him into conflict more frequently.

By January it became clear that Danny was not going to find a full-time job with health insurance. His "freelance" work repairing machines generated some income, but he was not eligible for insurance coverage. Danny's recent hospitalization made it clear to him and Marian that medical coverage was crucial for him, but he could not afford to pay the premiums on a policy for himself. It was at this time that Danny and Marian announced their engagement. Many couples who live together eventually marry because they plan to have children, but Danny wanted no more children. The decision to marry was primarily a solution to the problem of health-insurance coverage for Danny. Marian would have been happy to continue in their informal arrangement, fearing that a wedding would cause many family problems that she preferred to avoid. But necessity prevailed and a wedding date was set for March, when Danny would become eligible for coverage as her husband under Marian's policy.

Planning the wedding terrified Marian. Her mother had never been in her home during the five years Marian had lived there. Once her father came to deliver a piece of furniture he thought she might like, and her mother sat in the car, refusing to come into the house. Marian considered having a wedding without telling her mother. After much discussion, she planned a trip to the farm, alone, having resolved to make her mother acknowledge the choices she had made in life.

The meeting went well. Her mother was resigned to the marriage. In order to avoid problems, Danny and Marian had not asked her father to pay for the wedding; on their restricted funds, their wedding plans were modest. The wedding was to be small, a simple ceremony performed by a judge in the living room of Marian's house. No one in Danny's family was invited. Judy, Mat, Grandma, and Virginia had moved to Tennessee that fall, having sold the house after two years of waiting. Judy did not approve of the marriage, protesting still that Danny neglected his children. Marian felt that if neither Judy nor Danny's girls were to come to the wedding, they need not have a church service.

The wedding plans gave Danny new purpose and energy. He initiated a rash of plans to improve the house: he would build a patio in the back, pour new sidewalks in front, install new windows. He gave no thought to the more basic work that the house needed: painting, trimming, cleaning. The kitchen-cabinet doors stood in the basement waiting to be refinished, old wallpaper bulged from the walls, the woodwork in the bathroom had been partially stripped but never repainted or varnished. His new undertakings projected an appearance of industry, distracting attention from his otherwise idle existence.

For Marian there were invitations and the coordination of dresses with her sisters, who were to be bridesmaids. She arranged her vacation time to coincide with the wedding date. Her sister Laura had been married the previous December and comparison was inevitable, centering on what Marian would not have. Because the service and party were to be simple, the preparations were in reality negligible, and more time seemed to be spent explaining away the fact that some of Marian's relatives had declined her invitations.

On the day her vacation began, Marian came home with a curly permanent and a pink sweatshirt with the word "Physical" printed on the front. Her intention was to look like her sister, who had appeared at Marian's house shortly after she herself became engaged that summer wearing the same shirt and hairdo. Marian wanted to capture the look of the happy young bride. She also bought a box of chocolates and spent the first couple of days of her vacation eating them as she watched soap operas. "I'm going to do this right. Sit home, watch the soaps, and eat chocolates," she told me when I asked about her unusual behavior. To a woman who had worked all her adult life, the stereotype of the nonworking housewife was a glamorous ideal. Danny's chronic unemployment had made her realize that she might never attain that ideal, and she took this brief opportunity to live out her fantasy.

Danny had by this time removed the back porch from the house, leaving part of the understructure of the house exposed. He also dug ditches for the foundation of the patio he planned. He pulled out the bushes in front of the house and replaced them with scrawny young plants, which were never watered and so promptly died. Inside, he wallpapered a small hallway with a traditional yellow-flowered print but left the bathroom and kitchen untouched. In front of the house he removed the pavement and prepared the ground for the concrete. Work did not progress beyond that point until the day before the wedding. Marian scolded Danny, "My family is coming and it couldn't look worse—a mudhole in front and in the backyard."

On the night before the wedding we began to fix the food for the reception. Marian felt insecure about the preparations, never having thrown a large party before. "Danny's gone and invited everyone in town, and I have no idea who will be here," she complained fearfully. We worked most of the evening making hors d'oeuvres and planning the events of the next day. Danny worked in front of the house preparing for the cement, which had been promised for the next morning in exchange for electrical work he had done. Outside, neighbors stopped to congratulate him as he worked. Danny came in to taste the food, calling me Chef Boyardee, and relayed the greetings of the people who had stopped to talk. One neighbor woman said, "Well, you're finally gonna make her an honest woman." Marian was offended by the comment, but when we finished and I started upstairs to my room, she said, "My last night living in sin."

Early the next morning the friend with the cement finally came to pour and smooth the new sidewalks. Danny spent most of the morning supervising; Marian picked up the bouquets and the rented tuxedo. Marian's family arrived loaded down with food, metal trays, and clothes in garment bags. Mrs. Kessler opened drawers and closets. "I'm allowed to snoop; I'm the mother." Marian's two sisters and their husbands arrived. Danny invited one childhood friend to be present at the service.

The day was very hot, and overdressed as we were in our jackets and gowns, we all began to sweat. The windows could not be opened because Danny had sealed them the year before, hoping to install central air-conditioning. We opened the front and back doors and brought in two large floor fans to circulate the air. Neither door had a screen, and the back door looked out over a three-foot drop into the mud. Water had collected there, attracting flies, which had to be chased from the house.

The judge arrived on time at one o'clock. Marian had chosen some selections from the Bible which she asked her sisters to read. She herself read a poem about love that she had saved from an Ann Landers column. There was no music. Marian wore a simple pastel dress and carried yellow roses; white, she thought, would be inappropriate. Her sisters wore matching dresses, blue with printed flowers. The men all wore business suits except Danny, who wore a black tuxedo and a black cummerbund. When the short ceremony was over, Marian's mother embraced her and said enigmatically, "This isn't what I wanted to say to you, honey."

Guests were expected after six. The room began to cool, and we were happy to drink the slush punch heavy with alcohol. White mints in the form of flat roses perspired in the heat. Mixed nuts in bowls were distributed around the room. On the table was hard salami wrapped around horseradish, melon sections, cream cheese wrapped in ham, freshly cut vegetables; the bridal bouquet doubled as a table arrangement. The party succeeded in having a tone out of the ordinary, the quality of an occasion, almost gaiety. The guests soon found places on the chairs, on the front porch, spilling over onto the steps and into the yard. The men stood with their beers, commenting on the newly poured concrete. Danny's women friends from the diner spoke of their sadness at finally having actually lost him to another woman. The women from Marian's office came, all of them single. None had ever been in the house before, and few had known that she had been living with a man. In all there were fewer than fifteen guests.

The wedded couple left the party early for a motel in an unnamed place. Marian, who had had a good deal to drink, made a joke about going to see "dirty movies." Her parents spent the night in Danny and Marian's bedroom, where on the morning of the wedding Marian had hung a comical-looking doll from the ceiling fan. Confronting her mother with her choice, she displayed the doll as a symbol of her love match. On the shirt of the cross-eyed doll were printed the words "Too much sex ruins your vision."

The wedding had taken its shape and been precipitated by Danny's poor luck in the job market. The ceremony was necessitated by his need for health insurance. Circumstances had brought about the long-dreaded confrontation between Marian and her mother. Had Danny been able to find regular work, the wedding might never have taken place, or if it had, it would have been more formal, in a church, with music. A reception would have been catered in a rented hall for numerous guests. The simplicity and beauty of the day had affected me greatly, but I was reminded that the preparations were mostly a disappointment to the bride and groom. They had settled for simplicity and an anticeremonial approach because they could not afford an elaborate wedding like the ones their families and friends had had. Their wedding ceremony forced them into an awareness of the uncertainty and the compromised circumstances foisted on them by the changing economy, which they had been better able to deny in their everyday lives.

The stories of Mark's and Danny's efforts to adapt to plant closings reveal that in their own ways they perpetuated the conditions of their domination. They supported those conditions first as a matter of routine, by their involvement in institutions—unemployment insurance, training programs, public assistance. In a more profound way they allowed conditions to persist by their failure to struggle against them. It is the hundreds and thousands of individuals accepting their lot that in sum constitute current reality. As we shall see, individuals can also transform their world, if only within limits.

[7]

Cheese Politics

Unemployment takes on a political dimension when the unemployed come to view their personal problems in the context of social issues. They do so as groups mobilize to accomplish institutional ends and as individuals respond to the continuing exigencies of their lives. The citizens of Barberton have recognized plant closings and unemployment as a political problem, and those who enter the political arena must address it in some way.

The federal surplus cheese that became available in Barberton in 1983 became a pivotal item in the politics surrounding unemployment. It caused a great deal of indignation among the unemployed, and that indignation informed their mobilization for local political action. The process by which the problems of the unemployed lead to a change in consciousness and a political response is by no means automatic.

Initial Responses to Unemployment in Barberton

The closing of the Seiberling plant in 1980 was the event that signaled a new era in Barberton, in the way that the 1929 crash on Wall Street heralded the beginning of the Great Depression. Although unemployment had been a growing problem in the community for some years, the shutdown at the Seiberling plant marked the beginning of public recognition of the issue. Local newspapers gave the closing substantial coverage, and editorials began to ask if the magic was gone for good. A feature article on the Seiberling closing in the *New York Times Magazine* (Peterson 1980) put Barberton in the national public eye and heightened the sense of the significance of the shutdown. It was no longer assumed that anyone who wanted to work could find a job. The effect on the city's tax base was projected. Local merchants speculated about the consequences of the loss. Unemployment had emerged as a clearly public issue, drawing to it the political figures of the region.

Those who initially addressed the issue did so within the narrow framework of the well-established interests of powerful individuals and institutions. Local politicians, union officials, and philanthropic organizations spoke on behalf of the unemployed without addressing their actual needs or discussing their concerns. The United Rubber Workers was the first group to act as an advocate for the unemployed. One group from Local 18 organized a picket to protest the closing, and the nervous observers of the local labor scene anticipated a more forceful response to the corporate onslaught. Behind the scenes the international union found itself in an awkward situation: the union was in no position to protest the shutdown in any serious way. Because Local 18 had been working without a contract when the closing was announced, Firestone was technically not obligated to fulfill any of the previous contract's substantial provisions for benefits in the event of a shutdown: severance pay, the extension of health-insurance coverage, pension payments. The union had to agree to a smooth closing in return for those benefits; disgruntled workers might have cost the company lost production and damaged machinery. It is clear that the company benefited from the atmosphere of confusion and secrecy that surrounded the closing. Such a strategy, designed to dampen the immediate response to a plant closing, has been called "cooling out" (Lee 1985).

A few political leaders in Barberton were quick to realize that the closing represented potential disaster. Declining revenues and escalating problems (including decaying infrastructures and rising numbers of dependent citizens) remain the unsolved dilemma of many American cities (Ornstein 1983). William Judge, the energetic mayor of Barberton, took steps to investigate the possibility that the city might buy and

[155]

operate the plant, which was known to have been making a profit at the time of the closing.[1] The idea of community ownership of local steel foundries was being seriously considered in nearby Youngstown (Lynd 1982). A group of Barberton leaders traveled to Washington, D.C., to meet with representatives of the Department of Labor. No assistance was available for community-ownership schemes, but a small grant was offered to study other proposals for redevelopment. The mayor quickly turned his attention to finding a buyer for the plant, without success. In September 1980 a last effort was made to reopen the plant. The mayor called a meeting between the president of the URW, Peter Bommarito, and the chief executive officer of Firestone, John J. Nevin. At the meeting the mayor offered Firestone tax abatements and other incentives, to no avail. By October, Firestone had removed most of the machinery from the plant and sold the building to a small machine shop for use as a warehouse.

These efforts on the part of a city official were extraordinary, given the tradition and history of the city's politics. Local government in Barberton routinely concerns itself only with roads, sewers, and water. Despite the efforts of the Planning Department, the city has been unable to make any systematic improvements, to encourage new business, or to bring in major government funding for civic or industrial development. Most of the city politicians were small businessmen and had interests that they controlled and protected through their familiarity with city codes regulating such matters as inspections and licensing. When the attempt to reopen the Seiberling plant failed, city politics resumed its usual routine character.

Except in 1980, when Barbertonians joined the rush to Reagan, politics in Barberton has been controlled by the Democratic party since the 1940s. Barberton may accurately be called a one-party town. The Men's Democratic Club meets once a month in the American Legion Hall. Most of its members are councilmen and former councilmen. Here, too, small-business interests predominate. The group is static, organized seemingly to protect the political aspirations of its few regular members. Activities tend to attract the regular members, and they make no attempt to advertise broadly. There was some discussion of

---

[1]Pseudonyms are not used in this chapter. Many of the people mentioned are public figures who should be properly identified.

development of membership at each meeting I attended but no concrete proposal was ever made. I was the first new member of the group in five years. The Women's Democratic Club is larger and more active but plays no major role; Barberton has had not one female elected official in recent years. Nor has either club attempted to do any systematic voter registration. Politicians in Barberton claimed that the vast majority of the adults in town were voters. My own investigation revealed that only 50 percent of those eligible to vote did so in the 1980 presidential election, a bit less than the national average. This poor turnout reflects the failure of the clubs to generate interest and local participation in the political process.

Political competition after the closing tended to consist of attempts to discredit opponents or to usurp credit for popular actions. Unemployment and jobs were major issues. City council meetings were the usual arena where antagonists would square off. During the 1982 election year, several candidates made speeches from the council floor, drawing attention to the mayor's failure to bring new industry to the city and to deal with unemployment. In one particularly naive attempt a council candidate took the floor and waved the glossy promotional brochure of a nearby city as an example of what could be done by better leadership. In another maneuver, a city councilman contacted a Summit County official about grant money for road repair available through revenue sharing, and in so doing circumvented the appointed representative of the city who was to have made the contact. He was thus able to claim in his campaign that he had brought jobs to Barberton. This sort of infighting did little to clarify the issues or help formulate solutions to the problems that unemployment had created for the city.

Philanthropic organizations are very much a part of Barberton's political life through their cooperation with the city government and industry in addressing social needs. Although it did nothing to remedy the problems of the unemployed directly, the United Way's fundraising campaign of 1981 in Barberton emphasized unemployment and the recent crisis to such effect that it exceeded its goal for the year despite the fact that a large number of former contributors no longer had jobs. The organization's one specific service to the unemployed was the printing of a pamphlet that outlined some of the problems of the unemployed and listed the telephone number of the central information service for social-service programs in the county. No effort was made to distribute the almost useless pamphlets, which remained in a rack in the United Way office.

The United Way also carried out a research project designed to allow the people of Barberton themselves to initiate a new direction for the city. This project, Goals for Greater Barberton, was funded by the city with the money received from the Department of Labor, and was set up as a summer project by a graduate student in sociology. The director of the United Way spoke publicly about the project with enthusiasm, stressing that Barberton needed to examine alternative futures. "Perhaps we can become a high-tech center or a retirement community. The people have to decide." While the people's opportunity to make such a decision had no basis in reality, the project received a great deal of media coverage when it was begun. Local television stations covered a press conference held to publicize the mailing of the questionnaires to the residents of Barberton.

The project was largely unsuccessful. Only 10 percent of the questionnaires were returned. The graduate student returned to school in the fall, and the data were never collated or analyzed. The United Way committee made no recommendation or report, but its efforts gave the impression that something was being done about the dramatic changes taking place in Barberton and thus defused much of the public criticism of industry and government. Public discussion was thereby diverted from the actual events and the problems of unemployment and focused instead on some vague alternative future. Serious discussion might have raised questions concerning blame and responsibility for plant closings. The United Way of Barberton, controlled by the leaders of the city's major industries—Babcock and Wilcox, Ohio Brass, Pittsburgh Plate Glass, BankOhio—who used the philanthropic organization to further their own political interests, had no interest in clarifying these issues. Indeed, the United Way on several occasions acted directly on behalf of industry, to the detriment of local labor officials.[2]

Had the crisis passed, the ineffectual initial responses of the city's

[2]Two incidents illustrate the point. The director of the United Way attempted to reprimand an officer of Local 900 of the International Brotherhood of Boilermakers for leaking information to the press regarding the activities of Babcock and Wilcox. Later, the United Way named Mr. Wright, of Wright Tool and Forge, as director of its fund-raising drive, despite the protests of labor leaders that he had destroyed the union at his factory.

leaders would have provoked no criticism and might even have been considered successful. There had been no scandal or any embarrassing public incident associated with the closing; in general it had proceeded smoothly. But the crisis did not pass. The Seiberling shutdown was followed by other closings, and unemployment continued to increase in 1982 and 1983. There was some alarm among Barberton city officials as disturbing reports began to trickle into their offices concerning hungry families and mortgage foreclosures. The approaching winter raised the possibility that many impoverished people would have to make a choice between eating and staying warm. The mayor alerted the Red Cross to be prepared to move in with blankets and space heaters in the event of heat shutoffs. He was also concerned that the local hospital make good its commitment to meet the medical needs of the community. The hospital administration and the city health director gave assurances that provisions had been made.

Public expressions of concern about hunger in Barberton surfaced in 1982. In many other cities, food banks, soup kitchens, and similar programs began to appear. There was also a general awareness of the effects of the restrictions on eligibility for food stamps and of the increasing numbers of workers who could no longer collect unemployment benefits though they still had no work. It was the availability of federal surplus cheese that formed the basis of a food program in Barberton.

Federal Surplus Commodities and the Barberton Food Pantry

The first shipment of federal cheese and butter arrived in Barberton on 7 February 1983. During the following year over 10,000 pounds of butter and 30,000 pounds of cheese were distributed in the city. The federal surplus commodities were designated for low-income communities and areas hit by unemployment. The cheese came in five-pound bricks wrapped in plastic on which was printed "Department of Agriculture, Federal Surplus Commodities, Not for Resale."

The distribution of the cheese and butter made a great impression on the community, creating an awareness that hard times were upon them. That the proud people of Barberton would line up for a handout demonstrated that a need existed. Some citizens expressed fear that the food would be wasted; others were concerned about its quality. A joke circulated, especially among the older residents, about the effect of large quantities of cheese on the bowels. Many were embarrassed about taking the cheese while others were passive and accepted it willingly. Some people resented the fact that the cheese giveaway had been announced just before Christmas.

The discussion in the city council concerned the method of distributing the commodities. The first distribution was made directly from the refrigerated trucks in which they had arrived. Problems included the high cost of operating the trucks and the traffic snarls created in the parking lot of the shopping center where the distribution took place. Not everyone was pleased by the program. Councilman Pramuka charged that another councilman had personally given a bar of cheese to a man in a restaurant parking lot. The other members of council disregarded the charge, as by that time the program had gained widespread support.

The enthusiasm with which the community accepted the cheese meant obvious political capital and led to the development of similar programs. Mayor Judge floated the idea of establishing a food pantry in Barberton to provide free food for low-income and unemployed people. After a splashy announcement in the local newspapers, a community meeting was called to solicit volunteers. More than a hundred people turned out for the meeting, filling the city council chambers. The Salvation Army was to oversee the project, clearly stamping the pantry with the character of charity.

The $30,000 needed to open the pantry had first to be approved by the city council. The pantry was seen as a political coup for the mayor, and council members opposed to him attempted to block the project. Other people opposed it on other principles. Councilman Pramuka, a longtime conservative who owned a prosperous food store, dramatized his opposition by pulling a $500 bill out of his pocket and throwing it on the floor, declaring, "Now I challenge each of you do-gooders to match that as a contribution to the Salvation Army, who should be taking care of the problem. The city should stay out of the food business." A voice in the back of the room hooted, "Where'd you get all that money, Al?"

The measure carried 5 to 4, and the mayor got his pantry. He also got his name associated with the cheese. To simplify the distribution of the cheese, cards were issued to eligible recipients, then marked when they received their cheese. No card, no cheese. On each card was printed the name of the mayor.

The pantry opened with suitable fanfare in one of the empty storefronts downtown. A newspaper article carried a large picture of the outside of the building with a long line of people waiting, all facing away from the camera (*Barberton Herald* 16 February 1983). Observing the easy political capital to be made from the cheese distribution, other groups began to request permission to distribute the surplus commodities to their constituents. Various churches, unions, and senior citizens' groups in Akron had obtained some of the federal giveaways. In Barberton the request came from a recently formed grass-roots organization of unemployed people, which hoped to to attract new members with the food.

A National Movement among the Unemployed

The emergence of a grass-roots organization of the unemployed in Barberton was part of a national movement that had recently begun to take shape. By 1983 there was a full-fledged national group formally known as the National Unemployment Network (NUN). The seeds of the movement can be traced to the groups formed in the wake of the 1975 recession, when unemployment began to reach crisis proportions in communities that had previously enjoyed high rates of employment.

These groups began by setting up food banks and meeting other immediate needs of the unemployed and then attempted to organize on a broader political basis. One of the groups, the Mon (Monongehela) Valley Unemployment Committee, developed out of the activities of members of defunct local steel unions around Pittsburgh at the beginning of the dismantling of the American steel industry after 1975. The Philadelphia Unemployment Project (PUP) grew up during the same period. A small group with similar ideas had tried unsuccessfully to establish an organization by leafleting the OBES in Akron.

After 1980, groups of unemployed men and women sprang up in communities all over the Northeast and Midwest, offshoots of neighborhood organizations, defunct union locals, and church groups. Many began their efforts with small marches or demonstrations, as did the

Cleveland Council of Unemployed Workers, in whose activities I participated during 1982, its first year. The Cleveland council sponsored educational meetings, acted as an advocate for its members at the OBES, and staged protests of several kinds.

On 22 January 1983 the Mon Valley Unemployment Committee and PUP held a meeting to create a national organization among the many groups that had by then formed. The groups were contacted through a large informal network of union and community organizers. Representatives of various groups met in Homestead, Pennsylvania, site of the huge U.S. Steel works and the bloody events that surrounded the creation of the United Steel Workers of America (Brody 1960). More than seventy people representing thirty groups from seven states turned out for the meeting. Despite the fact that few people knew one another and that the group was large, the level of organization and the democratic spirit that prevailed were impressive. The most controversial part of the meeting was the establishment of demands for the group. The issues of the arms race and foreign imports were skirted, and the core issues emerged in three demands: the creation of jobs for all the unemployed, the extension of unemployment benefits until those jobs were created, and a moratorium on residential mortgage foreclosures and evictions. As one of the organizers said, "The rest can be discussed at the level of analysis."

The meeting also provided an opportunity for various groups to learn effective strategies from one another. In Pennsylvania, where the unemployment level had been very high for a long time, the number of mortgage foreclosures had increased alarmingly. Organizations in Homestead and in Philadelphia had blocked evictions by standing in front of houses to prevent sheriff's deputies from putting the families' possessions in the street. Similar tactics had been used by unemployment councils in the thirties (Rosenzweig 1976). Banks in the Pittsburgh area were picketed for their aggressive foreclosure policies. Lists of the names of attorneys who were most active in foreclosure cases— "vultures"—were printed in the local newspapers. These efforts led Pittsburgh's Judge Papadakos to declare a moratorium on foreclosures of owner-occupied homes (Feeley 1983).

The early success of the unemployment movement can be measured by the growth in the number of such groups by the summer of 1983. A national convention held in Erie, Pennsylvania, in June attracted over 250 activists representing sixty groups from sixteen states.

The first national political action of this movement took the form of a "People's Lobby" in Washington, D.C., on 15 March 1983. The Cleveland Council of Unemployed Workers sent two busloads of unemployed people, with local churches paying for the transportation. They joined 3,000 other unemployment activists from around the country to meet with their elected representatives and make their needs known. Specifically, they pressed for the passage of legislation for the extension of unemployment benefits (H.R. 233) and foreclosure aid (H.R. 1330).

The day culminated in a rally on the steps of the Capitol. Organizers from many states spoke; volunteers sang original songs. The crowd was stirred by the words of Linny Stovall from Pittsburgh, who addressed the leaders of the nation: "We came with Coxey's Army, we came in the thirties with our Hoovervilles, now we are here again. The unemployed are speaking for themselves today, and we are going to keep coming back until every American who wants to work can find a decent job."

A group performed a skit portraying the plight of the unemployed American. John and Joan Q. Public presented President Reagan with a pink slip, dismissing him from his job without notice. The Reagans were then subjected to a long series of indignities: they were denied unemployment insurance, had to sell Nancy's china, lost the ranch, and were denied welfare. Eventually the Reagans found themselves living on the beach. After each disappointment, Nancy burst into tears and wailed, "But Ronnie, what are we going to do?" Spontaneously the crowd broke into a chant: "Cheese! Cheese! Cheese!"

The rally failed to move the majority of congressmen—they defeated the measures supported by the movement—but those who attended had witnessed in action the character of working-class politics. The ideals and standards of self-reliance, opportunity, and equality were the values on which much of this protest was based. The political attitudes of the working class are not easily understood within the terms of the usual political continuum: discussion of the conservative or liberal nature of the American working class is misleading (Levinson 1980). On the one hand, working-class people have no deep sympathy for conservative economic plans that further empower large companies and weaken the position of workers. On the other hand, traditional liberal strategies to eradicate poverty do not command widespread support among the working class. This is not to say that Americans favor the abandonment of social programs, for they do not (Navarro

[163]

1985). The idea of direct public assistance in the form of welfare as a way to help people able to work has never been popular. Full employment and workers' rights are, in contrast, deeply and widely supported by the American working classes and are their preferred solution to economic inequities and insecurites (Levinson 1980; cf. Braverman 1974).

The New Deal, which had the strong support of the majority of Americans during the 1930s, was a response to widespread economic insecurity resulting from economic stagnation. The goal of that progressive tradition was full employment, and a basic level of economic security was seen as the right of every citizen. Contemporary demands for economic security through full employment represent a return to the terms of the New Deal tradition rather than a new development.

Organizing the Unemployed in Barberton

Politicization of the unemployed is a fitful process. The events in Barberton indicate the difficulties with which a mass movement develops. Sociological theories that hinge on the notion that abstract societal "systems" have "needs" and interests reveal little about why things happen as they do. In fact, it is individuals and groups of individuals within society that have needs and interests. At a more explicitly political level, we must understand that citizens do not spontaneously or automatically crowd into the streets or vote for a liberal candidate because the system requires change or simply because they feel deprivation. Nor does a lack of response imply that deprivation does not exist. The organized groups are indispensable to the genesis of mass movements (Piven and Cloward 1977).

The first step toward an organization of the unemployed in Barberton was taken by a group of former Seiberling workers. During my interviews with former union officials from 1980 to 1982, conversation often turned to political responses to unemployment, and I related my recent observations concerning the national movement of the unemployed. Carl Ashe, a former officer of URW Local 18, was interested in organizing the unemployed and called together a group of former rubber workers to discuss the idea. In February 1983 I met with his group to tell them about the efforts of the Cleveland Council of Unemployed Workers and the actions of NUN. The group sought the guidance and support of the United Rubber Workers International to pursue their initiative. With a staff member of the international office they generated a list of demands and some short-term plans. A meeting with regional organized labor leaders proved to be an ill-advised step.

That meeting killed the original initiative. One member of the regional labor organization, the labor representative to the United Way, opposed the idea, chiefly on the grounds that all needs were being met by the current system. The meeting degenerated into an unpleasant argument in which the representative to the United Way said, "We don't want a bunch of people marching around in the streets like the sixties." Finally, the fear of "Communist infiltration" was invoked, clearly a tactic to discourage the group from continuing. Carl Ashe was thoroughly demoralized by the meeting and failed to call his group together again, excusing himself on the grounds that he felt incompetent to identify infiltrators. "Getting a job is hard enough. If I got labeled a Communist I'd *never* get a job." My enthusiastic encouragement of his effort may have worked against him; my presence as an outsider and my association with NUN, a group outside of the AFL-CIO, were regarded with suspicion. (NUN was made up primarily of former union members but was not an official organ of a union.) In my later activities I was content to act simply as a source of information to organizers.

In May 1983 I received a telephone call from Rick Kepler, who was interested in forming an unemployment group. He had gotten my Barberton phone number from the coordinator of NUN at Mon Valley. *The Guardian,* a small political magazine covering labor news, had run an article about organizing the unemployed which included a contact number for NUN. Rick became one of the major participants in the organizing that followed.

Rick was born and raised in Barberton, the son of a beer-truck driver. Rick told me, "Drivers didn't make any money in those days, and with five kids we had to live in the projects to make it." His early experiences marked his life in a profound way, giving him an egalitarian spirit and a hatred of racism. (The project was mostly black; Rick is white).

Rick had grown up in what he called a "union town" and looked to the labor movement for strength. He had a long personal history of

[165]

union activism; however, it was his experience with the Vietnam War that first attracted him to politics. He had been married at the age of eighteen, then drafted at the height of the war. His disenchantment with the contemporary political situation, which he heard echoed in antiwar protests at home, helped to focus his political outlook. Later he worked briefly with the Community Action Agency, an outgrowth of the National Welfare Rights Organization, as an organizer. After a long history of job instability, union politics, and unemployment, Rick had developed a mature political perspective but little concrete experience.

During the spring of 1983 a particular local issue strongly attracted Rick's attention: the strike at the Wright Tool and Forge plant in Barberton, which was precipitated by the owner's demands for drastic concessions from the workers, including major losses in medical benefits, loss of vacation pay, substantial pay cuts, and termination of seniority rights. The concessions were a de facto denial of the existence of the union (AFL-CIO Boilermakers Local 1055) because they destroyed job security by allowing the company to lay off any worker, regardless of seniority, and hire another in his place. Most of the sixty-seven union employees had worked at the plant for more than twenty years and were over the age of forty. They feared that they would be replaced simply because of their age. To them the terms of the concessions clearly spelled union busting.

Rumors began to circulate that Mr. Wright, the owner, intended to end the strike by hiring "replacement workers," or scabs. To understand the events that followed, the deep emotional response of the workers in Barberton to the idea of crossing a picket line must be appreciated. To cross a picket line, to be a scab, was to take away another person's living.

Rick and I began to visit the picket line at the plant and attended the strike meetings to learn more. Rick's vocal and aggressive participation in the meetings drew suspicion from the union leadership, and again accusations of Communist affiliations were made. Because of my recent experiences with union leadership and Rick's abandonment of his original intention to organize the unemployed, I ended my participation. As the events unfolded, however, the issue of unemployment was at the center of the strike, and a local unemployment movement was in the making.

When the scabs were brought into the Wright plant, there was little the union was prepared to do. The leaders of the union were confined to the traditional tactics of the bargaining table, litigation, and the threat of a boycott. Mass unemployment, however, had created a new environment in which the old tactics were no longer effective. Replacement workers were brought into the plant on 1 June 1983. Striking workers stood by dumbly as the scabs drove past the picket line into the plant, with the Barberton police on hand to stop any violence. In a desperate attempt, one man, Charlie Lemon, lay down in the driveway to block the cars. The police removed him. Charlie was the vice-president of Local 900 of the International Brotherhood of Boilermakers, at Babcock and Wilcox. Like Rick, he had been raised in Barberton in a union family. He remembered having eaten beans for two weeks in a row while his father was on strike. "But we were so proud to eat them beans," he told me.

The thwarting of the strike led to the planning of a solidarity march to demonstrate community support for the Wright workers. Rick and Charlie took leading roles in organizing the march, despite the objection of higher-ranking union officials, who favored a boycott. The rally and parade on 23 July 1983 drew over 700 people, most of them members of other unions, and marked a turning point in labor organizing in Barberton. The spirit of the parade was militant and not one of celebration. Although Mayor Judge called the parade a "funeral march," the event forged strong new alliances and provided a training ground for the new leaders.[3] The Wright workers had lost their jobs, but some remained involved and became the first members of the Unemployment Council of Summit County.

After the march Rick took me up on my previous offer to assist him in organizing the unemployed. He had gathered together a group of industrial workers and unemployed workers interested in forming a grass-roots political organization of the unemployed. A group had set a date for a rally to protest a recent decision by the Pentagon to give a Scottish firm a contract that previously had been held by Babcock and Wilcox, thereby denying jobs to Barberton. Little planning had been done and time was short. I suggested that a press conference might be

[3]In 1985 the city council, with the backing of the mayor, made $900,000 in municipal bonds available to Wright Tool and Forge for economic development (Simonds 1986).

[167]

more easily organized and could be used to protest publicly the action of the Pentagon and kick off an organizing campaign. Speeches and press releases were written; arrangements were made for seating and for an amplification system. The lack of leadership in the group led to failure, however, for no one called the reporters. Inexperience and scarcity of resources were the frequent causes of failures in the early phase of the organizing in Barberton. Rick became discouraged, having no enthusiasm for "putting on a little show for the press." Disenchanted, he left town for a raft trip on the Mississippi River.

The Wright workers, still officially on strike, decided to march in the Barberton Labor Day Parade in 1983. The return of labor to the parade was a solemn affair, with the Wright workers marching in silence among the dance troupes and baton corps. A leaflet distributed to the crowds, announcing a meeting of the Unemployment Council of Summit County, drew two new members.

The events of the summer had made a deep impression on Charlie Lemon. The breaking of Boilermakers Local 1055 was a serious blow to all unions. The 40,000 unemployed people in Summit County potentially constituted a pool of scabs so large that virtually any union could be broken. The threat of unemployment had become the big stick that management used in contract talks to force concessions (Verespe 1982). With these concerns and his oath as a union officer to keep civic responsibility in mind, Charlie was driven to action. Foremost in his mind were the Wright workers, who did not qualify for unemployment benefits or food stamps because they were on strike.

Charlie first organized a food distribution for the unemployed, paid for with donations by unions, churches, and students. A meeting was planned, for the purpose of the giveaway was not only to help people but to create an organization of the unemployed. The union hall of Boilermakers Local 900 was decorated with signs reading "Jobs Now," "In Unity There Is Strength," and "Solidarity." The giveaway was announced for several days on a local radio station. When the day arrived, the organizers waited apprehensively, not knowing how many people would come for food.

Approximately 150 people were signed in and seated in the hall that day, 7 October 1983. Charlie opened the program with a speech about the need to organize in Barberton in order to survive the depression and to protect against further attacks on unions. Linda Watkins, organizer of the Cleveland Council of Unemployed Workers, spoke of the success of her group. Another Barberton organizer, Vlad Slomberg, spoke on the need for federal jobs and dollars to revive the Ohio economy. This and later meetings had the intensity of a revival meeting, with highly charged speeches and shouts of approval from the audience.

A follow-up meeting the next week was attended by twenty-eight people. Charlie appointed Vlad president of the Unemployment Council of Summit County. The meeting was not well planned, and little was accomplished. No project or action was proposed to give the group an immediate purpose. The newcomers were not welcomed into the group in such a way as to encourage them to return, and no means were established of contacting them for the next meeting.

I learned that Rick was back in Barberton and went to visit him. His trip had been a disappointment. After driving to Cincinnati, he had launched a small rubber raft into the river and begun his voyage. In three days he had gotten only as far as the Indiana border, fifteen miles downriver. "You couldn't get out in the main current because the barges would run you over. And along the bank, the river didn't move. Once my foot fell in the water and came out all silver. The river is like a big industrial sewer." Rick kicked his raft off into the river and hitchhiked back to his car. "Greg, I didn't find Huck Finn." I responded as had a philosophy professor of mine: "Sometimes you have to *be* Huck Finn." Rick's personal struggle for motivation to do political organizing was a recurrent problem, one I observed in many of the long-term unemployed. Pressing financial needs and discouragement were ever present.

Rick asked about the Unemployment Council. He responded to my encouragement and to the news of the success of the meeting. He chuckled about the large turnout. "There I was with my advanced political perspective, and Charlie comes along with a food giveaway, and bang he gets the people to come out."

Each successive meeting, however, drew fewer people. Vlad had gotten a part-time job and no longer had enough time to devote to the details of the organizing. No concrete project had yet emerged; meetings were chaotic because there was no agenda or sense of purpose. Charlie had lost faith in Rick because of his disappearance, and now Rick himself felt incapable of taking over the group. Loyalty was important to Charlie. He once reminded me of my own obligations to the group: "You better be there when the bear shits the buckwheat, buddy."

Leadership difficulties are a chronic problem for this sort of group and a structural weakness in the unemployment movement. There was a high rate of turnover of both organizers and volunteers. Membership status based on unemployment was inherently unstable, since most people who exhausted their benefits worked occasionally and might not think of themselves as unemployed.

Seeing the group foundering, Charlie developed another food giveaway, this one to include federal surplus cheese. After repeated requests, the Ohio AFL-CIO delivered cheese to Boilermakers Local 900. To announce the 9 November 1983 distribution of the cheese, Charlie handed out leaflets at the Norton OBES office, bearing a picture of a rat and a pig sitting at a table eating. The pig was labeled "The Rich" and the rat "Reagan." The caption read, "Reagan the Rat Says Let Them Eat Cheese." The meeting was well attended and rousing in the way earlier ones had been. A follow-up was scheduled, but again lack of effective leadership stalled the momentum. Without an agenda the meetings were chaotic, and a few members tended to dominate them. Vlad had stopped coming to scheduled meetings, and membership fell off again. Rick now took the initiative and gave the group a purpose: he proposed that they hold a Christmas party for the unemployed. They distributed fruit baskets, had a Santa to give toys to the children, and set up a free clinic where people could visit a doctor. The event was highly successful and gave the organizers confidence, which led to the creation of other projects.

While some details of this account may appear inconsequential, they point up the problems and tentative nature of community organizing among the unemployed. Lack of stable leadership, lack of funds, and mistakes can destroy the beginnings of political response. Simple techniques for creating organizations have to be learned, and concrete, immediate goals have to be decided upon, goals beyond a recognition of the global agenda for full employment. Funds have to be generated to pay for paper, printing, and later for a telephone line and staff. Styles of interpersonal relations need to be developed which stress commitment and avoid hierarchical relations inappropriate in a volunteer organization.

The issue of personal motivation among the organizers is also of importance if we are to understand the evolution of a local political response. When an organization depends on a handful of unpaid organizers who themselves face severe economic difficulties, the frustration and disappointment of political organizing frequently destroy the organization. Early failures so defeat and demoralize ad hoc leaders that they abandon their goals.

There had been a break in the political organizing tradition in Barberton. What politicians and unionists could once do well they could no longer do at all. Only after an effective leadership emerged in the group could the mistakes made during the early phases of the organizing be avoided and a real movement be built.

These events could not have occurred without leadership; the success and failure of movements depend on the strengths and weaknesses of their leader.[4] The efforts described here cannot be understood as arising from some need of the social system to return to a previous equilibrium or to transform itself. Human responses should be viewed not as adaptations by a system but rather as creative actions of people confronting their situations and redefining their resources.

A Free Clinic for Barberton

The Christmas party in 1983 marked the beginning of a movement that led to the creation of a health clinic for the unemployed in the Barberton area. To raise money for the party, volunteers collected donations at the gates of all the major plants in town during shift changes. This is a time-honored method of fund-raising in factory towns. With the money collected, the group planned their party and distributed announcements at the OBES office. Approximately sixty-five people attended, and the Unemployment Council members con-

---

[4]The role of the anthropologist as community activist is a matter of some interest. My own participation in these events must be acknowledged. I was actively involved in the events I describe here. While my efforts were appreciated, I served primarily as a resource for facts and figures, not as a leader. I helped to recruit physicians for the clinic and volunteered my own services. I guided the setting up of the small laboratory facility and the pharmacy. My role here should not be overestimated. Many of the volunteers had backgrounds in medicine as nurses; one was a physician's assistant. Other physicians soon became active in the organization.

[171]

sidered the event their greatest success to date. They were most impressed by the free clinic, staffed by volunteer doctors. A larger project to provide medical services seemed feasible.

The need for a free clinic for Barberton had been discussed frequently since 1980. Letters had appeared in the Akron and Barberton newspapers appealing to the leaders of the community to establish such a clinic to meet the needs of those unable to pay for medical services. The plight of people with no jobs and no health insurance was well covered by the local news media. A number of bills were introduced into Congress, including the Waxman Bill (H.R. 2552) and the Kennedy bills (S. 493 and S. 1154), which would have provided some form of health insurance for the unemployed. The bills failed to pass but made the issue highly public. It was estimated that between 10 and 15 million Americans lost health-insurance coverage as a result of the recession (Congressional Budget Office 1984).

Mayor Judge responded to the problem by creating a committee, whose members included the director of the city's Department of Health and hospital administrators, to study the possibility of founding a clinic. The committee concluded that a clinic was not necessary because according to their study the existing system of medical care delivery could meet the current demands. The director of the city Department of Health, George Harrison, dismissed the possibility of a free clinic; with doctors' office visits down by 25 percent, he said, it which be difficult to find volunteer doctors in the community. And many hospitals in the region provided free care. The Unemployment Council members knew that the care became free only after vigorous attempts to collect the bills proved to be unavailing.

The *Barberton Herald* printed a small announcement calling a meeting of citizens interested in founding a free clinic. The turnout was small—eight people—perhaps because the *Herald* did not accompany the notice by an article describing the project, as it had done in the case of the food pantry. Out of the meeting, however, emerged a core group committed to making the clinic a reality: Rick; Charlie and Becky Lemon; Nana Engle, president of Local 2317 of the American Federation of State, County, and Municipal Employees, from Barberton Citizens' Hospital; and Rosalie Denham, a union activist from the hospital. In a series of meetings the important first steps toward the opening of the clinic were taken.

After visiting a free clinic in Cleveland to gather information and understanding at last the magnitude of the project, the organizers considered scrapping the idea and instead mounting a protest movement to force the Barberton Citizens' Hospital to honor its Hill-Burton obligations. The Hill-Burton Act provided federal funds to build hospitals, which in return were responsible for the care of those unable to pay (Starr 1982). Rick reasoned that a free clinic would only take the pressure off the very people who should take responsibility for the problem. The group had several other considerations to weigh, however. The hospital workers felt that a picket of the hospital would endanger their own positions, in the face of threatened layoffs. Another objective of the group was to create a base for rebuilding the local labor movement. Charlie stressed the need to present the community with a positive alternative and in so doing to draw people into an organization. He saw the clinic as a way to have a political impact on the community as well as to provide a service for the unemployed. These planning meetings gave the clinic a political character, which was to distinguish it from charity organizations serving the unemployed.

For the kickoff, on 10 March 1984, a program was arranged, speakers were invited, speeches written, refreshments and music provided, and reporters from newspapers, radio, and television contacted. The tone of the program was calculated to embarrass the city officials and the professional community for their failure to act. The program excluded the usual political figures: the mayor, the director of the Department of Health, the director of the United Way. In his speech Rick stressed the fact that the clinic had been created by nonprofessionals. "If we had waited for the 'right people' to take care of the problem in Barberton, we would still be waiting." The issue of plant closings and unemployment was raised by speaker after speaker. Charlie spoke about the civic responsibility of the unions, and the commitment of the labor movement to work for national health insurance was affirmed. The festive event drew a large crowd. The organizers had matured to the point of developing relations with reporters, and the event received excellent coverage in all of the media.

The clinic opened four days later. Charlie arranged for the use of the hall of the Barberton Council of Labor, of which he was now president. The back half was transformed into a clinic. It looked a bit like a field hospital, with sheets hung from the ceiling to form cubicles in which patients could be examined. Beds, tables, a microscope, and other equipment had been donated by the Barberton Citizens' Hospital.

[173]

Charles Lemon, president of Local 900, International Brotherhood of Boilermakers

Rebecca Lemon, first director of the Barberton Free Clinic

Patient charts were prepared; volunteers were trained; doctors and nurses were solicited to volunteer. On the first night more than thirty patients were seen, many with serious medical problems.

Initial repercussions from the opening were minor. The Summit County unit of the American Medical Association called to register its disapproval of any services not on a "private practice model." There was muted criticism from the local United Way that the clinic was duplicating services, a statement that could hardly be taken seriously by those dealing with the health problems of the unemployed. The growing stream of unemployed men and women who came with their children to the free clinic during the following year settled the question about the need in the community.

The political character of the clinic was manifested in a variety of ways. Most obvious was the fact that the clinic was held in a labor hall. An important part of the organization of the clinic was the position of the "health advocates." These were volunteers who escorted the patients around the clinic and conducted interviews to learn what follow-up care each patient might need. The advocates informed patients about community resources that might help them pay for pharmaceuticals and the specialists to whom they might be referred. In some cases they helped those eligible to seek assistance from the welfare system. Patients who were not registered to vote were promptly given a registration form.

The clinic was set apart from charity organizations by other features as well. Patients were encouraged to become volunteers at the clinic. Most important, the clinic had no strict eligibility criteria and was open to anyone who could not afford a doctor. Much cynicism about eligibility had grown up when many of those who had lost their jobs discovered that they did not qualify for many services available in the community. The clinic's open eligibility was an affront to the charity organizations that were, like the leaders in Washington, in the process of stiffening their own requirements to stem the growing flood of demands for services.

The Politics of Indignation

Political indignation led to the creation of a free clinic in Barberton, but there has been no rising tide of dissent in this country. This lack of response to unemployment casts a new light on classic questions concerning political culture in America (De Brizzi 1979). The question "Why is there no working-class political movement in the United States?" can be reformulated to address the contemporary political response of the jobless to unemployment. Commentators have asked, "Why have the unemployed remained quiescent?" (Schlozman and Verba 1979, Friedman 1975).

One familiar answer to this question is that workers are quiescent because they have not suffered the sting of unemployment, thanks to the availability of unemployment insurance and other forms of support. The evidence presented here and in the many sources cited suggest that a different explanation must be sought. Deprivation and dissatisfaction due to unemployment have been well documented. To explain the puzzle of the quiescent unemployed, two political scientists, Kay Schlozman and Sidney Verba (1979:153), have posited the existence of an "invisible barrier between personal and abstract ideology." They observe that the everyday suffering of unemployed persons, while very real, did not affect their world view or general outlook during the 1975 recession. Underlying this formulation of the problem of quiescence is the assumption that political consciousness develops out of individual experience in some automatic way.

Political consciousness (or lack of it) is the result of far more complex circumstances than Schlozman and Verba's formulation suggests. Workers' knowledge about society and politics, about the way public policy affects everyday life, is not the simple reflection of individual experience. Consciousness is an interpretation of circumstances in particular social contexts. The interpretation of experience, indeed the visibility of facts themselves, depends on where, with whom, and under what circumstances the facts are discussed and given meaning.

Grass-roots organizing supplied a social context that transformed everyday experiences into political consciousness in Barberton. Barbertonians began to interpret unemployment, deprivation, and unmet health needs as politically significant facts through their participation in the free clinic.[5] The change in their outlook came not simply through

---

[5]The outcome of these efforts can be seen in the shift in political behavior in Barberton. Though Barberton had historically voted solidly Democratic, in the election of 1980 its voters favored Reagan over Jimmy Carter by a 5-to-4 margin. In 1984, other blue-collar communities in Ohio voted strongly for Reagan again. Barberton, on the contrary, voted for Walter Mondale. The efforts of the grass-roots movement described in this chapter have to be given partial credit for this turnaround.

suffering but through the efforts of community leaders to help them understand their suffering. The "invisible barrier between personal and abstract ideology" was overcome in Barberton through the efforts of community leaders to organize around the issue of unemployment.

The dominant trend in working-class America, the lack of political awareness of issues, must be understood in a similar way. Apolitical or antipolitical interpretations of reality are part of the general decline of participation in the political process, seen most clearly in the decline of the proportion of voters in the United States (Burnham 1982). The decline can be understood as a failure of the organizations that once encouraged political participation. Working-class consciousness today is a result of trends in the labor movement's leadership (Davis 1980a).

The American working class has a long tradition of active participation in political organizations that once gave workers a framework in which to interpret events and that encouraged political action. In the past, political clubs and local unions made politics an everyday affair for the men and women in Barberton. The mobilization of voters was the special talent of union organizers, which for a long time created a solid majority for the Democratic party. Political picnics, rallies, meetings, and marches were an important part of working-class life. The Labor Day parade in Barberton was the embodiment of that tradition, which created a link in the minds of people in the community between their everyday lives and political events of the day. This tradition of community organizing has faltered not only in Barberton but throughout the country.

The clearest example of the change in working-class political culture is the failure of unions to sustain voter participation even among their members (Edsall 1984). In 1982 only 50 percent of the members of the largest local union in Summit County, Boilermakers Local 900 in Barberton, had registered to vote. Once strong supporters of the ballot box and the democratic process, union leaders have lapsed in their efforts to motivate their members.

The failure of this tradition is due in part to neglect and in part to repression. The demobilization of the union movement in this country was a conscious goal of its leaders in the fifties (Davis 1982). The unintended consequence for the union movement has been the gradual dissolution of the political power base on which it was built. The oligarchy of the unions and the Democratic party proceeded on the assumption that the rank and file would passively continue to vote without the support of active local political institutions. This neglect led to the gradual erosion of union support. The trend continued in the seventies, further weakening the Democratic party and setting the stage for the ascent to power of the Republicans (Edsall 1984). Depoliticization of the base of the union movement was also the direction taken in England, with similar political consequences. In France, unions maintained their militant stance on the shop floor and in the community, creating a very different political climate in that country (Gallie 1984).

The suppression of militants and local political initiative during the fifties has been well documented (Piven and Cloward 1977). What is less well understood is the more subtle sort of repression that continues today. Politics is surrounded by an aura of fear in working-class communities. As one man in Barberton put it, "Every time you want to do something in this town it seems like you get called a Communist." My own experience confirms this sort of fear. Ignorance helps feed the fear. Frequently I heard statements like this one: "If I did anything like that [participate in a march], they might take away my unemployment insurance."

This analysis sheds light on the trend in American culture which has been called "privatization." Estrangement from political life, a specific type of privatization, is often discussed as if it were an autonomous force in society, an abstract historical process, or the manifestation of some systemic need. Criticism has made it clear that while privatization is an accurate description of many aspects of modern life, it does not explain the trend (Brittan 1977). The events that led to the depoliticization of shop-floor issues and repression of local political initiatives led to the alienation or privatization discussed here. The absence of local union political activity in many working-class communities has left a volatile, politically disaffected population without experienced, committed leadership. The failure of political leadership at the community level has left people without a way of making politics real, and without an everyday political context in which to interpret life, the base of the union movement has withered and died.

Two points remain. First, why is Barberton different, what accounts for the events there that run so much counter to the privatized responses of this era? The answer lies in the unique particulars of local

[179]

conditions, the personalities and energies of leaders, and local history and institutions. Effective leadership ends quiescence.

The second point pertains to action and failure. The personal and political failures we have observed in Barberton may seem to contradict my earlier emphasis on action. A definition of action must be qualified by the meaning captured in Marx's well-known aphorism: "Men [let us immediately say human beings] make history, but not in circumstances of their choosing" (trans. in Giddens 1985:xxi). To act is not always to succeed; to act is not always even to act in one's own best interest. Individuals and groups can act in ways that recreate and reinforce the conditions of their own exploitation. Finally, our actions have unintended consequences.

In the cases of Mark and Danny we have seen how their actions contributed in some ways to their own difficulties. Similarly the successes of the free clinic must be weighed against the wider failures. Some of the clinic organizers themselves acknowledged as much in moments of discouragement. "President Reagan," one of them observed bitterly, " would love to see clinics like this all over the United States." They realized that their efforts might help to obviate more radical responses. Their efforts to spur political responses in their community might be coopted by other forces. It may be too soon to judge their efforts. Their true success or failure will be borne out in the ultimate consequences of their actions for the history of their community.

The success or failure of the labor movement should be judged in the context of structure and action, of objective conditions and concrete responses. Its development is not part of some inexorable logic of history or the economy but is a result of deliberate tactical responses to conditions. When any movement we support succeeds, we must attribute its success in large part to our careful analysis and serious organizing. When it fails, we must acknowledge our faltering energies and flawed understanding of our own circumstances.

[8]

Epilogue: Some Observations on Working-Class Culture and Unemployment

A working-class culture survives in Barberton, but unemployment and plant closings have weakened it. Though the working class is highly diverse (Halle 1985), its members nonetheless share basic values and beliefs in at least four areas: the meaning of work, home, individualism, and community.

Each of these values is under attack. While motivation to work continues after loss of a job, a worker's commitment to a job or place of employment is often shaken. The immediate effects of economic losses on family values are both disintegrative and strengthening. One effect of economic decline has been the growing necessity of two incomes, along with the many associated changes in family values. The fabric of working-class culture has been placed under tremendous strain, and the outcomes are complex. Economic individualism is exaggerated by deprivation, but a countercurrent of revitalization of community values appears in grass-roots organizing among the unemployed.

Working-class people have met the cyclical changes in the economy—the booms and recessions after World War II—with a set of cultural values that have helped them survive. Earlier cycles of unemployment, however, were quite different from the dislocation caused by the plant closings since the late 1970s; most people successfully weathered periodic short-term layoffs with good unemployment-insurance benefits. The current restructuring of the economy is affecting the value system itself. Chronic job instability makes the perpetuation of the old culture more difficult. Disruption and dislocation are pressing old norms into new configurations.

The practical implication of these findings is that it is useless or cynical to call on people to solve the problems brought on them by unemployment through a simple "return to basic values." Calls for self-reliance, traditional family values, and old-style patriotism have ignored the fact that the social system that supported those values has been eroded. A generation has already redefined those terms.

Work

Meaning associated with employment is often called the "work ethic" and has been the subject of many writers concerned with the current economic malaise. The commitment of workers to secure, high-paying union jobs has been associated with their high levels of satisfaction and a measure of control of the work situation (cf. Applebaum 1982). Seiberling workers shared those benefits and that commitment. Among factory workers the willingness to work continues, but the motivational system that supports work is changing (Levitan and Johnson 1982).

The kind of work found by the men and women of Seiberling after the closing did not provide them with the same sort of identity and satisfaction. The necessity to work is ever present but is infused with different meanings under conditions of high unemployment and job instability. Workers with insecure jobs labor without much commitment to a particular industry or company. Without opportunity for advancement, workers find little incentive to improve at work. A job becomes an impersonal necessity, and fear of unemployment becomes a major factor in motivation.

The Seiberling workers had come to view their work in some ways like careers—stable situations, with a predictable transition of jobs in the plant, based on effort and achievements. They were commited to Seiberling. A recent analysis of the changing concept of career suggests an interesting comparison with the situation of industrial workers. "Career is . . . related to achievement and success and to progress, both of which are reenforced by notions of career ladders, career line and career commitment" (Portwood 1985:451). Professionals tend to lack ambition outside of a narrow range within the profession and a particular institution.

In his study of the closing of a school by the British government, Derek Portwood (1985) discussed sociology's need to revise the concept of career in the light of the experience of unemployment among professionals. The closing of the school brought an end to the jobs of the college professors and an end to their careers as careers had traditionally been conceptualized. Most lost tenure; some gave up academia altogether. Seniority proved to be a disadvantage; older professionals had greater difficulties becoming reestablished. Commitment to work became a handicap, because most had never given much thought to alternative careers.

In similar ways, plant closings, high levels of unemployment, and job instability have changed the way industrial workers think about work. One's commitment to a place of work is lost when that place closes. The personal identity and pride that had been derived from participation in the rubber industry was canceled for the Seiberling workers. Commitment to their new jobs was difficult to develop, especially given the marginal nature of many of those jobs. The dull necessity of earning a living is the only thing left to replace their previous involvement. The trajectory of work life is disrupted and expectations of future rewards are brought into question. Seiberling workers felt a security not unlike that of the professors before the closing and experienced a similar sense of loss.

Home

When we examine the fate of family values, we must consider both the immediate effects of unemployment on families and the overall consequences of the restructuring of the economy. The disruptive and integrative effects of the closing of the Seiberling plant on the family values of its workers were similar to those observed during the Great Depression (Elder 1979). Organization within families—the role of breadwinner, housework responsibilities, child-care strategies—is changing also as a result of the job insecurity that is so much a part of the economic changes brought by plant closings (cf. Morris 1985).

The hardship that unemployment and job instability bring to a family

[183]

has been well documented (Rubin 1976). The experiences of many of the Seiberling workers and their families add to this sad picture. Unemployment can also bring families together. A man becomes increasingly dependent on his wife when her job supplies the only income or provides the family with health insurance and other benefits. The ties that bind are often underwritten by these sorts of substantial financial support. During economically tight periods, when divorce may lead to bankruptcy or welfare dependency, there are powerful incentives for a couple to work out their differences and stay together.

During periods of unemployment people depend on their family networks in numerous ways. Financial support is the most obvious sort of assistance, and extended families are brought more closely together by this sort of dependency. Working-class families have for a long time supplied a network of contacts for information about job openings and informal sources of income. Susan Gore (1976) observed that family support (group cohesion, participation, norms of obligation) tends to lessen the negative impact of job loss on the worker's sense of well-being.

Unemployment and plant closings also have a more general affect on family values. The need of families to have more than one member working outside the home threatens the cultural ideal of the husband who supports the domestic work of the wife. Working-class marriage in our society has been founded on the stable employment of husbands (Harris 1983). Families in Barberton tend to hold to the traditional arrangement of domestic work for women and wage earning for men. While many married women worked in the past, their incomes had been regarded as secondary or supplementary. The wife as a second wage earner had become important in the effort to maintain and raise the family's standard of living; job insecurity today is making the two-wage family a preferred strategy that stabilizes the family unit. Unemployment and job insecurity have led to a change in the meaning of the increasing numbers of married women entering the work force (Mitchell 1980, Kline 1983).

A set of values in regard to domestic work is developing which stresses equal sharing of household responsibilities. Cleaning, cooking, shopping, and child rearing are no longer universally considered the sole responsibility of the women. When women provide the primary income for a home, men tend to pick up domestic tasks, often to mutual dissatisfaction (Redclift and Mingione 1985). This change is by no means a smooth process and is the source of much tension and disruption in family life.

Individualism

What it means to be an individual is a central theme in American culture. Utilitarianism, usually associated with individualism, hinges on an economic understanding of one's place in the world. It is the responsibility of individuals to pursue their greatest fortune, and according to this philosophy the goods of society will then be most justly distributed and apportioned. The conditions created by unemployment lead to the development of an exaggerated utilitarianism. Many of the unemployed respond to savage conditions by developing more competitive attitudes and values. The unemployed often adopt a hyperindividualistic, cynical view of the world. The dog-eat-dog view of the world is reinforced when workers are shaken out of the other traditions that give them a place as an individual in the world.

Other American cultural traditions also have defined individualism. The individualism of religion and the individualism of civil society are well represented in Barberton but have been weakened by unemployment and job insecurity. Individualism based on religion understands the individual as having been placed on earth for a reason and having moral obligations to a community. The civil-society tradition stresses the relation of the individual to the state. This tradition, the peculiarly American expression of Enlightenment philosophy, is maintained through activities in local politics and volunteer organizations. The individual has a civic duty to participate in a self-governing society, and thus to maintain freedom. In their study of national culture, Robert Bellah and a group of co-workers (1985) have called these two traditions *biblical individualism* and *civic republicanism.*

The republican and biblical traditions blend and remain strong among the working-class people of Barberton with whom I lived. There persists a strong belief in democracy and an understanding of the responsibilities of living in a free society, despite cynicism about particular elections or officials. This attitude extends to participation in union activities, which are understood as a stake in the democratic

[185]

process. Similarly, the many neighborhood and community organizations, including the free clinic, represent the vitality of the republican individual.

Biblical individualism in Barberton is difficult to disentangle from civic republicanism. Religion among working-class Americans tends to be a set of vague sentiments (Halle 1985), biblical metaphor blending easily with the civic ethic. (This is not true of members of evangelical movements, whose leaders are fundamentally hostile to a secular, ethical view of the world. Antidemocratic sentiments can be found at the center of the attack on "secular humanism.")

People in Barberton frequently talk about a "calling" in life, but the calling is usually not understood strictly in religious terms. Many people believe that they are on earth for a purpose. Purposes tend to be simple: responsibilities toward children, spouses, and family. People also talk about the importance of leading a good life and helping others. Models of decent and good lives, however, tend to be found more in popular culture than in biblical characters.

While biblical individualism and civic republicanism remain strong elements of working-class culture, utilitarianism may be exaggerated under conditions of economic insecurity. In the wake of the economic downturn, a widening segment of the population has become dependent on food stamps, training programs, and public assistance. Help is sought with a variety of motives, some applicants requesting assistance as a right, others thinking of it as an option, still others adopting a cynical get-all-I-can attitude. Help-seeking behavior is, however, clearly an action taken by an economic individual.

Some observers have mistakenly interpreted these facts as a weakening of individualism. Charles Murray (1985) has charged that the fiber of American individualism has been disrupted by the development of dependency on federal assistance programs. Murray argues that these programs may be to blame for the persistence of poverty in this country. The very nature of these programs, he claims, undermines what the poor need most—the individualistic drive to pursue their best interests.

Aside from its faulty psychological and economic assumptions (cf. Reich 1984), the argument fails to understand the cultural values of individualism in the working class in its diversity. It fails to see the ironic or cynical ways in which people accepted federal cheese or the pragmatism in their acceptance of such a program as one resource among many. A request for assistance need not be the passive sort of phenomenon conjured up by "dependency." Prolonged unemployment may exaggerate the utilitarian stream of these traditions. During tough economic times, economic individualism is translated into striving to "get by." One gets by as one can, whether by taking assistance or by selling drugs. "Getting by" can be just as strenuous for a person weathering a recession as "rowing your own boat" is during good times.

Community

Barbertonians have a sense of the existence of a community of working people, which includes most of the people in the town. "Community" refers to the sense of belonging to some group or collectivity. Drawing on their history, people in Barberton have revitalized their community values in the face of the stress brought on by economic dislocation. This movement is the countercurrent to the exaggerated individualism that is also a response to the insecurity of the era.

The creation of the free clinic was in part an expression of the need for community and stands in sharp contrast to utilitarian individualism. Volunteers repeatedly told me that they never felt they were part of the community until they started volunteering at the clinic. The clinic exemplifies a certain view of community, drawing on a democratic tradition, framed in terms of democratic rights. The clinic and the organizing efforts among the unemployed drew on the traditions of important social movements in this country, including the labor movement, the civil rights movement, and the feminist movement (Bowles and Gintis 1986).

This democratic tradition can be seen in both the mission and the structure of the free clinic. There is among working people a general sense that health care is a right. The free clinic differs in important ways from charity organizations. The organization itself is voluntary and democratic; the leaders are directly accountable to the members of the clinic. While there is a clear division of labor inherited from the institution of medicine, the relationships are much less hierarchical because all members have equal status as volunteers. There is no clear distinction between patients and volunteers. Patients are systematically asked to work as volunteers in the clinic, and patients help make up its board. The volunteers, therefore, tend to treat patients without the stigmatization that sometimes goes with charity. The clinic is an authentic expression of the communal values that have grown out of the disruption caused by plant closings.

The revival of community values in Barberton must be understood as one of the varied responses to the insecurity brought on by economic disruption. Identification with a collectivity is fragile in contemporary culture. Anthropologists have frequently commented on the strong communal values that attach people to the group in tribal and village societies. In traditional societies, existence is infused with morality by tradition and kinship, the institutions that organize daily life. In contemporary society there has been little in day-to-day living that binds people to the group, little that makes communal values seem important.

Community rituals are deeply felt only when they are given meaning in everyday life. The changing meaning of the Labor Day parade illustrates the point. With the current eclipse of the power of the labor movement, there has been little in the lived experience of people to give the parade any special meaning. The unemployed often feel alienated from the unions. The union's active part in the daily lives of working-class people has shrunk. The parade, once a symbol of solidarity and power, has become a mere spectacle.

In the absence of communal values, participation in the routines of work and consumption tend to take their place. While the work and consumerism of a capitalist society supply the much-needed psychological security once supplied by community, they have stripped much of modern life of its moral significance. Routinization and the habitual quality of everyday life provide only an attenuated experience of being part of a collectivity. A certain amount of security is produced by the familiarity of a job and of buying habits. With plant closings and large-scale economic disruption, these thin strands—the strands that bind the individual to the community—are broken.

The insecurity brought on by the loss of a sense of attachment to a community has had profound consequences for modern society (Harris 1981). The psychological need for community has been expressed in a variety of ways in this century—the rise of nationalism, the growth of social movements, and spread of religious fanaticism. These developments represent a "re-moralization of spheres of life denuded of 'moral meaning' by the impact of technology and of the 'created' environments more generally" (Giddens 1985:320). A notable example of this sort of development was the rise of fascism during the Great Depression. The widespread insecurity brought on by that major disruption made many people susceptible to all sorts of calls for unity, no matter how undemocratic the tone of some of them. Unemployment brings to the fore the insecurity of modern society and exposes the tenuousness of our links with our community.

Bibliography

Abbott, William, and Joe Glazer. 1961. *Twenty-Five Years of the URW.* Akron: Exchange Printing Co.

Adams, Leonard P. 1971. *Public Attitude towards Unemployment Insurance.* Kalamazoo, Mich.: W. E. Upjohn Institute for Employment Research.

AFL-CIO News. 1983a. "Poverty Rate Up to 15%, Real Family Income Down." 28 (31), 6 August, p. 1.

———. 1983b. "Twenty Million Jobs." 28 (23), 11 July, pp. 1–3.

Allen, Hugh. 1979. *Rubber's Home Town: The Real-Life Story of Akron.* New York: Stratford.

American Legion. 1922. *Historical Souvenir: American Legion Circus and Industrial Exposition.* Barberton, O.

Applebaum, Herbert A. 1981. *Royal Blue.* New York: Holt, Rinehart & Winston.

———. 1982. "The Anthropology of Work in Industrial Society." *Anthropology of Work Review* 7 (3): 5–32.

Applebaum, Richard, Peter Dreier, and Michael Harrington. 1981. "A Faded Dream: Housing in America." *Dissent,* Winter, p. 21.

Bakke, E. W. 1940a. *Citizens without Work: A Study of the Effects of Unemployment upon the Worker's Social Relations and Practice.* New Haven: Yale University Press.

———. 1940b. *The Unemployed Worker: A Study of the Task of Making a Living without a Job.* New Haven: Yale University Press.

Barrett, Michelle, and Mary McIntosh. 1982. *The Anti-social Family.* London: Verso.

Bednarzik, Robert W. 1983. "Layoffs and Permanent Job Losses: Workers, Traits, and Patterns." *Monthly Labor Review* 106 (5): 3.

——, Maryllyn A. Hewson, and Michael A. Urguhart. 1981. "New Recession Takes Its Toll." *Monthly Labor Review* 105 (3): 3–14.

Bell, Daniel. 1960. *The Coming of the Post-industrial Society.* New York: Basic Books.

Bellah, Robert, Richard Madsen, William M. Sullivan, Ann Swidler, and Steven M. Tipton. 1985. *Habits of the Heart.* Berkeley: University of California Press.

Berger, Bennett M. 1960. *Working-Class Suburb: A Study of Auto Workers in Suburbia.* Berkeley: University of California Press.

Bluestone, Barry, and Bennett Harrison. 1982. *The De-industrialization of America: Plant Closings, Community Abandonment, and the Dismantling of Basic Industry.* New York: Basic Books.

Boryczka, Raymond, and Lorin Lee Cary. 1982. *No Strength without the Union: An Illustrated History of Ohio Workers.* Columbus: Ohio Historical Society.

Bowles, Samuel, and Herbert Gintis. 1986. *Democracy and Capitalism: Property, Community, and the Contradictions of Modern Social Theory.* New York: Basic Books.

Bowles, Samuel, David Gordon, and Thomas Weisskopf. 1983. *Beyond the Wasteland: A Democratic Alternative to Economic Decline.* New York: Anchor/ Doubleday.

Boyer, Richard O., and Herbert M. Morais. 1972. *Labor's Untold Story.* New York: United Electrical, Radio, and Machine Workers of America.

Brand, H. 1981. "On the Economic Conditions of American Workers." *Dissent,* Summer, pp. 331–35.

Braverman, Harry. 1974. *Labor and Monopoly Capitalism: The Degradation of Work in the Twentieth Century.* New York: Monthly Review Press.

Brenner, M. Harvey. 1973. *Mental Illness and the Economy.* Cambridge: Harvard University Press.

Brittan, Arthur. 1977. *The Privatised World.* London: Routledge & Kegan Paul.

Brody, David. 1960. *Steelworkers in America: The Nonunion Era.* Cambridge: Harvard University Press.

Brooks, Geraldine. 1983. "Left Behind: Despite the Recovery, Some Lose Jobs Now, and It's a Hard Blow." *Wall Street Journal,* 5 August, p. 1.

Bureau of National Affairs. 1982. "Recession: Job Losses and Concession Bargaining." *Labor Relations Report* 110 (23).

Burnham, Walter Dean. 1982. *The Current Crisis in American Politics.* New York: Oxford University Press.

Buss, Terry F., and F. Steven Redburn. 1983a. *Unemployment: Plant Closings and Community Mental Health.* Beverly Hills: Sage.

——. 1983b. *Shutdown at Youngstown: Public Policy for Mass Unemployment.* Albany: State University of New York Press.

Carey, Max L. 1981. "Occupational Employment Growth through 1990." *Monthly Labor Review* 104 (8): 42–55.

Cetron, Marvin J. 1984. "Getting Ready for the Jobs of the Future." *The Futurist* 17 (3): 24–30.

Cleveland Council of Unemployed Workers. 1986a. "Candidates Lie about Jobs." 4 (6): 2.

———. 1986b. "Home Foreclosures at All-Time High." 4 (3): 2.

Cobb, Sidney, and Stanislav Kasl. 1977. *Termination: The Consequences of Job Loss.* Report prepared for U.S. Department of Health, Education, and Welfare, National Institute of Occupational Health and Safety. Washington, D.C.: Government Printing Office.

Congressional Budget Office. 1984. "Estimated Number of Unemployed Who Were without Health Coverage Because of Job Loss in Dec. 1983." Memorandum to Andy Scheider from Tom Buchberger, January 25.

Criminal Justice Commission. 1980. *Summit County: Criminal Justice Commission 1980 Comprehensive Justice Plan.* Akron.

DaVanzo, Julie. 1977. "Why Do Families Move?" Research and Development Monograph 48, pp. 76–79. Washington, D.C.: Employment and Training Administration, U.S. Department of Labor.

Davis, George. 1962. "The Story of Barberton, Ohio: The Magic City, 1891–1962." Barberton: Barberton Public Library. Mimeo.

Davis, Mike. 1980a. "Why the United States Working Class Is Different." *New Left Review* 123 (September–October): 3–46.

———. 1980b. "The Barren Marriage of American Labor and the Democratic Party." *New Left Review* 124: 43–84.

———. 1982. "The AFL-CIO's Second Century." *New Left Review* 136 (November–December): 43–54.

Devens, Richard M. 1986. "Displaced Workers: One Year Later." *Monthly Labor Review* 109 (7): 40–43.

Dooley, D., and R. Catalano. 1979. "Economic, Life, and Disorder Changes: Time-Series Analysis." *American Journal of Community Psychology* 7 (4): 381–96.

Edsall, Thomas Byrne. 1984. *The New Politics of Inequality.* New York: W. W. Norton.

Edwards, Richard C. 1979. *Contested Terrain: Transformation of the Work Place in the 20th Century.* New York: Basic Books.

Ehrbar, A. F. 1983. "Jobs." *Fortune,* 16 May, pp. 107–12.

Elder, Glen H. 1979. *Children of the Great Depression.* Chicago: University of Chicago Press.

Etzioni, Amitai. 1983. *An Immodest Agenda.* New York: McGraw-Hill.

Eyer, Joseph. 1977. "Does Unemployment Cause the Death Rate Peak in Each Business Cycle?" *International Review of Health Services* 7 (4): 625–62.

Feeley, Diana. 1983. "Unemployment Grows, a New Movement Stirs." *Monthly Review* 35 (7): 14–27.

Feldstein, Martin. 1973. "The Economics of the New Unemployment." *The Public Interest* 37 (Fall): 3–42.

Ferman, Louis A., and Jeanne P. Gordus, eds. 1979. *Mental Health and the Economy.* Kalamazoo, Mich.: W. E. Upjohn Institute for Employment Research.

Fleming, Willian Franklin. 1981. *America's Match King, Ohio Columbus Barber, 1841–1920*. Barberton: Barberton Historical Society.

Freud, Sigmund. 1930. *Civilization and Its Discontents*. Trans. Joan Riviere. London: Hogarth.

Friedman, Milton. 1975. "Where Has the Hot Summer Gone." *Newsweek*, 4 August, p. 63.

—— and Rose Friedman. 1979. *Free to Chose*. New York: Harcourt Brace Jovanovich.

Fullerton, Howard N. 1980. "The 1995 Labor Force: A First Look." *Monthly Labor Review* 103 (12): 11–21.

Gallie, Duncan. 1984. *Social Inequality and Class Radicalism in France and Britain*. London: Cambridge University Press.

Gans, Herbert. 1962. *Urban Villages: Group and Class in the Life of Italian-Americans*. New York: Free Press.

Garraty, John A. 1978. *Unemployment in History*. New York: Harper & Row.

Gaventa, John. 1980. *Power and Powerlessness: Quiescence and Rebellion in an Appalachian Village*. Urbana: University of Illinois Press.

Giddens, Anthony. 1975. "Classical Social Theory and Origins of Modern Sociology." *American Journal of Sociology* 81 (4): 703–29.

——. 1979. *Central Problems in Social Theory*. Berkeley: University of Calfornia Press.

——. 1985. *The Nation-State and Violence*. Berkeley: University of California Press.

Gilder, George. 1981. *Wealth and Poverty*. New York: Basic Books.

Ginzberg, Eli. 1968. *Manpower Agenda*. New York: McGraw-Hill.

Gluckman, Max. 1958. *Analysis of a Social Situation in Modern Zululand*. Manchester: Manchester University Press.

Gordon, David M. 1972. *Theories of Poverty and Unemployment*. Lexington, Mass.: Lexington Books.

——, Richard Edwards, and Michael Reich. 1984. *Segmented Work, Divided Workers*. Cambridge: Cambridge University Press.

Gordus, Jeanne P., Paul Jarley, and Louis Ferman. 1981. *Plant Closings and Economic Dislocation*. Kalamazoo, Mich.: W. E. Upjohn Institute for Employment Research.

Gore, Susan. 1976. "The Influence of Social Support and Variables Ameliorating the Consequences of Job Loss." Ph.D. diss., University of Pennsylvania.

Gotbaum, Victor. 1984. "Our Unions under Attack." *Dissent*, Spring, p. 136.

Green, James R. 1980. *The World of the Workers*. New York: Hill & Wang.

Grismer, Karl Hiram. 1952. *Akron and Summit County*. Akron: Summit County Historical Society.

Hacker, Andrew. 1983. *U/S: A Statistical Portrait of the American People*. New York: Viking.

Halle, David. 1985. *America's Working Man: Work, Home, and Politics among Blue-Collar Property Owners*. Chicago: University of Chicago Press.

Harrington, Michael. 1984a. *The New American Poverty*. New York: Holt, Rinehart & Winston.

——. 1984b. "The New Gradgrinds." *Dissent*, Spring, p. 177.

Harris, C. C. 1983. "Social Transition and the Deconstruction of the Family: Reflections on Research into the Domestic Circumstances of the Victims of Economic Change." Paper presented at the Tocqueville Society Seminar on Work and the Family in Europe and the U.S., Arc-et-Sinans, June.

Harris, Marvin. 1981. *America Now: The Anthropology of a Changing Culture*. New York: Simon & Schuster.

Haye, John, and Peter Nutman. 1981. *Understanding the Unemployed: The Psychological Effects of Unemployment*. New York: Tavistock.

Henson, Rich. 1983. "Can the Magic Ever Come Back?" *Beacon: The Sunday Magazine of the Akron Beacon Journal*, 15 May.

Illich, Ivan. 1978. *The Right to Useful Unemployment*. London: Boyar.

Jahoda, Marie. 1984. *Employment and Unemployment: A Social-Psychological Analysis*. Cambridge: Cambridge University Press.

——, Paul Lazarsfeld, and Hans Zeisel. 1971. *Marienthal: The Sociography of an Unemployed Community*. Chicago: Aldine/Atherton.

Johnston, W. A., and O. E. Olin. 1976. *Barberton and Kenmore: The Golden Years*. Barberton: Barberton Historical Society.

Keyserling, Leon H. 1979. *Liberal and Conservative National Economic Policies and Their Consequences, 1919–75*. Washington, D.C.: Conference on Economic Progess. September.

Kline, Deborah Pisetzner. 1983. "Trends in Employment and Unemployment in Families." *Monthly Labor Review* 106 (12): 21.

Komarosky, Mirra. 1964. *Blue-Collar Marriage*. New York: Random House.

Kornblum, William. 1974. *Blue-Collar Community*. Chicago: University of Chicago Press.

Lee, James A. 1979. *Employment, Unemployment, and Health Insurance: Behavioral and Descriptive Analysis of Health Insurance Loss Due to Unemployment*. Cambridge: Abbott Books.

Lee, Raymond M. 1985. "Redundancy, Labour Markets, and Informal Relations." *Sociological Review* 33 (3): 469–91.

Lekachman, Robert. 1984. "High Unemployment—What Will the Democrats Say?" *Dissent*, Spring, pp. 137–40.

Lens, Sidney. 1973. *The Labor Wars*. Garden City, N.Y.: Doubleday.

Leventman, Paula Goldman. 1981. *Professionals Out of Work*. New York: Free Press.

Levinson, Andrew. 1980. *The Full Employment Alternative*. New York: Coward, McCann & Geoghegan.

Levitan, Sar A. 1971. *Blue-Collar Workers: A Symposium on Middle America*. New York: McGraw-Hill.

—— and Clifford M. Johnson. 1982. *Second Thoughts on Work*. Kalamazoo, Mich.: W. E. Upjohn Institute for Employment Research.

Li Hsiao Fang. 1948. "The Geographic Structure of Barberton's Industry." Master's thesis, Kent State University.

Liebow, Elliot. 1967. *Tally's Corner.* Boston: Little, Brown.

Lief, Alfred. 1951. *The Firestone Story: A History of the Firestone Tire and Rubber Company.* New York: McGraw-Hill.

Linn, M. W., R. Sandifer, and S. Stein. 1985. "Effects of Unemployment on Mental and Physical Health." *American Journal of Public Health* 75: 502–6.

Lynd, Robert S., and Helen M. Lynd. 1929. *Middletown: A Study in American Culture.* New York: Harcourt Brace.

—— and ——. 1937. *Middletown in Transition: A Study of Cultural Conflict.* New York: Harcourt Brace.

Lynd, Staughton. 1982. *The Fight against Shutdowns: Youngstown's Steelmill Closings.* San Pedro: Singlejack Books.

Marx, Karl. 1971. *Grundrisse.* Trans. David McLellan. New York: Harper & Row.

Mitchell, Olivia S. 1980. "Labor Force Activity of Married Women as a Response to Changing Jobless Rates." *Monthly Labor Review* 103 (6): 32–33.

Monheit, Alan C., Michael M. Hagan, Marc L. Berk, and Gail R. Wilensky. 1983. *Unemployment, Health Insurance, and Medical Care Utilization.* Washington D.C.: National Center for Health Services Research, Department of Health and Human Services, November 3.

Monthly Review. 1983. "Unemployment: The Failure of Private Enterprise." 35 (2): 1–9.

Morris, Lydia. 1985. "Local Social Networks and Domestic Organizations: A Study of Redundant Steel Workers and Their Wives." *Sociological Review* 33 (22): 327–41.

Munts, Raymond, and Irwin Garfinkel. 1979. "The Work Disincentive Effects of Unemployment Insurance." Kalamazoo, Mich.: W. E. Upjohn Institute for Employment Research.

Murray, Charles. 1985. *Losing Ground: American Social Policy, 1951–1980.* New York: Basic Books.

Murray, Merrill G. 1974. *The Duration of Unemployment Benefits.* Kalamazoo, Mich.: W. E. Upjohn Institute for Employment Research.

Navarro, Vincente. 1985. "The 1980–1984 U.S. Elections and the New Deal: An Alternative Interpretation." *International Review of Health Services* 15 (3): 359–94.

New York Times Supplement. 1982. "Employment Outlook in High Tech." 28 March, sec. 12, p. 1.

Ohio Chamber of Commerce. 1975. *Ohio and Its Resources: Bicentennial Issue.* Columbus.

Ohio Public Interest Campaign. 1980. *Blacks and Women Hit Hard by Plant Closings.* Akron, March.

Ornstein, Allan C. 1983. "Decline of the Frost Belt." *Dissent,* Summer, pp. 366–74.

Padilla, Arthur. 1981. "The Unemployment Insurance System: Its Financial Structure." *Monthly Labor Review* 104 (12): 32–37.

Parnes, Herbert S. 1982. *Unemployment Experience of Individuals over a Decade: Variation by Sex, Race, and Age.* Kalamazoo, Mich.: W. E. Upjohn Institute for Employment Research.

Parsons, Talcott. 1960. "Durkheim's Contribution to the Theory of Integration of Social Systems." In *Emile Durkheim, 1858–1917*, ed. Kurt Wolf. Columbus: Ohio State University Press.

Peterson, Iver. 1980. "Magic City Losing Firestone, Fights to Stay Alive." *New York Times Magazine*, 25 March.

Pfeiffer, Richard. 1979. *Working for Capitali$m.* New York: Columbia University Press.

Pierson, Frank C. 1980. *The Minimum Level of Unemployment and Public Policy.* Kalamazoo, Mich.: W. E. Upjohn Institute Employment Research.

Piven, Francis Fox, and Richard A. Cloward. 1977. *Poor People's Movements: Why They Succeed, How They Fail.* New York: Pantheon.

—— and ——. 1982. *The New Class War: Reagan's Attack on the Welfare State.* New York: Pantheon.

Portwood, Derek. 1985. "Careers and Redundancy." *Sociological Review* 33 (3): 449–62.

Raines, John C., Leonora E. Berson, and David M. Gracie. 1982. *Community and Capital in Conflict.* Philadelphia: Temple University Press.

Redclift, Nanneke, and Enzo Mingione. 1985. *Beyond Employment: Household, Gender, and Subsistence.* Oxford: Basil Blackwell.

Reich, Robert B. 1985. "Prescription from the Right." *Dissent* 4 (Spring): 237–40.

Renninger, Terry. 1932. "Industrial Survey of Barberton: A City in Its Youth." B.A. thesis, University of Akron.

Riche, Richard W., Daniel E. Hecker, and John U. Burgan. 1983. "High Tech Today and Tomorrow: A Small Slice of Employment." *Monthly Labor Review* 106 (11): 50.

Roberts, Harold S. 1944. *The Rubber Workers.* New York: Harper.

Roberts, Markley. 1984. "Unemployment." *AFL-CIO American Federationist* 91 (2), 21 April.

Rones, Phillip L. 1980. "Moving to the Sun: Regional Job Growth." *Monthly Labor Review* 103 (3): 12–19.

Rosenzweig, Roy. 1976. "Organizing the Unemployed: The Early Years of the Great Depression, 1929–1933." *Radical America* 10 (July): 37–60.

Rubin, Lillian B. 1976. *Worlds of Pain.* New York: Basic Books.

Rumberger, Russell W. 1981. *Overeducation in the U.S. Labor Market.* New York: Praeger.

Runner, Diana. 1982. "Unemployment Insurance Law: Change in 1981." *Monthly Labor Review* 105 (2): 16.

Sawhill, Isabel, and Charles Stone. 1986. *The Reagan Record.* Washington, D.C.: Urban Institute.

Scase, Richard. 1982. "The Petty Bourgeoisie and Modern Capitalism: A Consideration of Recent Theories." In *Social Class and the Division of Labor*, ed. A. Giddens and G. Mackenzie. Cambridge: Cambridge University Press.

Schlozman, Kay L., and Sidney Verba. 1979. *Insult to Injury: Unemployment, Class, and Political Response.* Cambridge: Harvard University Press.

Shrake, Richard W., III. 1974. "Working Class Politics in Akron Ohio: The U.R.W. and the Failure of the Farm Labor Party." Ph.D. diss., University of Akron.

Simonds, Jack. 1986. "Council Allows Bonding for Wright Tool Company." *Barberton Herald*, 4 February.

Stack, Carol B. 1974. *All Our Kin: Strategies for Survival in a Black Community.* New York: Harper & Row.

Stone, Milan. 1983. Speech before Subcommittee on Commerce, Transportation, and Tourism, Committee on Energy and Commerce, U.S. House of Representatives, on H.R. 1234, 5 May.

Strange, Walter G. 1977. *Job Loss: A Psychosocial Study of Workers' Reaction to a Plant Closing in a Company Town in Southern Appalachia.* Washington, D.C.: National Technical Information Service.

Susser, Ida. 1982. *Norman Street: Poverty and Politics in an Urban Neighborhood.* New York: Oxford University Press.

Terry, Sylvia. 1982. "Unemployment and Its Effects on Family Income in 1981." *Monthly Labor Review* 105 (4): 35.

Tiffany, Donald W., James R. Cowan, and Phyllis M. Tiffany. 1970. *The Unemployed: A Social-Psychological Portrait.* Englewood Cliffs, N.J.: Prentice-Hall.

United Rubber Workers. 1975. *URW United for Freedom.* Akron: United Rubber, Cork, Linoleum, and Plastics Workers of America.

U.S. Bureau of the Census. 1982. *Census of 1980: General Social and Economic Characteristics.* Washington, D.C.: Government Printing Office.

U.S. Department of Health, Education, and Welfare. 1973. *Work in America: Report of a Special Task Force.* Boston: MIT Press.

——. 1980. *Effect of the 1974–75 Recession on Health Care for the Disadvantaged.* Washington D.C.: National Center for Health Services Research, January.

Verespe, Michael A. 1982. "Labor Concessions: A New Era or a Long Fuse?" *Industry Week*, 4 October, pp. 33–38.

Wales, R. 1893. *Barberton, Ohio.* Akron: Barberton Land Company. Promotional brochure.

Wallace, Anthony. 1970. *Culture and Personality.* New York: Random House.

Wall Street Journal. 1969. "Firestone Dayton Tire to Build Plant Capable of Building 17,000 Tires Per Day." 20 March.

Wilson, James Q. 1983. "Thinking about Crime." *Atlantic* 252 (3): 72–79.

Zinn, Howard. 1980. *A People's History of the United States.* New York: Harper & Row.

Index

Library of Congress Cataloging-in-Publication Data
Pappas, Gregory, 1952–
  The magic city.

  (Anthropology of contemporary issues)
  Bibliography: p.
  Includes index.
  1. Plant shutdowns—Ohio—Barberton. 2. Unemployment Structural—Ohio—Barberton. 3. Barberton (Ohio)—Economic conditions. I. Title. II. Series.
  HD5708.55.U62B376   1989   331.13′7977136   88–47935
  ISBN 0–8014–2277–9
  ISBN 0–8014–9548–2 (pbk.)